Cyrus Townsend

Commodore Paul Jones

Cyrus Townsend Brady

Commodore Paul Jones

1st Edition | ISBN: 978-3-75234-887-3

Place of Publication: Frankfurt am Main, Germany

Year of Publication: 2020

Outlook Verlag GmbH, Germany.

Reproduction of the original.

COMMODORE
PAUL JONES

BY

CYRUS TOWNSEND BRADY

PREFACE.

In preparing this work I began, I admit, with an ardent admiration for John Paul Jones, born of long study of his career. I have endeavored, however, so far as possible, to lay aside my preconceived opinions and predisposition in his favor, and I have conscientiously gone over the immense mass of material bearing upon him, *de novo*, in an attempt to be absolutely and strictly impartial. Perhaps I have not altogether succeeded, but if it be found that I have erred in Jones' favor, I shall be glad that I have followed the impulses of affection rather than those of depreciation. I have not, I trust, been blind to the faults in the character of the great sailor, nor to the mistakes he committed, nor to the wrongdoings in his career to which I have called attention; but, in spite of these things, which I have most reluctantly recorded, I am happy that renewed investigation, careful study, and much thought have only endeared him the more to me. I lay down the pen with a higher respect, with a more affectionate regard, with a greater admiration for him than ever.

In Miss Seawell's fine phrase, "It may be said of him as of the great Condé: 'This man was born a captain.'" His place among the great sea kings as a strategist, a tactician, and a fighter is now unquestioned by the most calumnious of his defamers; but the wound he inflicted upon British pride still rankles after the lapse of more than a century, and his professional status and personal character are still bitterly aspersed. So doth prejudice blind the eyes of truth. I have devoted some space to the old charge that he was a pirate, which was renewed recently in an article in the London Academy, one of the leading journals of England, and I trust that the reader will find that I have finally disposed of that absurd statement, and the other slanders concerning him, in these pages. And I have tried to be fair to the enemy as well.

Wherever it has been possible, without clogging the narrative or letting it assume the form of a mere collection of letters, Paul the sailor, like Paul the Apostle, hath been permitted to speak for himself. Contrary to some of his biographers, I have made it a rule to accept Jones' own statements unless they were controverted by adequate evidence. It is proper to call attention to the fact that the intent of the series, of which this is one, which deals primarily with the subjects of the different volumes as great commanders, naturally emphasizes their public exploits rather than their private life. This will account for a lack of amplification in certain directions, and for the omission of details of certain periods of his life which, were the circumstances other than they are, would probably be treated of at greater length. However, it is believed that enough appears in the pages to complete the picture and exhibit the man.

There is a great amount of matter available for the study of his life, in the shape of lives, essays, sketches, and general histories, and contemporary memoirs, and an immense mass of manuscript reports and correspondence, and Jones himself left several interesting accounts of his career and services, which are of great value to his biographers. I have freely used all sources of information to which I could gain access, and they have not been few. It will be only justice, however, if I acknowledge that among the authorities consulted I have found the excellent life by Commodore Alexander Slidell Mackenzie, U. S. N., published in 1841, the most useful. Mackenzie was an officer and seaman of wide experience and fine talents, whose life covered the period of our naval development succeeding the War of 1812, and his comments from a sailor's point of view are instructive and invaluable. His work is marred by an unfortunate bias against Jones, which appears in several instances; in a desire to be accurate and just he has gone to a censurable extreme. Two other books have been most helpful: the life by John Henry Sherburne, sometime Register of the United States Navy, published in 1825, with its valuable collection of reports of participants in different actions, and statements and official documents not otherwise preserved; and the life compiled from the manuscript furnished by Miss Janette Taylor, a niece of the great commodore, published in 1830. I may also add that I have found Captain Mahan's admirable papers upon the subject, in Scribner's Magazine, of great value. Indeed, there are facts, observations, and deductions in these articles which appear nowhere else, so sure is the touch of a genius for historical accuracy and investigation like his. Among other essayists, Miss Molly Elliott Seawell, whose facile pen has done so much to exploit our early naval heroes, has written a notable and interesting paper which appeared in the Century Magazine; while Professor John Knox Laughton, the English naval expert, in his celebrated but scandalous and utterly unjustifiable attack, gives us a modern British estimate of the commodore. I shall pay my respects to his contribution later. No extended life has been published for fifty years.

My thanks are due to General Horace Porter and the Honorable Charlemagne Tower, LL.D., ambassadors of the United States to France and Russia respectively, for investigations in answers to inquiries, and for suggestions; to Dr. Talcott Williams, of Philadelphia, for valuable suggestions as to sources of possible information; to the Rev. Dr. William Elliot Griffis, of Ithaca, New York, for much interesting matter connected with the Baron van der Capellen, for unpublished manuscript notes on North Holland, the Helder, and the Texel, and for the rare copy of the old Dutch song, "Hir komt Pauwel Jones aan," which appears in the appendix; to Lieutenant-General O. V.

Stubendorff, Chief of the Topographical Section of the Imperial Russian General Staff, and to Major-General E. Sarantchof, of the Russian army, for maps, reports, and other data concerning the campaign on the Dnieper-Liman, not accessible in any American books; to Mr. Charles T. Harbeck, of New York, for generous permission to make use of rare books and pamphlets relating to Paul Jones in his valuable collection of Americana; to Messrs. W. M. Cumming and Junius Davis, of Wilmington, N. C., and Mrs. A. I. Robertson, of Columbia, S. C., for information concerning the assumption of the name of Jones by John Paul, not hitherto published in book form; to Mr. E. G. McCollin and the Misses Mabel S. Meredith, Edith Lanigan, and Bertha T. Rivailles for much important work in translation; and to Miss Isabel Paris for invaluable assistance in transcribing the manuscript.

Lest any of the above should be involved in possible criticisms which may be made of the book, I beg to close this preface with the assurance that for everything which follows I alone am responsible.

CYRUS TOWNSEND BRADY.

PHILADELPHIA, PA., *July, 1900.*

CHAPTER I.

ANCESTRY—BIRTH—EARLY YEARS—PROFESSION—SUCCESS
—CHANGE OF NAME.

Of the three great captains whose magnificent fighting has added such glorious chapters to the history of our naval campaigns, but one, George Dewey, the last of them all, is purely an American by birth and generations of ancestors. Farragut, the greatest of the three, was but one remove from a Spaniard. John Paul Jones, first of the group in point of time and not inferior to the others in quality and achievement, was a Scotsman. Only the limitation in means necessitated by the narrow circumstances of his adopted country during his lifetime prevented his surpassing them all. He remains to this day a unique character among the mighty men who trod the deck and sailed the ocean—a strange personality not surpassed by any in the long line of sea fighters from Themistocles to Sampson. In spite of, nay, because of, his achievements, he was among the most calumniated of men. What follows is an attempt to tell his story and to do him justice.

Near the close of the fifth decade of the eighteenth century, George I reigned in England, by the grace of God and because he had succeeded in putting down the rebellion of 1745; Frederick the Great was tenaciously clutching the fair province of Silesia which Maria Theresa, with equal resolution but with faint prospect of success, was endeavoring to retain; Louis XV (the well beloved!) was exploiting the privileges and opportunities of a king with Madame de Pompadour and the *Parc aux Cerfs*; and the long war of the Austrian succession was just drawing to a close, when there was born on July 6, 1747, to a Scots peasant, named John Paul, and to Jean MacDuff, his wife, a son, the fifth child of a large family.[1]

The youngster was duly christened John Paul, Junior, after his sire. He is the hero of this history. He first saw the light on the estate of Arbigland, in the parish of Kirkbean, in the county of Kirkcudbright, a province once called the Royal Stewartry of Kirkcudbright (pronounced "Kircoobree"), because it had been governed formerly by a steward or deputy, appointed by the crown, of which the county had been an appanage.

The father of the subject of this memoir filled the modest situation of a master gardener, a precursor of the modern and scientific landscape gardener, or engineer, in a small scale, in the employ of a Scots bonnet laird named Craik. His remote family—peasants, yeomen always—had come from the ancient lands of the Thanes of Fife, whence his grandfather had removed to Leith, where he kept a mail garden or wayside inn—in short, a tavern. It is to the credit of Master John Paul, Senior—evidently a most honest and capable man in that humble station in life into which it had pleased God to call him— that he forsook the tavern and clung to the garden. When he had finished his apprenticeship as gardener he removed to Arbigland, where he married Jean MacDuff, the daughter of a sturdy yeoman farmer of the neighboring parish of New Abbey, whose family had been established in their present location from time immemorial.

The marriage was blessed with seven children, the two youngest sons dying in infancy. The first was a boy named William; the next three were girls, named Elizabeth, Janet, and Mary Ann; and the fifth and last, considering the death of the infants, the boy named John, after his father. *En passant*, there must have been something favorable to the development of latent possibilities in gardeners' sons in that corner of Scotland, for in the neighboring county of Ayr, a few years later was born of similar bucolic stock the son of another tiller of the soil, known to fame as Robbie Burns!

The cottage in which young Paul made his first appearance was a little stone building in a verdant glade in a thriving wood hard by the north shore of the Solway. In front of the cottage whose whitewashed walls were in full view of the ships which entered the Firth there was a patch of greensward. The country of that section of bonnie Scotland in which is the parish of Arbigland is rugged and broken. To the east and to the west, huge, craggy mountains shut in a thickly wooded plateau, diversified by clear, rapid streams abounding in fish. The fastnesses in the hills even then were covered with romantic ruins of decayed strongholds of feudal times, reminiscent of the days of the Black Douglasses and their men. The coast line, unusually stern and bold, is broken by many precipitous inlets, narrow and deep. At the foot of the cliffs at low tide broad stretches of sand are exposed to view, and the rapid rise of the tide makes these shelving beaches dangerous places upon which to linger. The water deepens abruptly beyond the beaches, and vessels under favorable circumstances are enabled to approach near the shore.

Amid such scenes as these the childhood of young Paul was passed. Like every thrifty Scots boy of the period, he had plenty of work to do in assisting his mother and father. The life of a Scots peasant of that time was one of hard and incessant toil; his recreations were few, his food meager, his opportunities limited, and the luxuries absent. Young John Paul ate his porridge and did his work like the rest. It would probably now be considered a sad and narrow life, which the stern and rigid austerity of the prevailing form of Calvinism did nothing to lighten. That gloomy religion, however, did produce men.

It was the parish school which shaped and molded the minds of the growing Scots, and it was the Kirk which shaped and directed the schools, and the one was not more thorough than the other. I doubt if anywhere on earth at that day was the standard of education among the common people higher and more universally reached than in Scotland. During the short school year Paul was sent religiously to the nearest parish school, where he was well grounded in the rudiments of solid learning with the thoroughness which made these little schools famous. No demands of labor were allowed to interfere with the claims of education. On Sunday he was religiously and regularly marched to the kirk to be duly inducted into the mysteries of the catechism, and thoroughly indoctrinated with the theory of predestination and its rigorous concomitants.

Of him, as of other boys, it is veraciously stated that he conceived a great fondness for the sea, and it is related that all his plays were of ships and sailors—a thing easily understood when it is remembered that his most impressionable hours were spent in sight and sound of the great deep, and that the white sails of ships upon the horizon were quite as familiar a picture to his youthful vision as the tree-clad hills and valleys of his native land. It is evident that he had no fancy for the garden. A man of action he, from his bib-and-tucker days. His chroniclers have loved to call attention to the fact that even as a lad he manifested the spirit of one born to rule, for in the sports and games it was his will which dominated his little group of comrades—and the Scotsman, even when he is a child, is not easily dominated, be it remembered. His was a healthy, vigorous boyhood.

His desire for the sea must have been stronger than the evanescent feeling which finds a place sooner or later in the life of most boys, for in 1759, with the full consent of his parents, he crossed the Solway to Whitehaven, the principal port of the Firth, where he was regularly bound apprentice to a merchant named Younger, who was engaged in the American trade. He was immediately sent to sea on the ship Friendship, Captain Benson, and at the tender age of twelve years he made his first voyage to the new land toward whose freedom and independence he was afterward destined to contribute so much. The destination of the ship happened to be the Rappahannock River. As it fortunately turned out, his elder brother, William, had some years before migrated to Virginia, where he had married and settled at Fredericksburg, and by his industry and thrift finally amassed a modest fortune. Young Paul at once conceived a great liking for America which never faltered; long afterward he stated that he had been devoted to it from his youth.

The ship duties in port not being arduous, the young apprentice, through the influence of his brother, was permitted to spend the period of the vessel's stay in America on shore under the roof of his kinsman. There he continued his studies with that zeal for knowledge which was one of his distinguishing characteristics, and which never left him in after life; for it is to be noted that he was always a student; indeed, had he not been so, his subsequent career would have been impossible. It was largely that habit of application, early acquired, that enabled him to advance himself beyond his original station. He especially applied himself to the science of navigation, the intricacies of which he speedily mastered, so that he became subsequently one of the most expert navigators that sailed the sea.

His natural inclination for the sea stood him in good stead, and he finally acquired a complete knowledge of the details of his trying profession. Upon the failure of Mr. Younger, who surrendered the indentures of young Paul to him as the only thing he could do for him in his present circumstances, he was sufficiently capable to receive an appointment as third mate on the slaver King George, of Whitehaven. A few years after, in 1766, being then but nineteen years of age, he was appointed to the most responsible position of chief mate of the slaver Two Friends, a brigantine of Jamaica. The contrast between the old and the new *régime* is brought vividly before us when we learn that to-day a cadet midshipman—the lowest naval rank at present—of the same age has still a year of schooling to undergo before he can even undertake the two years' probationary cruise at sea required before he can be commissioned in the lowest grade.

Slave trading was a popular and common vocation in that day, not reprehended as it would be at present. Gentlemen of substance and station did not scruple to engage in it, either as providing money and receiving profit, or as actually participating as master or supercargo of ships in the traffic. It is interesting to note that young Paul, as he grew in years and acquired character, became intensely dissatisfied with slaving. The sense of the cruelties, iniquities, and injustice of the trade developed in him with coming manhood, and gradually took such possession of him that, as was stated by his relatives and himself, he finally resolved to withdraw from it.

This determination, scarcely to be expected from one of his birth and circumstances, was greatly to his credit. The business itself was a most stirring and lucrative one, and for a young man to have attained the rank he enjoyed so early in life was evidence that he need have no fear but that the future would bring him further advancement and corresponding pecuniary reward. In this decision he was certainly in advance of his time as well; but that love of liberty which had been bred in him by the free air of the bold hills of his native land, and which afterward became the master passion of his life, for which he drew his sword, was undoubtedly heightened and intensified by this close personal touch with the horrors of involuntary servitude.

In the year 1768, therefore, giving up his position on the Two Friends, he sailed as a passenger in the brigantine John, bound for Kirkcudbright. It happened that the captain and mate of the vessel both died of fever during the voyage, and at the request of the crew Paul assumed command and brought the vessel safely to her port. Currie, Beck & Co., the owners of the John, were so pleased with this exploit that they appointed young Paul master and supercargo of the vessel, in which he made two voyages to the West Indies. He was a captain, therefore, and a merchant at the age of twenty-one. The owners of the John dissolved partnership on the completion of his second voyage, and disposed of the ship, giving Paul the following honorable certificate upon his discharge from their employ:

"These do certify to whom it may concern, that the bearer, Captain John Paul, was two voyages master of a vessel called the John, in our employ in the West India trade, during which time he approved himself every way qualified both as a navigator and supercargo; but as our present firm is dissolved, the vessel was sold, and of course he is out of our employ, all accounts between him and the owners being amicably adjusted. Certified at Kirkcudbright this 1st April, 1771.

"CURRIE, BECK & CO."

One incident in his West Indian service is worthy of mention, because it afterward crept out in a very ugly manner. On the second voyage of the John the carpenter, a man named Mungo Maxwell, formerly of Kirkcudbright, who had been mutinous, was severely flogged by the order of Paul. Maxwell was discharged at the island of Tobago. He immediately caused Paul to be summoned before the judge of the vice-admiralty court for assault. The judge, after hearing the testimony and statement of Captain Paul, dismissed the complaint as frivolous. Maxwell subsequently entered on a Barcelona packet, and in a voyage of the latter ship from Tobago to Antigua died of a fever. Out of this was built up a calumny to the effect that Maxwell had been so badly punished by Paul that he died from his injuries. When Paul was in the Russian service years afterward the slander was enhanced by the statement that Maxwell was his nephew. There was nothing whatever in the charge.

After his retirement from the command of the John he engaged in local trading with the Isle of Man. It has been charged that he was a smuggler during this period; but he specifically and vehemently denied the allegation, and it is certain that the first entry of goods shipped from England to the Isle of Man, after it was annexed to the crown, stands in his name on the custom-house books of the town of Douglas. Soon after this he commanded a ship, the Betsy, of London, in the West India trade, in which he engaged in mercantile speculations on his own account at Tobago and Grenada, until the year 1773, when he went to Virginia again to take charge of the affairs of his brother William, who had died intestate, leaving neither wife nor children.

Very little is known of his life from this period until his entry into the public service of the United States. From remarks in his journal and correspondence, it is evident, in spite of his brother's property, to which he was heir, and some other property and money which he had amassed by trading, which was invested in the island of Tobago, West Indies, that he continued for some time in very straitened circumstances. He speaks of having lived for nearly two years on the small sum of fifty pounds. It is probable that his poverty was due to his inability to realize upon his brother's estate, and the difficulty of getting a return of his West Indian investments, on account of the unsettled political conditions, though they were of considerable value. During this period, however, he took that step which has been a puzzle to so many of his biographers, and which he never explained in any of his correspondence that remains. He came to America under the name of John Paul; he reappeared after this period of obscurity under the name of John Paul Jones.

It is claimed by the descendants of the Jones family of North Carolina that while in Fredericksburg the young mariner made the acquaintance of the celebrated Willie (pronounced Wylie) Jones, one of the leading attorneys and politicians of North Carolina. Jones and his brother Allen were people of great prominence and influence in that province. It was Jones' influence, by the way, which in later years postponed the ratification of the proposed Constitution of the United States by North Carolina. Willie Jones seems to have attended to the legal side of Paul's claims to his deceased brother's estate, and a warm friendship sprang up between the two young men, so dissimilar in birth and breeding, which, it is alleged, ended in an invitation to young Paul to visit Jones and his brother on their plantations.

The lonely, friendless little Scotsman gratefully accepted the invitation—the society of gentle people always delighted him; he ever loved to mingle with great folk throughout his life—and passed a long period at "The Grove," in Northampton County, the residence of Willie, and at "Mount Gallant," in Halifax County, the home of Allen. While there, he was thrown much in the society of the wife of Willie Jones, a lady noted and remembered for her graces of mind and person, and who, by the way, made the famous answer to Tarleton's sneer—wholly unfounded, of course—at the gallant Colonel William A. Washington for his supposed illiteracy. Morgan and Washington had defeated Tarleton decisively at the Cowpens, and in the course of the action Washington and Tarleton had met in personal encounter. Washington had severely wounded Tarleton in the hand. The Englishman had only escaped capture by prompt flight and the speed of his horse. "Washington," said the sneering partisan to Mrs. Jones, "why, I hear he can't even write his name!" "No?" said the lady quietly and interrogatively, letting her eyes fall on a livid scar across Tarleton's hand, "Well, he can make his mark, at any rate."

The Jones brothers were men of culture and refinement. They were Eton boys, and had completed their education by travel and observation in Europe. That they should have become so attached to the young sailor as to have made him their guest for long periods, and cherished the highest regard for him subsequently, is an evidence of the character and quality of the man. Probably for the first time in his life Paul was introduced to the society of refined and cultivated people. A new horizon opened before him, and he breathed, as it were, another atmosphere. Life for him assumed a different complexion. Always an interesting personality, with his habits of thought, assiduous study, coupled with the responsibilities of command, he needed but a little contact with gentle people and polite society to add to his character those graces of manner which are the final crown of the gentleman, and which the best of his contemporaries have borne testimony he did not lack. The impression made upon him by the privilege of this association was of the deepest, and he gave to his new friends, and to Mrs. Jones especially, a warm-hearted affection and devotion amounting to veneration.

It is not improbable, also, that in the society in which he found himself—and it must be remembered that North Carolina was no less fervidly patriotic, no less desirous of independence, than Massachusetts: it was at Mecklenburg that the first declaration took place—the intense love of personal liberty and independence in his character which had made him abandon the slave trade was further developed, and that during this period he finally determined to become a resident of the new land; a resolution that made him cast his lot with the other colonists when the inevitable rupture came about.

It is stated that in view of this determination on his part to begin life anew in this country, and as a mark of the affection and gratitude he entertained for the family of his benefactors, he assumed the name of Jones. It was a habit in some secluded parts of Scotland and in Wales to take the father's Christian name as a surname also, and this may have been in his mind at the time. He did not assume the name of Jones, however, out of any disregard for his family or from any desire to disguise himself from them, for, although he last saw them in 1771, he ever continued in correspondence with them, and found means, whatever his circumstances, to make them frequent remittances of money during his busy life. To them he left all his property at his death. It is certain, therefore, that for no reason for which he had cause to be ashamed did he affix the name of Jones to his birth name, and it may be stated that whatever name he took he honored. Henceforth in this volume he will be known by the name which he made so famous.[2]

One other incident of this period is noteworthy. During his visit to North Carolina he was introduced by the Jones brothers to Joseph Hewes, of Edenton, one of the delegates from North Carolina to the first and second Provincial Congresses, and a signer of the great Declaration of Independence. In Congress Hewes was a prominent member of the Committee on Naval Affairs, upon which devolved the work of beginning and carrying on the navy of the Revolution. When the war broke out Paul Jones was still living in Virginia. But when steps were taken to organize a navy for the revolted colonies, attracted by the opportunities presented in that field of service in which he was a master, and glad of the chance for maintaining a cause so congenial to his habit of life and thought, he formally tendered his services to his adopted country. The influence of Willie Jones and Hewes was secured, and on the 7th of December, 1775, Jones was appointed a lieutenant in the new Continental navy.

Additional note on the assumption of the name of Jones.

Mr. Augustus C. Buell, in his exhaustive and valuable study of Paul Jones, published since this book was written, states that the name was assumed by him in testamentary succession to his brother, who had added the name of Jones at the instance of a wealthy planter named William Jones, who had adopted him. Mr. Buell's authority rests on tradition and the statements made by Mr. Louden, a great-grandnephew of the commodore (since dead), and of the sometime owner of the Jones plantation. On the other hand, in addition to the letters quoted in the Appendix, I have received many others from different sources, tending to confirm the version given by me. Among them is one from a Fredericksburg antiquarian, who claims that William Paul never bore the name of Jones in Fredericksburg. General Cadwallader Jones (who died in 1899, aged eighty-six), in a privately published biography, also states explicitly that he heard the story from Mrs. Willie Jones herself. Mr. Buell, in a recent letter to me, calls attention to the fact—and it is significant—that absolutely no reference to the North Carolina claim appears in any extant letter of the commodore, and claims that

Hewes and Jones were acquainted before John Paul settled in America. As the official records have all been destroyed, the matter of the name will probably never be absolutely determined.

CHAPTER II.

COMMISSIONED IN THE NAVY—HOISTS THE FIRST FLAG— EXPEDITION TO NEW PROVIDENCE—ENGAGEMENT WITH THE GLASGOW.

The honor of initiative in the origin of the American navy belongs to Rhode Island, a doughty little State which, for its area, possesses more miles of seaboard than any other. On Tuesday, October 3, 1775, the delegates from Rhode Island introduced in the Continental Congress a resolution which had been passed by the General Assembly of the province on August 26th of the same year, in which, among other things, the said delegates were instructed to "use their whole influence, at the ensuing Congress, for building, at the Continental expense, a fleet of sufficient force for the protection of these colonies, and for employing them in such manner and places as will most effectually annoy our enemies, and contribute to the common defense of these colonies."

Consideration of the resolution was twice postponed, but it was finally discussed on the 7th of October and referred to a committee. On the 13th of October the committee reported, and Congress so far accepted the Rhode Island suggestion that the following resolution was passed:

"*Resolved*, That a swift sailing vessel, to carry ten carriage guns and a proportionate number of swivels with eighty men, be fitted with all possible dispatch for a cruise of three months, and that the commander be instructed to cruise eastward for intercepting such transports as may be laden with warlike stores and other supplies for our enemies, and for such other purposes as the Congress shall direct." Another vessel was also ordered fitted out for the same purpose.

Messrs. Deane, Langden, and Gadsden were appointed a committee to carry out the instructions embodied in the resolution. When the committee submitted a report, on the 30th of October, it was further resolved "that the second vessel ordered to be fitted out on the 13th inst. be of such size as to carry fourteen guns and a proportionate number of swivels and men." Two other vessels were also ordered to be put into service, one to carry not more than twenty and the other not more than thirty-six guns, "for the protection and defense of the United Colonies, as the Congress shall direct."

This may be considered as the real and actual beginning of the American navy. There had been numerous naval encounters between vessels of war of the enemy and private armed vessels acting under the authority of the various colonies; and Washington himself, with the approval of the Congress, which passed some explicit resolutions on the subject on October 5th, had made use of the individual colonial naval forces, and had issued commissions to competent men empowering them to cruise and intercept the transports and other vessels laden with powder and supplies for the enemy, but no formal action looking to the creation of a regular naval force had been taken heretofore.

Congress had long clung to the hope of reconciliation with the mother country, and had been exceedingly loath to take the radical step involved in the establishment of a navy, for in the mind of the Anglo-Saxon, who always claimed supremacy on the sea, a navy is primarily for offense. To constitute a navy for defense alone is to invite defeat. Aggression and initiative are of the essence of success in war on the sea. Now, in the peculiar condition in which the United Colonies found themselves, a naval force could be used for no other purpose than offense. The capacity of any navy which the colonies could hope to create, for defensive warfare, would be so slender as to be not worth the outlay, and the creation of a navy to prey upon the enemy's commerce and to take such of his armed vessels as could be overcome would controvert the fiction that we were simply resisting oppression. It would be making war in the most unmistakable way.

It is a singular thing that men have been willing to do, or condone the doing of, things on land which they have hesitated to do or condone on the sea. The universal diffusion of such sentiments is seen in the absurdly illogical contention on the part of the British Government subsequently, that, although a soldier on land was a rebel, he could be treated as a belligerent; while a man who stood in exactly the same relation to the King of England whose field of action happened to be the sea was of necessity a pirate.

At any rate, by the acts of Congress enumerated, a navy was assembled, and the plan of Rhode Island was adopted. It was Rhode Island, by the way, which, by preamble and resolution, sundered its allegiance to Great Britain just two months to a day before the Declaration of Independence. To the naval committee already constituted, Stephen Hopkins, Richard Henry Lee, John Adams, and Joseph Hewes were soon added. The committee at once undertook the work of carrying out the instructions they had received. On the 5th of November they selected for the command of the proposed navy Esek Hopkins, of Rhode Island, a brother of the famous Stephen Hopkins who was a member of the committee and one of the most influential members of the Congress. Other officers were commissioned from time to time as selections were made, and commissions and orders were issued to them by the committee, subject, of course, to the ratification or other action by the Congress. Paul Jones' commission as a lieutenant, as has been stated, was dated the 7th of December, 1775.

Esek Hopkins, who was born in 1718, was therefore fifty-seven years of age. He had been a master mariner for thirty years. He was a man of condition and substance who had traded in his own ships in all the then visited parts of the globe. As a commander of privateers and letters of marque he was not without experience in arms. He had been created a brigadier general of the Rhode Island militia on the threatened outbreak of hostilities, a position he resigned to take command of the navy. On the 22d of December Congress confirmed the nomination of Hopkins as commander-in-chief, and regularly appointed the following officers:

Captains:	Dudley Saltonstall, Abraham Whipple, Nicholas Biddle, John Burroughs Hopkins.	First Lieutenants:	John Paul Jones, Rhodes Arnold, — Stansbury, Hoysted Hacker, Jonathan Pitcher.
Second Lieutenants:	Benjamin Seabury, Joseph Olney, Elisha Warner, Thomas Weaver, — McDougall.	Third Lieutenants:	John Fanning, Ezekiel Burroughs, Daniel Vaughan.

These were, therefore, the forerunners of that long line of distinguished naval officers who have borne the honorable commission of the United States.

In addition to the regular course pursued, other action bearing upon the subject of naval affairs was had. On Saturday, November, 25th, Congress, enraged by the burning of Falmouth, adopted radical resolutions, looking toward the capture and confiscation of armed British vessels and transports, directing the issuance of commissions to the captains of cruisers and privateers, and creating admiralty courts and prescribing a scheme for distributing prize money. On November 28th resolutions prescribing "Regulations for the Government of the Navy of the United Colonies" were adopted, the first appearance of that significant phrase in the records, by the way.

On December 5th the seizure of merchant vessels engaging in trade between the Tories of Virginia and the West Indies under the inspiration of Lord Dunmore, was ordered. On December 11th a special committee to devise ways and means for "furnishing these colonies with a naval armament" was appointed. Two days later the report of the committee was adopted, and thirteen ships were ordered built, five of thirty-two, five of twenty-eight, and three of twenty-four guns. They were to be constructed one in New Hampshire, two in Massachusetts, one in Connecticut, two in Rhode Island, two in New York, four in Pennsylvania, and one in Maryland; the maximum cost of each of them was sixty-six thousand six hundred and sixty-six dollars and sixty-six and two thirds cents. They had a fine idea of accuracy in the construction corps of that day.

But, while Congress had been therefore preparing to build the navy, the regular marine committee had not been idle. By strenuous effort the committee assembled a squadron. A merchant vessel called the Black Prince, which had lately arrived from London under the command of John Barry (afterward a famous American commodore), was purchased and renamed the Alfred, after King Alfred the Great, who is commonly believed to be the founder of the British navy. She was a small, stanch trading vessel, very heavily timbered, and with unusually stout scantlings for a ship of her class, although of course not equal to a properly constructed ship of war. The committee armed her with twenty 9-pounders on the main deck, and four smaller guns, possibly 6- or 4-pounders, on the forecastle and poop, and she was placed under the command of Captain Dudley Saltonstall. Jones, whose name stood first on the list of first lieutenants, was appointed her executive officer. Hopkins selected her for his flagship. Jones had been offered the command of one of the smaller vessels of the squadron, but elected to fill his present station, as presenting more opportunities for acquiring information and seeing service. His experience in armed vessels had been limited; he knew but little of the requirements of a man-of-war, and deemed he could best fit himself for that higher command to which he aspired and determined to deserve by beginning his service under older and more experienced officers— a wise decision.

The next important vessel was another converted merchantman, originally called the Sally, now named the Columbus, after the great discoverer. She was a full-rigged ship of slightly less force and armament than the Alfred, commanded by Captain Abraham Whipple, already distinguished in a privateering way. In addition to these there were two brigs called the Andrea

Doria and the Cabot, commanded by Captains Nicholas Biddle and John Burroughs Hopkins, a son of the commander-in-chief. The Andrea Doria and Cabot carried fourteen 4-pounders each.

Hopkins arrived at Philadelphia in December, 1775, in the brig Katy, of the Rhode Island navy, which was at once taken into the Continental service and renamed the Providence, after the commander's native town. She carried twelve light guns, 4-pounders. There were also secured a ten-gun schooner called the Hornet, and the Wasp and Fly, two eight-gun schooners or tenders, one of which Jones had refused. The work of outfitting these ships as generously as the meager resources of the colonies permitted had been carried on assiduously before the arrival of the commander-in-chief, whose first duty, when he reached Philadelphia, was formally to assume the command.

This assumption of command entailed the putting of the ships in commission by publicly reading the orders appointing the commodore, and assigning him to command, and hoisting and saluting the flags. The officers previously appointed had been proceeding somewhat irregularly, doubtless, by going on with their preparations prior to this important ceremony. At any rate, in the latter part of December, 1775, or the early part of January, 1776— the date not being clear, the authorities not only differing, but in no single case venturing upon a definite statement—all things having been made ready, Commodore Hopkins with his staff officers entered the commodore's barge, lying at the foot of Walnut Street, and was rowed to the flagship. The wharves and houses facing the river were crowded with spectators to witness so momentous a ceremony as the commissioning of the first American fleet.

It has been recorded that it was a bright, cold, clear winter morning. The barge picked its way among the floating ice cakes of the Delaware, and finally reached the Alfred. The commodore mounted the side, followed by his staff, and was received with due honors in the gangway by the captain and his officers in such full dress as they could muster. The crew and the marines were drawn up in orderly ranks in the waist and on the quarter deck. After the reading of the commodore's commission and the orders assigning him to the command of the fleet, Captain Dudley Saltonstall nodded his head to John Paul Jones, his executive officer. The young Scotsman, with, I imagine, a heart beating rarely, stepped forward and received from the veteran quartermaster the end of the halliards, to which, in the shape of a neatly rolled-up ball, was bent a handsome yellow silk flag, bearing the representation of a rattlesnake about to strike (and perhaps a pine tree also), with the significant legend "Don't tread on me." With his own hands the young lieutenant hauled the rolled-up ensign to the masthead, and then, with a slight twitch, he broke the stops and there blew out in the morning breeze, before the eyes of the commodore, his officers, the men of the ships, and the delighted spectators on shore, the first flag that ever flew from a regularly commissioned war ship of the United Colonies. The grand union flag, a red and white striped ensign with the English cross in the canton, was also hoisted. The flags were saluted by the booming of cannon from the batteries of the ships, and with cheers from the officers and men of the squadron and the people on the shore, and thus the transaction was completed, and the navy of the United States began to be.

The ships were slight in force, their equipments meager and deficient, and of inferior quality at best. The men had but little experience in naval warfare, and their officers scarcely much more. There were men of undoubted courage and capacity among them, however, and several to whom the profession of arms was not entirely new. At least two of them, Jones and Biddle, were to become forever famous for their fighting. Compared with the huge and splendid navy of England, the whole force was an unconsidered trifle, but it was a beginning, and not a bad one at that, as the mother country was to find out. The outfitting of the squadron was by no means complete, and, though the commodore with the others labored hard, the work proceeded slowly and with many hindrances and delays; it was never properly done. Then the ships were ice-bound in Delaware Bay, and it was not until nearly two months had elapsed that they were able to get to sea.

The principal difficulty in the rebellious colonies, from the standpoint of military affairs, was the scarcity of powder. There were guns in respectable numbers, but without powder they were necessarily useless. The powder mills of the colonies were few and far between, and their output was inadequate to meet the demand. It is now well known that although Washington maintained a bold front when he invested the British army in Boston, at times his magazines did not contain more than a round or two of powder for each of his guns. His position was a magnificent specimen of what in modern colloquialism would have been called a "bluff." There was, of course, but little powder to spare for the improvised men-of-war, and most of what they had was borrowed from the colony of Pennsylvania. To get powder was the chief end of military men then.

On February 17, 1776, the little squadron cleared the capes of the Delaware, and before nightfall had disappeared from view beneath the southeast horizon. It appears that the orders were for Hopkins to sail along the coast toward the south, disperse Dunmore's squadron, which was marauding in Virginia, pick up English coasting vessels, and capture scattered English ships cruising between Pennsylvania and Georgia to break up the colonial coasting trade and capture colonial merchantmen. But it also appears from letters of the Marine Committee that another object of the expedition was the seizure of large stores of powder and munitions of warfare which had been allowed to accumulate at New Providence, in the Bahama group, and that Hopkins sailed with much discretion as to his undertaking and the means of carrying it out. The Bahama project was maintained as a profound secret between the naval committee and its commodore, the matter not being discussed in Congress even.

With that end in view the commander-in-chief, by orders published to the fleet before its departure, appointed the island of Abaco, one of the most northerly of the Bahama group, as a rendezvous for his vessels in case they became separated by the usual vicissitudes of the sea. The scattered ships were directed to make an anchorage off the southern part of the island, and wait at least fourteen days for the other vessels to join them before cruising on their own account in such directions as in the judgment of their respective commanders would most annoy, harass, and damage the enemy.

Shortly after leaving the capes the squadron ran into a severe easterly gale off Hatteras, then, as now, one of the most dangerous points on the whole Atlantic seaboard. The ships beat up against it, and all succeeded in weathering the cape and escaping the dreaded perils of the lee shore. If lack of training prevented the officers from claiming to be naval experts, there were prime seamen among them at any rate. When the gale abated Hopkins cruised along the coast for a short time, meeting nothing of importance in the way of a ship. Rightly concluding that the fierce winter weather would have induced the enemy's vessels to seek shelter in the nearest harbors, and his cruise in that direction, if further continued, would be profitless, he squared away for the Bahamas, to carry out the second and secret part of his instructions.

It was for a long time alleged that he took this action on his own account, and one of the charges against him in the popular mind was disobedience of orders in so doing; but he was undoubtedly within his orders in the course which he took, and it is equally certain that the enterprise upon which he was about to engage was one in which more immediate profit would accrue to the colonies than in any other. He should be held not only guiltless in the matter, but awarded praise for his decision. On the 1st of March the squadron, with the exception of the Hornet and the Fly, which had parted company in the gale, reached the island of Abaco, about forty miles to the northward of New Providence.

No part of the western hemisphere had been longer known than the Bahamas. Upon one of them Columbus landed. The principal island among them, not on account of its size, which was insignificant, but because it possessed a commodious and land-locked harbor, is the island of New

Providence. No island in the great archipelago which forms the northeastern border of the Caribbean had enjoyed a more eventful history. From time immemorial it had been the haunt of the buccaneer and the pirate. From it had sailed many expeditions to ravage the Spanish Main. It had been captured and recaptured by the successive nationalities which had striven for domination in the Caribbean, and in their brutal rapacity had made a hell of every verdant tropic island which lifted itself in the gorgeous beauty peculiar to those latitudes, above the deep blue of that lambent sea. It had come finally and definitely under the English crown, and a civilized government had been established by the notorious Woodes Rogers, who was himself a sort of Jonathan Wild of the sea, but one remove—and that not a great one—from the gentry whose nests he broke up and whose ravages he had put down. It had been taken since then by the Spaniards, but had been restored to the British.

The town of Nassau, which lies upon the northern face of the island, is situated upon the side of a hill which slopes gently down toward the water. The harbor, which is sufficiently deep to accommodate vessels drawing not more than twelve feet, is formed by a long island which lies opposite the town. There are two entrances to the harbor, only one of which was practicable for large ships, though both were open for small vessels. At the ends of the harbor, commanding each entrance, two forts had been erected: Fort Montague on the east and Fort Nassau on the west. Through culpable negligence, in spite of the quantity of military stores it contained, there was not a single regular soldier on the island at that time, and no preparations for defense had been made.

It was proposed to make the descent upon the western end of the island and then march up and take the town in the rear. Paul Jones, however, in the council which was held on the Alfred before the debarkation, pointed out the greater distance which the men would have to march in that case, the alarm which would be given by the passage of the ships, and advised that a landing be effected upon the eastern end of the island, whence the attack could be more speedily delivered, and, as the ships would not be compelled to advance, no previous alarm would be given. Hopkins demurred to this plan on the ground that no safe anchorage for the ships was afforded off the eastern end. The Alfred had taken two pilots from some coasting vessels which had been captured, and from them it was learned that about ten miles away was a small key which would afford the larger vessels safe anchorage. As Hopkins hesitated to trust the pilots, Jones, at the peril of his commission, offered in conjunction with them to bring the ships up himself. His suggestions were agreed to, his offer accepted, and when the vicinity of the key was reached he took his station on the fore-topmast crosstrees of the Alfred. He had sailed in the West Indian waters many times, and was familiar with the look of the sea and the indications near the shore. With the assistance of the pilots, after a somewhat exciting passage, he succeeded in bringing all the ships to a safe anchorage. That he was willing to take the risk, and, having done so, successfully carry out the difficult undertaking, gives a foretaste of his bold and decisive character, and of his technical skill as well.

Preparations for attack were quickly made. Commodore Hopkins, having impressed some local schooners, loaded them with two hundred and fifty marines from the squadron, under the command of Captain Samuel Nichols, the ranking officer of the corps, and fifty seamen under the command of Lieutenant Thomas Weaver of the Cabot, and on March 2d the transports with this attacking force were dispatched to New Providence.[3] They were convoyed by the Providence and the Wasp, and a landing was effected under the cover of these two ships of war. Unfortunately, however, some of the other larger vessels got under way at the same time, and their appearance alarmed the town.

It never seems to have occurred to any one but Jones that the west exit from the harbor should be guarded by stationing two of the smaller vessels off the channel to close it while the rest of the squadron took care of the eastern end. It seems probable from his correspondence that he ventured upon the suggestion, for he specifically referred in condemnatory terms to the failure to do so. At any rate, if he did suggest it, and from his known capacity it is extremely likely that the obvious precaution would have occurred to him, his suggestion was disregarded, and the western pass from the harbor was left open—a fatal mistake.

The point where the expedition landed without opposition was some four and a half miles from Fort Montague. It was a bright Sunday morning when the first American naval brigade took up its march under Captain Nichols' orders. The men advanced steadily, and, though they were met by a discharge of cannon from Fort Montague, they captured the works by assault without loss, the militia garrison flying precipitately before the American advance. The marines behaved with great spirit on this occasion, as they have ever done. Instead of promptly moving down upon the other fort, however, they contented themselves during that day with their bloodless achievement, and not until the next morning did they advance to complete the capture of the place.

The inhabitants of the island were in a state of panic, and when the marines and sailors marched up to attack Fort Nassau they found it empty of any garrison except Governor Brown, who opened the gates and formally surrendered it to the Americans. During the confusion of the night Brown seems to have preserved his presence of mind, and rightly divining that the powder would be the most precious of all the munitions of warfare in his charge, he had caused a schooner which lay in the harbor to be loaded with one hundred and fifty barrels, the limit of its capacity, and before daybreak she set sail and made good her escape through the unguarded western passage. A dreadful misfortune that, which would not have occurred had Jones been in command.

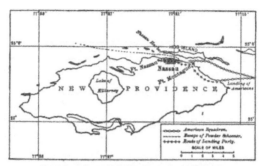

Map of attack on New Providence in the Bahamas.

However, a large quantity of munitions of war of great value to the struggling colonies fell into the hands of Hopkins' men, including eighty-eight cannon, ranging in size from 9- to 36-pounders, fifteen large mortars, over eleven thousand round shot, and twenty precious casks of powder. The Americans behaved with great credit in this conquest. None of the inhabitants of the island were harmed, nor was their property touched. It was a noble commentary on some of the British forays along our own coast. Hopkins impressed a sloop, promising to pay for its use and return it when he was through with it, which promise was faithfully kept, and the sloop was loaded with the stores, etc., which had been captured.

His own ships were also heavily laden with these military stores, the Alfred in particular being so overweighted that it was almost impossible to fight her main-deck guns, so near were they to the waterline, except in the most favorable circumstances of wind and weather.

Taking Governor Brown, who was afterward exchanged for General Lord Stirling, and one or two other officials of importance as hostages on board his fleet, Hopkins set sail for home on the 17th of March. He had done his work expeditiously and well, but through want of precaution which had been suggested by Jones, he had failed in part when his success might have been complete. Still, he was bringing supplies of great value, and his handsome achievement was an auspicious beginning of naval operations. The squadron pursued its way toward the United Colonies without any adventures or happenings worthy of chronicle until the 4th of April, when off the east end of Long Island they captured the schooner Hawk, carrying six small guns. On the 5th of April the bomb vessel Bolton, eight guns, forty-eight men, filled with stores of arms and powder, was captured without loss.

On the 6th, shortly after midnight, the night being dark, the wind gentle, the sea smooth, and the ships very much scattered, swashing along close-hauled on the starboard tack between Block Island and the Rhode Island coast, they made out a large ship, under easy sail, coming down the wind toward the squadron. It was the British sloop of war Glasgow, twenty guns and one hundred and fifty men, commanded by Captain Tyringham Howe. She was accompanied by a small tender, subsequently captured. The nearest ships of the American squadron luffed up to have a closer look at the stranger, the men being sent to quarters in preparation for any emergency. By half after two in the morning the brig Cabot had come within a short distance of her. The stranger now hauled her wind, and Captain John Burroughs Hopkins, the son of the commodore, immediately hailed her. Upon ascertaining who and what she was he promptly poured in a broadside from his small guns, which was at once returned by the formidable battery of the Glasgow. The unequal conflict was kept up with great spirit for a few moments, but the Cabot alone was no match for the heavy English corvette, and after a loss of four killed and several wounded, including the captain severely, the Cabot, greatly damaged in hull and rigging, fell away, and her place was taken by the Alfred, still an unequal match for the English vessel, but more nearly approaching her size and capacity.

The Andrea Doria now got within range and joined in the battle. For some three hours in the night the ships sailed side by side, hotly engaged. After a time the Columbus, Captain Whipple, which had been farthest to leeward, succeeded in crossing the stern of the Glasgow, and raked her as she was passing. The aim of the Americans was poor, and instead of smashing her stern in and doing the damage which might have been anticipated, the shot flew high and, beyond cutting the Englishman up aloft, did no appreciable damage. The Providence, which was very badly handled, managed to get in long range on the lee quarter of the Glasgow and opened an occasional and ineffective fire upon her. But the bulk of the fighting on the part of the Americans was done by the Alfred.

Captain Howe maneuvered and fought his vessel with the greatest skill. During the course of the action a lucky shot from the Glasgow carried away the wheel ropes of the Alfred, and before the relieving tackles could be manned and the damage repaired the American frigate broached to and was severely raked several times before she could be got under command. At daybreak Captain Howe, who had fought a most gallant fight against overwhelming odds, perceived the hopelessness of continuing the combat, and, having easily obtained a commanding lead on the pursuing Americans, put his helm up and ran away before the wind for Newport.

Hopkins followed him for a short distance, keeping up a fire from his bow-chasers, but his deep-laden merchant vessels were no match in speed for the swift-sailing English sloop of war, and, as with every moment his little squadron with its precious cargo was drawing nearer the English ships stationed at Newport, some of which had already heard the firing and were preparing to get under way, Hopkins hauled his wind, tacked and beat up for New London, where he arrived on the 8th of April with his entire squadron and the prizes they had taken, with the exception of the Hawk, recaptured.

The loss on the Glasgow was one man killed and three wounded; on the American squadron, ten killed and fourteen wounded, the loss being confined mainly to the Alfred and the Cabot, the Columbus having but one man wounded. During this action Paul Jones was stationed in command of the main battery of the Alfred. He had nothing whatever to do with the maneuvers of the ships, and was in no way responsible for the escape of the Glasgow and the failure of the American force to capture her.

The action did not reflect credit on the American arms. The Glasgow, being a regular cruiser and of much heavier armament than any of the American ships, was more than a match for any of them singly, though taken together, if the personnel of the American squadron had been equal to, or if it even approximated, that of the British ship, the latter would have been captured without difficulty. The gun practice of the Americans was very poor, which is not surprising. With the exception of a very few of the officers, none of the Americans had ever been in action, and they knew little about the fine art of hitting a mark, especially at night. They had had no exercise in target practice and but little in concerted fleet evolution. There seems to have been no lack of courage except in the case of the captain of the Providence, who was court-martialed for incapacity and cowardice, and dismissed from the service. Hopkins' judgment in withdrawing from the pursuit for the reasons stated can not be questioned, neither can he be justly charged with the radical deficiency of the squadron, though he was made to suffer for it.

While the Glasgow escaped, she did not get off scot free. She was badly cut up in the hull, had ten shot through her mainmast, fifty-two through her mizzen staysail, one hundred and ten through her mainsail, and eighty-eight through her foresail. Her royal yards were carried away, many of her spars badly wounded, and her rigging cut to pieces. This catalogue tells the story. The Americans in their excitement and inexperience had fired high, and their shot had gone over their mark. The British defense had been a most gallant one, and the first attack between the ships of the two navies had been a decided triumph for the English.

Paul Jones' conduct in the main battery of the Alfred had been entirely satisfactory to his superior officers. He, with the other officers of that ship, was commended, and subsequent events showed that he still held the confidence of the commodore.

CHAPTER III.

The British fleet having left Newport in the interim, on the 24th of April, 1776, the American squadron got under way from New London for Providence, Rhode Island. The ships were in bad condition; sickness had broken out among their crews, and no less than two hundred and two men out of a total of perhaps eight hundred and fifty—at best an insufficient complement—were left ill at New London. Their places were in a measure supplied by one hundred and seventy soldiers, lent to the squadron by General Washington, who had happened to pass through New London, *en route* to New York, on the day after Hopkins' arrival. There was a pleasant interview between the two commanders, and it was then that Jones caught his first glimpse of the great leader.

The voyage to New London was made without incident, except that the unfortunate Alfred grounded off Fisher's Island, and had to lighten ship before she could be floated. This delayed her passage so that she did not arrive at Newport until the 28th of April. The health of the squadron was not appreciably bettered by the change, for over one hundred additional men fell ill. Many of the seamen had been enlisted for the cruise only, and they now received their discharge, so that the crews of the already undermanned ships were so depleted from these causes that it would be impossible for them to put to sea. Washington, who was hard pressed for men, and had troubles of his own, demanded the immediate return to New York of the soldiers he had lent to the fleet. The captain of the Providence being under orders for a court-martial for his conduct, on the 10th of May Hopkins appointed John Paul Jones to the command of the Providence.

The appointment is an evidence of the esteem in which Jones was held by his commanding officer, and is a testimony to the confidence which was felt in his ability and skill; for he alone, out of all the officers in the squadron, was chosen for important sea service at this time. Having no blank commissions by him, Hopkins made out the new commission on the back of Jones' original commission as first lieutenant. It is a matter of interest to note that he was the first officer promoted to command rank from a lieutenancy in the American navy. His first orders directed him to take Washington's borrowed men to New York. After spending a brief time in hurriedly overhauling the brig and preparing her for the voyage, Jones set sail for New York, which he reached on the 18th of May, after thirty-six hours. Having returned the men, Jones remained at New York in accordance with his orders until he could enlist a crew, which he presently succeeded in doing. Thereafter, under supplemental orders, he ran over to New London, took on board such of the men left there who were sufficiently recovered to be able to resume their duties, and came back and reported with them to the commander-in-chief at Providence. He had performed his duties, routine though they were, expeditiously and properly.

He now received instructions thoroughly to overhaul and fit the Providence for active cruising. She was hove down, had her bottom scraped, and was entirely refitted and provisioned under Jones's skillful and practical direction. Her crew was exercised constantly at small arms and great guns, and every effort made to put her in first-class condition. In spite of the limited means at hand, she became a model little war vessel. On June 10th a sloop of war belonging to the enemy appeared off the bay, and in obedience to a signal from the commodore Jones made sail to engage. Before he caught sight of the vessel she sought safety in flight. On the 13th of June the Providence was ordered to Newburyport, Massachusetts, to convoy a number of merchant vessels loaded with coal for Philadelphia. Before entering upon this important duty, however, Jones was directed to accompany the tender Fly, loaded with cannon, toward New York, and, after seeing her safely into the Sound, convoy some merchant vessels from Stonington to Newport.

There were a number of the enemy's war vessels cruising in these frequented waters, and the carrying out of Jones' simple orders was by no means an easy task; but by address and skill, and that careful watchfulness which even then formed a part of his character, he succeeded in executing all his duties without losing a single vessel under his charge. He had one or two exciting encounters with English war ships, the details of which are unfortunately not preserved. In one instance, by boldly interposing the Providence between the British frigate Cerberus and a colonial brigantine loaded with military stores from Hispaniola, he diverted the attention of the frigate to his own vessel, and drew her away from the pursuit of the helpless merchantman, which thereby effected her escape. Then the Providence, a swift little brig admirably handled, easily succeeded in shaking off her pursuer, although she had allowed the frigate to come within gunshot range. The brigantine whose escape Jones had thus assured was purchased into the naval service and renamed the Hampden.

The coal fleet had assembled at Boston instead of Newburyport, and in pursuance of his original orders Jones brought them safely to the capes of the Delaware on the 1st of August. The run to Philadelphia was soon made, and Hopkins' appointment, under which he was acting, was ratified by the

Congress, and the commission of captain was given him, dated the 8th of August, 1776.

Hitherto Jones, like all the others engaged in the war, had been a subject of England, a colonist in rebellion against the crown. By the Declaration of Independence he had become a citizen of the United States engaged in maintaining the independence and securing the liberty of his adopted country. The change was most agreeable to him. It added a dignity and value to his commission which could not fail to be acceptable to a man of his temperament. It was pleasant to him also to have the confidence of his commander-in-chief, which had been shown in the appointment to the command of the Providence, justified by the government in the commission which had been issued to him.

Jones had made choice of his course of action in the struggle between kingdom and colony deliberately, not carried away by any enthusiasm of the moment, but moved by the most generous sentiments of liberty and independence. He had much at stake, and he was embarked in that particular profession fraught with peculiar dangers not incident to the life of a soldier. It must have been, therefore, with the greatest satisfaction that he perceived opportunities opening before him in that cause to which he had devoted himself, and in that service of which he was a master. A foreigner with but scant acquaintance and little influence in America, he had to make his way by sheer merit. The value of what has been subsequently called "a political pull" with the Congress was as well known then as it is now, and nearly as much used, too. He practically had none. Nevertheless, his foot was already upon that ladder upon which he intended to mount to the highest round eventually. He was not destined to realize his ambition, however, without a heartbreaking struggle against uncalled-for restraint, and a continued protest against active injustice which tried his very soul.

It was first proposed by the Marine Committee that he return to New England and assume command of the Hampden, but he wisely preferred to remain in the Providence for the time being. He thoroughly knew the ship and the crew, over which he had gained that ascendency he always enjoyed with those who sailed under his command. Not so much by mistaken kindness or indulgence did he win the devotion of his men—for he was ever a stern and severe, though by no means a merciless, disciplinarian—but because of his undoubted courage, brilliant seamanship, splendid audacity, and uniform success. There is an attraction about these qualities which is exercised perhaps more powerfully upon seamen than upon any other class. The profession of a sailor is one in which immediate decision, address, resource, and courage are more in evidence than in any other. The seaman in an emergency has but little time for reflection, and in the hour of peril, when the demand is made upon him, he must choose the right course instantly—as it were by instinct.

With large discretion in his orders, which were practically to cruise at pleasure and destroy the enemy's commerce, the Providence left the Delaware on the 21st of August. In the first week of the cruise she captured the brigs Sea Nymph, Favorite, and Britannia; the first two laden with rum, sugar, etc., and the last a whaler. These rich prizes were all manned and sent in.

On the morning of the 1st of September, being in the latitude of the Bermudas, five vessels were sighted to leeward. The sea was moderately smooth, with a fresh breeze blowing at the time, and the Providence immediately ran off toward the strangers to investigate. It appeared to the observers on Jones' brig that the largest was an East Indiaman and the others ordinary merchant vessels. They were in error, however, in their conclusions, for a nearer approach disclosed the fact that the supposed East Indiaman was a frigate of twenty-eight guns, called the Solebay. Jones immediately hauled his wind and clapped on sail. The frigate, which had endeavored to conceal her force with the hope of enticing the Providence under her guns, at once made sail in pursuit. The Providence was a smart goer, and so was the Solebay. The two vessels settled down for a long chase. On the wind it became painfully evident that the frigate had the heels of the brig. With burning anxiety Jones and his officers saw the latter gradually closing with them. Shot from her bow-chasers, as she came within range, rushed through the air at the little American sloop of war, which now hoisted her colors and returned the fire. Seeing this, the Solebay set an American ensign, and fired one or two guns to leeward in token of amity, but Jones was not to be taken in by any transparent ruse of this character. He held on, grimly determined. As the Solebay drew nearer she ceased firing, confident in her ability to capture the chase, for which, indeed, there appeared no escape.

An ordinary seaman, even though a brave man, would probably have given up the game in his mind, though his devotion to duty would have compelled him to continue the fight until actually overhauled, but Jones had no idea of being captured then. Already a plan of escape had developed in his fertile brain. Communicating his intentions to his officers, he completed his preparations, and only awaited the favorable moment for action. The Solebay had crept up to within one hundred yards of the lee quarter of the Providence. If the frigate yawed and delivered a broadside the brig would be sunk or crippled and captured. Now was the time, if ever, to put his plan in operation. If the maneuver failed, it would be all up with the Americans. As usual, Jones boldly staked all on the issue of the moment. As a preliminary the helm had been put slightly a-weather, and the brig allowed to fall off to leeward a little, so bringing the Solebay almost dead astern—if anything, a little to windward. In anticipation of close action, as Jones had imagined, the English captain had loaded his guns with grape shot, which, of course, would only be effective at short range. Should the Englishman get the Providence under his broadside, a well-aimed discharge of grape would clear her decks and enable him to capture the handsome brig without appreciably damaging her.

From his knowledge of the qualities of the Providence, Jones felt sure that going free—that is, with the wind aft, or on the quarter—he could run away from his pursuer. The men, of course, had been sent to their stations long since. The six 4-pounders, which constituted the lee battery, were quietly manned, the guns being double-shotted with grape and solid shot. The studding sails—light sails calculated to give a great increase in the spread of canvas to augment the speed of the ship in a light breeze, which could be used to advantage going free and in moderate winds—were brought out and prepared for immediate use. Everything having been made ready, and the men cautioned to pay strict attention to orders, and to execute them with the greatest promptitude and celerity, Jones suddenly put his helm hard up.

The handy Providence spun around on her heel like a top, and in a trice was standing boldly across the forefoot of the onrushing English frigate. When she lay squarely athwart the bows of the Solebay Jones gave the order to fire, and the little battery of 4-pounders barked out its gallant salute and poured its solid shot and grape into the eyes of the frigate. In the confusion of the moment, owing to the suddenness of the unexpected maneuver, and the raking he had received, the English captain lost his head. Before he could realize what had happened, the Providence, partially concealed by the smoke from her own guns, had drawn past him, and, covered with great wide-reaching clouds of light canvas by the nimble fingers of her anxious crew, was ripping through the water at a great rate at a right angle to her former direction.

When the Solebay, rapidly forging ahead, crossed the stern of the saucy American a few moments after, she delivered a broadside, which at that range, as the guns were loaded with grape shot, did little damage to the brig and harmed no one. The distance was too great and the guns were badly aimed. By the time the Solebay had emulated the maneuvers of the Providence and had run off, the latter had gained so great a lead that her escape was practically effected. The English frigate proved to be unable to outfoot the American brig on this course, and after firing upward of a hundred shot at her the Solebay gave over the pursuit. This escape has ever been counted one of the most daring and subtle pieces of seamanship and skill among the many with which the records of the American navy abound. As subsequent events proved, the failure to capture Jones was most unfortunate on the part of the English.

Jones now shaped his course for the Banks of Newfoundland, to break up the fishing industry and let the British know that ravaging the coast, which they had begun, was a game at which two could play. On the 16th and 17th of the month he ran into a heavy gale, so severe in character that he was forced to strike his guns into the hold on account of the rolling of the brig. The gale abated on the 19th, and on the 20th of September, the day being pleasant, the Providence was hove to and the men were preparing to enjoy a day of rest and amusement, fishing for cod, when in the morning two sail appeared to windward. As Jones was preparing to beat up and investigate them, they saved him that trouble by changing their course and running down toward him. They proved to be a merchant ship and a British frigate, the Milford, 32.

Jones kept the Providence under easy canvas until he learned the force of the enemy, and then made all sail to escape. Finding that he was very much faster than his pursuer, he amused himself during one whole day by ranging ahead and then checking his speed until the frigate would get almost within range, when he would run off again and repeat the performance. It was naturally most tantalizing to the officers of the Milford, and they vented their wrath in futile broadsides whenever there appeared the least possibility of reaching the Providence. After causing the enemy to expend a large quantity of powder and shot, having tired of the game, Jones contemptuously discharged a musket at them and sailed away.

On the 21st of September he appeared off the island of Canso, one of the principal fishing depots of the Grand Banks. He sent his boat in that night to gain information, and on the 22d he anchored in the harbor. There were three fishing schooners there, one of which he burned, one he scuttled, and the third, called the Ebenezer, he loaded with the fish taken from the two he had destroyed, and manned as a prize. After replenishing his wood and water, on the 23d he sailed up to Isle Madame, having learned that the fishing fleet was lying there dismantled for the winter. Beating to and fro with the Providence off the island, on that same evening he sent an expedition of twenty-five men in a shallop which he had captured at Canso, accompanied by a fully manned boat from the Providence. Both crews were heavily armed. The expedition captured the fishing fleet of nine vessels without loss. The crews of most of them, numbering some three hundred men, were ashore at the time, and the vessels were dismantled. Jones promised that if the men ashore would help to refit the vessels he desired to take with him as prizes, he would leave them a sufficient number of boats to enable them to regain their homes. By his ready address he actually persuaded them to comply with his request, and the unfortunate Englishmen labored assiduously to get the ships ready for sea.

On the 25th of September their preparations were completed, but a violent autumn gale blew up, and their situation became one of great peril. The Providence, anchored in Great St. Peter Channel, rode it out with two anchors down to a long scope of cable. The ship Alexander and the schooner Sea Flower, which were heavily laden with valuable plunder, had also reached the same channel. The Alexander succeeded in making an anchorage under a point of rocks which sheltered her, and enabled her to sustain the shock of the gale unharmed. The Sea Flower was driven on the lee shore, and, being hopelessly wrecked, was scuttled and fired the next day. The Ebenezer, loaded with fish from Canso, was also wrecked. The gale had abated about noon, when, after burning the ship Adventure, dismantled and in ballast, and leaving a brig and two small schooners to enable the English seamen to reach home, the Providence, accompanied by the Alexander and the brigs Kingston Packet and Success, got under way for home. On the 27th the Providence, in spite of the fact that she was now very short-handed on account of the several prizes she had manned, chased two armed transports apparently bound in for Quebec, which managed to make good their escape. The little squadron resumed its course, and arrived safely at Rhode Island without further mishap on the 7th of October.

On this remarkable cruise Jones had captured sixteen vessels, eight of which he manned and sent in as prizes, destroying five of the remainder, and generously leaving three for the unfortunate fishermen to reach their homes. He had carried out his orders to sink, burn, destroy, and capture with characteristic thoroughness, but without needless cruelty and oppression. He burned no dwelling houses, and turned no non-combatants out of their homes in the middle of winter, as Mowatt had done at Falmouth. He had entirely broken up the fishery at Canso, had escaped by the exercise of the highest seamanship from one British frigate, and had led another a merry dance in impotent pursuit. Property belonging to the enemy had been destroyed to the value of perhaps a million of dollars in round numbers, not to speak of the effect upon their pride by the bold cruising of the little brig of twelve 4-pound guns and seventy men.

CHAPTER IV.

THE CRUISE OF THE ALFRED.

When his countrymen heard the story of this daring and successful cruise, Jones immediately became the most famous officer of the new navy. The *éclat* he had gained by his brilliant voyage at once raised him from a more or less obscure position, and gave him a great reputation in the eyes of his countrymen, a reputation he did not thereafter lose. But Jones was not a man to live upon a reputation. He had scarcely arrived at Providence before he busied himself with plans for another undertaking. He had learned from prisoners taken on his last cruise that there were a number of American prisoners, at various places, who were undergoing hard labor in the coal mines of Cape Breton Island, and he conceived the bold design of freeing them if possible.

We are here introduced to one striking characteristic, not the least noble among many, of this great man. The appeal of the prisoner always profoundly touched his heart. The freedom of his nature, his own passionate love for liberty and independence, the heritage of his Scotch hills perhaps, ever made him anxious and solicitous about those who languished in captivity. It was but the working out of that spirit which compelled him to relinquish his participation in the lucrative slave trade. In all his public actions, he kept before him as one of his principal objects the release of such of his countrymen as were undergoing the horrors of British prisons.

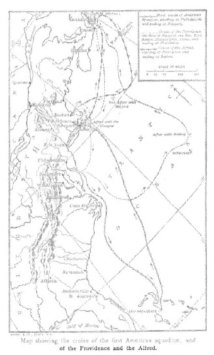

Map showing the cruise of the first American squadron,
and of the Providence and the Alfred.

Map showing the cruise of the first American squadron,
and of the Providence and the Alfred.

The suggested enterprise found favor in the mind of Commodore Hopkins, who forthwith assigned Jones to the command of a squadron comprising the Alfred, the Providence, and the brigantine Hampden. Jones hoisted his flag on board the Alfred and hastened his preparations for departure. He found the greatest difficulty in manning his little squadron, and finally, in despair of getting a sufficient crew to man them all, he determined to set sail with the Alfred and the Hampden only, the latter vessel being commanded by Captain Hoysted Hacker. He received his orders on the 22d of October, and on the 27th the two vessels got under way from Providence. The wind was blowing fresh at the time, and Hacker, who seems to have been an indifferent sailor, ran the Hampden on a ledge of rock, where she was so badly wrecked as to be unseaworthy. Jones put back to his anchorage, and, having transferred the crew of the Hampden to the Providence, set sail on the 2d of November.

Both vessels were very short-handed. The Alfred, whose proper complement was about three hundred, which had sailed from Philadelphia with two hundred and thirty-five, now could muster no more than one hundred and fifty all told. The two vessels were short of water, provisions, munitions, and everything else that goes to make up a ship of war. Jones made up for all this deficiency by his own personality.

On the evening of the first day out the two vessels anchored in Tarpauling Cove, near Nantucket. There they found a Rhode Island privateer at anchor. In accordance with the orders of the commodore, Jones searched her for deserters, and from her took four men on board the Alfred. He was afterward sued in the sum of ten thousand pounds for this action, but, though the commodore, as he stated, abandoned him in his defense, nothing came of the suit.

On the 3d of November, by skillful and successful maneuvering, the two ships passed through the heavy British fleet off Block Island, and squared away for the old cruising ground on the Grand Banks. In addition to the release of the prisoners there was another object in the cruise. A squadron of merchant vessels loaded with coal for the British army in New York was about to leave Louisburg under convoy. Jones determined to intercept them if possible.

On the 13th, off Cape Canso again, the Alfred encountered the British armed transport Mellish, of ten guns, having on board one hundred and fifty soldiers. After a trifling resistance she was captured. She was loaded with arms, munitions of war, military supplies, and ten thousand suits of winter clothing, destined for Sir Guy Carleton's army in Canada. She was the most valuable prize which had yet fallen into the hands of the Americans. The warm clothing, especially, would be a godsend to the ragged, naked army of Washington. Of so much importance was this prize that Jones determined not to lose sight of her, and to convoy her into the harbor himself. Putting a prize crew on board, he gave instructions that she was to be scuttled if there appeared any danger of her recapture.

About this time two other vessels were captured, one of which was a large fishing vessel, from which he was able to replenish his meager store of provisions. On the 14th of November a severe gale blew up from the northwest, accompanied by a violent snowstorm. Captain Hacker bore away to the southward before the storm and parted company during the night, returning incontinently to Newport. The weather continued execrable. Amid blinding snowstorms and fierce winter gales the Alfred and her prizes beat up along the desolate iron-bound shore. Jones again entered the harbor of Canso, and, finding a large English transport laden with provisions for the army aground on a shoal near the mouth of the harbor, sent a boat party which set her on fire. Seeing an immense warehouse filled with oil and material for whale and cod fisheries, the boats made a sudden dash for the shore, and, applying a torch to the building, it was soon consumed.

Beating off the shore, still accompanied by his prizes, he continued up the coast of Cape Breton toward Louisburg, looking for the coal fleet. It was his good fortune to run across it in a dense fog. It consisted of a number of vessels under the convoy of the frigate Flora, a ship which would have made short work of him if she could have run across him. Favored by the impenetrable fog, with great address and hardihood Jones succeeded in capturing no less than three of the convoy, and escaped unnoticed with his prizes.

Two days afterward he came across a heavily armed British privateer from Liverpool, which he took after a slight resistance. But now, when he attempted to make Louisburg to carry out his design of levying on the place and releasing the prisoners, he found that the harbor was closed by masses of ice, and that it was impossible to effect a landing. Indeed, his ships were in a perilous condition already. He had manned no less than six prizes, which had reduced his short crew almost to a prohibitive degree. On board the Alfred he had over one hundred and fifty prisoners, a number greatly in excess of his own men; his water casks were nearly empty, and his provisions were exhausted. He had six prizes with him, one of exceptional value. Nothing could be gained by lingering on the coast, and he decided, therefore, to return.

The little squadron, under convoy of the Alfred and the armed privateer, which he had manned and placed under the command of Lieutenant Saunders, made its way toward the south in the fierce winter weather. Off St. George's Bank they again encountered the Milford. It was late in the afternoon when her topsails rose above the horizon. The wind was blowing fresh from the northwest; the Alfred and her prizes were on the starboard tack, the enemy was to windward. From his previous experience Jones was able fairly to estimate the speed of the Milford. A careful examination convinced him that it would be impossible for the latter to close with his ships before nightfall. He therefore placed the Alfred and the privateer between the English frigate lasking down upon them and the rest of his ships, and continued his course. He then signaled the prizes, with the exception of the privateer, that they should disregard any orders or signals which he might give in the night, and hold on as they were.

The prizes were slow sailers, and, as the slowest necessarily set the pace for the whole squadron, the Milford gradually overhauled them. At the close of the short winter day, when the night fell and the darkness rendered sight of the pursued impossible, Jones showed a set of lantern signals, and, hanging a top light on the Alfred, right where it would be seen by the Englishmen, at midnight, followed by the privateer, he changed his course directly away from the prizes. The Milford promptly altered her course and pursued the light. The prizes, in obedience to their orders, held on as they were. At daybreak the prizes were nowhere to be seen, and the Milford was booming along after the privateer and the Alfred.

To run was no part of Paul Jones' desires, and he determined to make a closer inspection of the Milford, with a view to engaging if a possibility of capturing her presented itself; so he bore up and headed for the oncoming British frigate. The privateer did the same. A nearer view, however, developed the strength of the enemy, and convinced him that it would be madness to attempt to engage with the Alfred and the privateer in the condition he then was, so he hauled aboard his port tacks once more, and, signaling to the privateer, stood off again. For some reason—Jones imagined that it was caused by a mistaken idea of the strength of the Milford—Saunders signaled to Jones that the Milford was of inferior force, and disregarding his orders foolishly ran down under her lee from a position of perfect safety, and was captured without a blow. The lack of proper subordination in the nascent navy of the United States brought about many disasters, and this was one of them. Jones characterized this as an act of folly; it is difficult to dismiss it thus mildly. I would fain do no man an injustice, but if a man wanted to be a traitor that is the way he would act. Jones' own account of this adventure, which follows, is of deep interest:

"This led the Milford entirely out of the way of the prizes, and particularly the clothing ship, Mellish, for they were all out of sight in the morning. I had now to get out of the difficulty in the best way I could. In the morning we again tacked, and as the Milford did not make much appearance I was unwilling to quit her without a certainty of her superior force. She was out of shot, on the lee quarter, and as I could only see her bow, I ordered the letter of marque, Lieutenant Saunders, that held a much better wind than the Alfred, to drop slowly astern, until he could discover by a view of the enemy's side whether she was of superior or inferior force, and to make a signal accordingly. On seeing Mr. Saunders drop astern, the Milford wore suddenly and crowded sail toward the northeast. This raised in me such doubts as determined me to wear also, and give chase. Mr. Saunders steered by the wind, while the Milford went lasking, and the Alfred followed her with a pressed sail, so that Mr. Saunders was soon almost hull down to windward. At last the Milford tacked again, but I did not tack the Alfred till I had the enemy's side fairly open, and could plainly see her force. I then tacked about ten o'clock. The Alfred being too light to be steered by the wind, I bore away two points, while the Milford steered close by the wind, to gain the Alfred's wake; and by that means he dropped astern, notwithstanding his superior sailing. The weather, too, which became exceedingly squally, enabled me to outdo the Milford by carrying more sail. I began to be under no apprehension from the enemy's superiority, for there was every appearance of a severe gale, which really took place in the night. To my great surprise, however, Mr. Saunders, toward four o'clock, bore down on the Milford, made the signal of her inferior force, ran under her lee, and was taken!"

With the exception of one small vessel, which was recaptured, the prizes all arrived safely, the precious Mellish finally reaching the harbor of Dartmouth. The Alfred dropped anchor at Boston, December 15, 1776. The news of the captured clothing reached Washington and gladdened his heart— and the hearts of his troops as well—on the eve of the battle of Trenton.

The reward for this brilliant and successful cruise, the splendid results of which had been brought about by the most meager means, was an order relieving him of the command of the Alfred and assigning him to the Providence again. When he arrived at Philadelphia the next spring he found that by an act of Congress, on the 10th of October, 1776, which had created a number of captains in the navy, he, who had been first on the list of lieutenants, and therefore the sixth ranking sea officer, was now made the eighteenth captain. He was passed over by men who had no claim whatever to superiority on the score of their service to the Commonwealth, which had been inconsiderable or nothing at all. Indeed, there was no man in the country who by merit or achievement was entitled to precede him, except possibly Nicholas Biddle.

If the friendless Scotsman had commanded more influence, more political prestige, so that he might have been rewarded for his auspicious services by placing him at the head of the navy, I venture to believe that some glorious chapters in our marine history would have been written.

CHAPTER V.

SUPERSEDED IN RANK—PROTESTS VAINLY AGAINST THE INJUSTICE—ORDERED TO COMMAND THE RANGER—HOISTS FIRST AMERICAN FLAG.

The period between the termination of his last cruise and his assignment to his next important command was employed by Jones in vigorous and proper protests against the arbitrary action of Congress, which had deprived him of that position on the navy list which was his just due, were either merit, date of commission, or quality of service considered. To the ordinary citizen the question may appear of little interest, but to the professional soldier or sailor it is of the first importance. Indeed, it is impossible to conceive of properly maintaining an army or navy without regular promotion, definitive station, and adequate reward of merit. To feel that rank is temporary and position is at the will of unreasonable and irresponsible direction is to undermine service.

The same injustice drove John Stark, of New Hampshire, to resign the service with the pithy observation that an officer who could not protect his own rights was unfit to be trusted with those of his country. It did not prevent his winning the fight at Bennington, though. The same treatment caused Daniel Morgan to seek that retirement from which he was only drawn forth by his country's peril to win the Battle of the Cowpens. And, lastly, it was the same treatment which, in part at least, made Arnold a traitor. Then, as ever, Congress was continually meddling with matters of purely military administration, to the very great detriment of the service.

Jones has been censured as a jealous stickler for rank, a quibbler about petty distinctions in trying times. Such criticisms proceed from ignorance. If there were nothing else, rank means opportunity. The range of prospective enterprises is greater the higher the rank. The little Scotsman was properly tenacious of his prerogatives—we could not admire him if he were not so— and naturally exasperated by the arbitrary course of Congress, against which he protested with all the vehemence of his passionate, fiery, and—it must be confessed—somewhat irritable nature. On this subject he thus wrote to the Marine Board at Philadelphia:

"I am now to inform you that by a letter from Commodore Hopkins, dated on board the Warren, January 14, 1777, which came to my hands a day or two ago, I am superseded in the command of the Alfred, in favour of Captain Hinman, and ordered back to the sloop in Providence River. Whether this order doth or doth not supersede also your orders to me of the 10th ult. you can best determine; however, as I undertook the late expedition at his (Commodore Hopkins') request, from a principle of humanity, I mean not now to make a difficulty about trifles, especially when the good of the service is to be consulted. As I am unconscious of any neglect of duty or misconduct, since my appointment at the first as eldest lieutenant of the navy, I can not suppose that you have intended to set me aside in favour of any man who did not at that time bear a captain's commission, unless, indeed, that man, by exerting his superior abilities, hath rendered or can render more important services to America. Those who stepped forth at the first, in ships altogether unfit for war, were generally considered as frantic rather than wise men, for it must be remembered that almost everything then made against them. And although the success in the affair with the Glasgow was not equal to what it might have been, yet the blame ought not to be general. The principal or principals in command alone are culpable, and the other officers, while they stand unimpeached, have their full merit. There were, it is true, divers persons, from misrepresentation, put into commission at the beginning, without fit qualification, and perhaps the number may have been increased by later appointments; but it follows not that the gentleman or man of merit should be neglected or overlooked on their account. None other than a gentleman, as well as a seaman both in theory and practice, is qualified to support the character of a commission officer in the navy; nor is any man fit to command a ship of war who is not also capable of communicating his ideas on paper, in language that becomes his rank. If this be admitted, the foregoing operations will be sufficiently clear; but if further proof is required it can easily be produced.

"When I entered into the service I was not actuated by motives of self-interest. I stepped forth as a free citizen of the world, in defense of the violated rights of mankind, and not in search of riches, whereof, I thank God, I inherit a sufficiency; but I should prove my degeneracy were I not in the highest degree tenacious of my rank and seniority. As a gentleman I can yield this point up only to persons of superior abilities and superior merit, and under such persons it would be my highest ambition to learn. As this is the first time of my having expressed the least anxiety on my own account, I must entreat your patience until I account to you for the reason which hath given me this freedom of sentiment. It seems that Captain Hinman's commission is No. 1, and that, in consequence, he who was at first my junior officer by eight, *hath expressed himself as my senior officer* in a manner which doth himself no honour, and which doth me signal injury. There are also in the navy persons who have not shown me fair play after the service I have rendered them. I have even been blamed for the civilities which I have shown to my prisoners, at the request of one of whom I herein inclose an appeal, which I must beg leave to lay before Congress. Could you see the appellant's accomplished lady, and the innocents their children, arguments in their behalf would be unnecessary. As the base-minded only are capable of inconsistencies, you will not blame my free soul, which can never stoop where I can not also esteem. Could I, which I never can, bear to be superseded, I should indeed deserve your contempt and total neglect. I am therefore to entreat you to employ me in the most enterprising and active service, accountable to your honourable board only for my conduct, and connected as much as possible with gentlemen and men of good sense."

The letter does credit to his head and heart alike. Matter and manner are both admirable. In it he is at his best, and one paragraph shows that the generous sympathy he ever felt for a prisoner could even be extended to the enemies of his country, so that as far as he personally was concerned they should suffer no needless hardship in captivity. Considered as the production of a man whose life from boyhood had been mainly spent upon the sea in trading ships and slavers, with their limited opportunities for polite learning, and an entire absence of that refined society without which education rarely rises to the point of culture, the form and substance of Jones' letters are surprising. Of this and of most of the letters hereafter to be quoted only words of approbation may be used. A just yet modest appreciation of his own dignity, a proper and resolute determination to maintain it, a total failure to truckle to great men, an absence of sycophancy and hypocrisy, a clear insight into the requirements of a gentleman and an effortless rising to his own high standard without unpleasant self-assertion, are found in his correspondence. Considering the humble source from which he sprang, his words, written and spoken, equally with his deeds, indicate his rare qualities.

It is probable that no disposition existed in Congress to do him an injustice —quite the reverse, in fact; but the claims of the representatives of the several States, which were insistently put forth in behalf of local individuals aspiring to naval station from the various colonies in which the different ships were building, were too strong to be disregarded. The central administration was at no time sufficiently firm for a really strong government, and conciliation and temporization were necessary. It was only by the very highest quality of tact that greater difficulties were overcome, and that more glaring acts of injustice were not perpetrated. So sensible were the authorities of Jones' conduct, so valuable had been his services on his last two cruises, that while they were unable at that time, in spite of his protests, to restore him to his proper place in the list, as a concession to his ability and merit orders were given him assigning him to the command of the squadron consisting of the Alfred, Columbus, Cabot, Hampden, and Providence, to operate against Pensacola.

This was virtually creating him commander-in-chief of the naval forces, for outside the ships mentioned there were but few others worthy of consideration. Natural jealousy had, however, arisen in the mind of Hopkins, the commander-in-chief, at being thus superseded and ignored through one of his own subordinates by Congress, with which his relations had become so strained that he affected to disbelieve the validity of the order assigning Jones to this duty, and, refusing to comply therewith, retained the ships under his command. The matter thereupon fell through.

Finding all efforts to secure the squadron and carry out these orders fruitless, Jones journeyed to Philadelphia for the purpose of emphatically placing before the Marine Committee his grievances. There a further shock awaited him.

"My conduct hitherto," he writes on this subject in the memorial addressed to Congress from the Texel years after, "was so much approved of by Congress that on the 5th of February, 1777, I was appointed, with unlimited orders, to command a little squadron of the Alfred, Columbus, Cabot, Hampden, and sloop Providence. Various important services were pointed out, but I was left at free liberty to make my election. That service, however, did not take place; for the commodore, who had three of the squadron blocked in at Providence, affected to disbelieve my appointment, and would not at last give me the necessary assistance. Finding that he trifled with my applications as well as the orders of Congress, I undertook a journey from Boston to Philadelphia, in order to explain matters to Congress in person. I took this step also because Captain Hinman had succeeded me in the command of the Alfred, and, of course, the service could not suffer through my absence. I arrived at Philadelphia in the beginning of April. But what was my surprise to find that, by a new line of navy rank, which had taken place on the 10th day of October, 1776, all the officers that had stepped forth at the beginning were superseded! I was myself superseded by thirteen men, not one of whom did (and perhaps some of them durst not) take the sea against the British flag at the first; for several of them who were then applied to refused to venture, and none of them has since been very happy in proving their superior abilities. Among these thirteen there are individuals who can neither pretend to parts nor education, and with whom, as a private gentleman, I would disdain to associate.

"I leave your excellency and the Congress to judge how this must affect a man of honour and sensibility.

"I was told by President Hancock that what gave me so much pain had been the effect of a multiplicity of business. He acknowledged the injustice of that regulation, said it should make but a nominal and temporary difference, and that in the meantime I might assure myself that no navy officer stood higher in the opinion of Congress than myself."

The complete news of his displacement and supersession in rank does not appear to have reached him before this. His efforts to secure the restoration of his rank proving useless, he applied for immediate sea duty. The next attempt on the part of the Marine Committee to gratify Jones's wish for active service, and avail themselves of his ability at the same time, took the shape of a resolution of Congress authorizing him to choose the best of three ships which it was proposed to purchase in Boston, which he was to command until some better provision could be made for him. He was ordered to that point to fit out the ship. During this period of harassing anxiety he gave great attention to formulating plans and making suggestions looking to a more effective organization of the new naval establishment.

To Robert Morris, chairman of the committee, on different occasions, he communicated his views on this important subject in a series of valuable letters, of which the following are pertinent extracts:

"As the regulations of the navy are of the utmost consequence, you will not think me presumptuous, if, with the utmost diffidence, I venture to communicate to you such hints as, in my judgment, will promote its honor and good government. I could heartily wish that every commissioned officer were to be previously examined; for, to my certain knowledge, there are persons who have already crept into commission without abilities or fit qualifications; I am myself far from desiring to be excused. From experience in ours, as well as from my former intimacy with many officers of note in the British navy, I am convinced that the parity of rank between sea and land or marine officers is of more consequence to the harmony of the sea service than has generally been imagined... I propose not our enemies as an example for our general imitation; yet, as their navy is the best regulated of any in the world, we must, in some degree, imitate them, and aim at such further improvement as may one day make ours vie with and exceed theirs."

With regard to the difficulty of recruiting seamen, some of whom, finding the merchant service or coasting trade was broken up, had entered the army at the beginning of the war, while many more had engaged in privateering—a much more profitable vocation than the regular service—he says:

"It is to the least degree distressing to contemplate the state and establishment of our navy. The common class of mankind are actuated by no nobler principle than that of self-interest; this, and this alone, determines all adventurers in privateers—the owners, as well as those whom they employ. And while this is the case, unless the private emolument of individuals in our navy is made superior to that in privateers, it can never become respectable, it will never become formidable. And without a respectable navy—alas!

America. In the present critical situation of affairs human wisdom can suggest no more than one infallible expedient: enlist the seamen during pleasure, and give them all the prizes. What is the paltry emolument of two thirds of prizes to the finances of this vast continent? If so poor a resource is essential to its independence, in sober sadness we are involved in a woeful predicament, and our ruin is fast approaching. The situation of America is new in the annals of mankind; her affairs cry haste, and speed must answer them. Trifles, therefore, ought to be wholly disregarded, as being, in the old vulgar proverb, penny wise and pound foolish. If our enemies, with the best establishment and most formidable navy in the universe, have found it expedient to assign all prizes to the captors, how much more is such policy essential to our infant fleet! But I need use no arguments to convince you of the necessity of making the emoluments of our navy equal, if not superior, to theirs. We have had proof that a navy may be officered on almost any terms, but we are not so sure that these officers are equal to their commissions; nor will the Congress ever obtain such certainty until they in their wisdom see proper to appoint a board of admiralty competent to determine impartially the respective merits and abilities of their officers, and to superintend, regulate, and point out all the motions and operations of the navy."

In another letter to Robert Morris he writes:

"There are no officers more immediately wanted in the marine department than commissioners of dockyards, to superintend the building and outfits of all ships of war; with power to appoint deputies, to provide, and have in constant readiness, sufficient quantities of provisions, stores, and slops, so that the small number of ships we have may be constantly employed, and not continue idle, as they do at present. Besides all the advantages that would arise from such appointments, the saving which would accrue to the continent is worth attending to. Had such men been appointed at the first, the new ships might have been at sea long ago. The difficulty now lies in finding men who are deserving, and who are fitly qualified for an office of such importance."

We are surprised at the clear insight of this untrained, inexperienced Scotsman, whom, by the way, I shall hereafter call an American. Most of his recommendations have long since been adopted in our own navy and other navies of the world. His conclusions are the results of his long and thorough professional study, his habits of application, his power of comprehension and faculty of clear and explicit statement. His observations would do credit to the most trained observer with large experience back of his observation.

Another curious letter to a former friend on the island of Tobago, written at this time, which deals with certain investments in property with balances due him from his various trading ventures, contains the following statement:

"As I hope my dear mother is still alive, I must inform you that I wish my property in Tobago, or in England, after paying my just debts, to be applied for her support. Your own feelings, my dear sir, make it unnecessary for me to use arguments to prevail with you on this tender point. Any remittances which you may be enabled to make, through the hands of my good friend Captain John Plainer, of Cork, will be faithfully put into her hands; she hath several orphan grandchildren to provide for."

All of which plainly indicates that, though a citizen of another country and the bearer of another name, he still retained those natural feelings of affection which his enemies would fain persuade us were not in his being.

While waiting at Boston for the purchase of the ships referred to, he was selected by Congress to command a heavy ship of war, a frigate to be called the Indien, then building at Amsterdam, which undoubtedly would be the most formidable vessel in the American service. This would be not only a just tribute to his merit, but would also solve the difficulty about relative rank, for he would be the highest ranking officer in Continental waters, and there could be no conflict of authority. He was directed to proceed at once to Europe to take command of this ship. The Marine Committee sent the following letter, addressed to the commissioners of the United States in Europe, to Paul Jones, for him to present to them on his arrival in France:

"PHILADELPHIA, *May 9, 1777.*

"HONOURABLE GENTLEMEN: This letter is intended to be delivered to you by John Paul Jones, Esquire, an active and brave commander in our navy, who has already performed signal services in vessels of little force; and, in reward for his zeal, we have directed him to go on board the Amphitrite, a French ship of twenty guns, that brought in a valuable cargo of stores from Messrs. Hortalez & Co.,[4] and with her to repair to France. He takes with him his commission, and some officers and men, so that we hope he will, under that sanction, make some good prizes with the Amphitrite; but our design of sending him is, with the approbation of Congress, that you may purchase one of those fine frigates that Mr. Deane writes us you can get, and invest him with the command thereof as soon as possible. We hope you may not delay this business one moment, but purchase, in such port or place in Europe as it can be done with most convenience and dispatch, a fine, fast-sailing frigate, or larger ship. Direct Captain Jones where he must repair to, and he will take with him his officers and men toward manning her. You will assign him some good house or agent, to supply him with everything necessary to get the ship speedily and well equipped and manned; somebody that will bestir himself vigorously in the business, and never quit it until it is accomplished.

"If you have any plan or service to be performed in Europe by such a ship, that you think will be more for the interest and honour of the States than sending her out directly, Captain Jones is instructed to obey your orders; and, to save repetition, let him lay before you the instructions we have given him, and furnish you with a copy thereof. You can then judge what will be necessary for you to direct him in; and whatever you do will be approved, as it will undoubtedly tend to promote the public service of this country.

"You see by this step how much dependence Congress places in your advices; and you must make it a point not to disappoint Captain Jones' wishes and expectations on this occasion."

At the same time the committee sent the following letter to Jones himself:

"PHILADELPHIA, *May 9, 1777.*

"SIR: Congress have thought proper to authorize the Secret Committee to employ you on a voyage in the Amphitrite, from Portsmouth to Carolina and France, where it is expected you will be provided with a fine frigate; and as your present commission is for the command of a particular ship, we now send you a new one, whereby you are appointed a captain in our navy, and of course may command any ship in the service to which you are particularly ordered. You are to obey the orders of the Secret Committee, and we are, sir, etc."

The Amphitrite, which was to carry out Jones and the other officers and seamen to man the proposed frigate, was an armed merchantman. The French commander of the Amphitrite, however, made great difficulty with regard to surrendering his command to Jones, and even to receiving him and his men on board the ship, and through his persistent and vehement objections this promising arrangement likewise fell through. Jones continued his importunities for a command, however, his desire being then, as always, for active service. Finally, by the following resolutions passed by Congress on the 14th of June, he was appointed to the sloop of war Ranger, then nearing completion at Portsmouth, New Hampshire:

"*Resolved,* That the flag of the thirteen United States be thirteen stripes, alternate red and white; that the union be thirteen stars, white in a blue field, representing a new constellation.

"*Resolved,* That Captain Paul Jones be appointed to command the ship Ranger.

"*Resolved,* That William Whipple, Esquire, member of Congress and of the Marine Committee, John Langdon, Esquire, Continental agent, and the said John Paul Jones be authorized to appoint lieutenants and other commissioned and warrant officers necessary for the said ship; and that blank commissions and warrants be sent them, to be filled up with the names of the persons they appoint, returns whereof to be made to the navy board in the Eastern Department."

At last, having received something tangible, he hastened to Portsmouth as soon as his orders were delivered to him, and assumed the command. It is claimed, perhaps with justice, that his hand was the first to hoist the new flag of the Republic, the Stars and Stripes, to the masthead of a war ship, as it had been the first to hoist the first flag of any sort at the masthead of the Alfred, not quite two years before. The date of this striking event is not known.

It is interesting to note the conjunction of Jones with the flag in this resolution; an association justified by his past, and to be further justified by his future, conduct, and by the curious relationship in which he was brought to the colors of the United States by his opportune action upon various occasions. The name of no other man is so associated with our flag as is his.

CHAPTER VI.

THE FIRST CRUISE OF THE RANGER—SALUTE TO THE

In spite of the most assiduous effort on the part of Jones, he was unable to get the Ranger ready for sea before October, and the following extract from another letter to the Marine Committee shows the difficulties under which he labored, and the inadequate equipment and outfit with which he finally sailed.

"With all my industry I could not get the single suit of sails completed until the 20th current. Since that time the winds and weather have laid me under the necessity of continuing in port. At this time it blows a very heavy gale from the northeast. The ship with difficulty rides it out, with yards and topmasts struck, and whole cables ahead. When it clears up I expect the wind from the northwest, and shall not fail to embrace it, although I have not a spare sail nor materials to make one. Some of those I have are made of hissings.[5] I never before had so disagreeable service to perform as that which I have now accomplished, and of which another will claim the credit as well as the profit. However, in doing my utmost, I am sensible that I have done no more than my duty."

The instructions under which Jones sailed for Europe are outlined in the following orders from the Marine Committee:

"As soon as these instructions get to hand you are to make immediate application to the proper persons to get your vessel victualed and fitted for sea with all expedition. When this is done you are to proceed on a voyage to some convenient port in France; on your arrival there, apply to the agent, if any, in or near said port, for such supplies as you may stand in need of. You are at the same time to give immediate notice, by letter, to the Honourable Benjamin Franklin, Silas Deane, and Arthur Lee, Esquires, or any of them at Paris, of your arrival, requesting their instructions as to your further destination, which instructions you are to obey as far as it shall be in your power.

"You are to take particular notice that while on the coast of France, or in a French port, you are, as much as you conveniently can, to keep your guns covered and concealed, and to make as little warlike appearance as possible."

In the original plan the ship was heavily over-armed, being pierced for twenty-six guns. Considering her size and slight construction, Jones exercised his usual good judgment by refusing to take more than eighteen guns, the ordinary complement for a ship of her class. These were 6-pounders manufactured in the United States and ill proportioned, being several calibres short in the length of the barrel, according to a statement of the captain—a most serious defect. To all these disabilities was added an inefficient and insubordinate first lieutenant named Simpson, who probably had been appointed to this responsible position on account of the considerable family influence which was back of him. He was related to the Hancocks among others. The crew was a fair one, but was spoiled eventually by the example of Simpson and other officers. On the first of November, 1777, the imperfectly provided Ranger took her departure from Portsmouth bound for Europe. Her captain laments the fact that she had but thirty gallons of rum aboard for the men to drink, a serious defect in those grog-serving days. Before sailing, Jones made large advances from his private funds to the men, the Government being already in his debt to the amount of fifteen hundred pounds, for previous advances to the men of the Alfred and the Providence. None of these advances were repaid until years after. These facts are evidence, by the way, that he had finally realized considerable sums of money from his brother's estate, for he had no other financial resource save his West Indian investments, which were worth nothing to him at this time.

Wickes, Johnston, and Cunningham, in the Reprisal, Lexington, Surprise, and Revenge, insignificant vessels of inferior force, had by their brilliant and successful cruising in the English Channel demonstrated the possibility of operations against British commerce in that supposedly safe quarter of the ocean. Paul Jones was now to undertake, upon a larger scale, similar operations with much more astounding results.

On the way over, two prizes, both brigantines, laden with wine and fruit, were captured. Nearing the other side, the Ranger fell in with ten sail of merchantmen from the Mediterranean, under convoy of the line of battle ship Invincible, 74. Jones made strenuous efforts to cut out one of the convoy, but they clung so closely to the line of battle ship that he found it impossible to bring about his design, though he remained in sight of the convoy during one whole day. Had the Ranger been swifter or handier, he might have effected something, but she was very crank and slow as well.

On the 2d of December the sloop of war dropped anchor in the harbor of Nantes. Jones sent his letters and instructions to the commissioners, and had the pleasure of confirming to them the news of the surrender of Burgoyne and his army, which was probably the most important factor in bringing about the subsequent alliance between America and France. While awaiting a reply to his letters he busied himself in repairing the defects and weaknesses of his ship so far as his limited means permitted. Her trim was altered, ballast restowed, and a large quantity of lead taken on board; the lower masts were shortened several feet, and every other change which his skill and experience dictated was made on the ship. The results greatly conduced to her efficiency. It may be stated here that Jones was a thorough and accomplished seaman, and no man was capable of getting more out of a ship than he. From a slow, crank, unwieldy vessel he developed the sloop of war into a handy, amenable ship, and very much increased her speed.

In January, 1778, in obedience to instructions from the commissioners, he visited them in Paris and explained to them in detail his proposed plan of action. Alone among the naval commanders of his day does he appear to have appreciated that commerce destroying can be best carried on and the enemy most injured by concentrated attacks by mobile and efficient force upon large bodies of shipping in harbors and home ports, rather than by sporadic cruising in more or less frequented seas. He had come across with the hope of taking command of the fine frigate Indien, then building in Holland, and then, with the Ranger and such other ships as might be procured, carrying out his ideas by a series of bold descents upon the English coasts. But while the ministers of the King of France were hesitating, or perhaps better perfecting their plans preparatory to announcing an alliance offensive and defensive with this country, it was deemed of the utmost importance that no occasion should be given the British which would enable them unduly to hasten the course of events. The suspicion of the British Government was aroused with respect to the Indien, however, and it was thought best, under the circumstances, to pretend that she was being made for the Government of France, with which England was then nominally at peace. In any event, work upon her had been so delayed that she was very far from completion, and would not have been available for months.

Thus was Jones deprived of the enjoyment of this command, to his great personal regret, to the disarrangement of his plans, and to the detriment of the cause he was so gallantly to support. There was no other ship nor were any smaller vessels then available for him, and he was therefore of necessity continued in the command of the Ranger.

This in itself was annoying, and produced a sequence of events of a most unfortunate character. Lieutenant Simpson had been promised the command of the Ranger when Jones took over the Indien, and the failure to keep this promise entailed by the circumstances mentioned, embittered Simpson to such a degree that his efficiency—never of the first order—was greatly impaired, and so long as he remained under the command of Jones he was a smoldering brand of discontent and disobedience.

On the 10th of January Jones, who had rejoined his ship, wrote at great length to Silas Deane, one of the commissioners, suggesting a plan whereby, in case the proposed alliance between France and the rebellious colonies were consummated, a magnificent blow might be struck against England, and the cause of the Revolution thereby greatly furthered. He urged that Admiral D'Estaing should be dispatched with a great fleet to pen up and capture Lord Howe, then operating in the Delaware with an inferior fleet. There is no doubt that this conception was essentially sound, and if he himself could have been intrusted with the carrying out of the plan the results would have been most happy; but, in order to effect anything, in peace or war, prompt action is as necessary as careful planning and wise decision.

When the French did finally adopt the plan they found that their dilatory proceedings, their failure to take immediate advantage of past preparation, and their substitution of Toulon for Brest as a naval point of departure, doomed the enterprise to failure. Lord Howe, hearing of the attempt, and realizing his precarious and indefensive position in the Delaware, made haste to return to his old anchorage in New York. When D'Estaing, urged by Washington, arrived off the harbor, he was deterred from attacking Lord Howe's inferior force by the representations of the pilots, who stated that there was not enough water on the bar for the greater ships of the line. While, therefore, Jones' suggestion came to nothing, it is interesting and instructive to contemplate this project of his fertile brain. Another enterprise proposed by him involved an expedition to take the island of St. Helena, and with it as a base of attack attempt the capture of the numerous Indiamen which either stopped at Jamestown or passed near the island. This too was unheeded.

While these matters were under consideration, the Ranger sailed from Nantes to Quiberon Bay early in February, 1778, having under convoy several American trading ships which were desirous of joining a great fleet of merchant vessels assembling at that point. These vessels were to be convoyed past Cape Finisterre on their way across the Atlantic by a heavy French squadron of five line of battle ships and several frigates and sloops under the command of La Motte Piquet.

On the 13th of February the Ranger hove to off the bay. The wind was blowing furiously, as it frequently does on the rocky confines of that bold shore, off which a few years before the great Lord Hawke had signally defeated Conflans; but, instead of running to an anchorage immediately, Jones sent a boat ashore, and through the American resident agent communicated to the French commander his intention of entering the bay next day and saluting him; asking, as was customary, that the salute be returned. The

French admiral courteously replied that he would return four guns less than the number he received, his instructions being to that effect, and in accordance with the custom of his navy when an interchange of sea courtesies took place between the fleets of France and those of a republic. This was not satisfactory to the doughty American, and he addressed the following letter to the American agent for the French commander:

"February 14, 1778.

"DEAR SIR: I am extremely sorry to give you fresh trouble, but I think the admiral's answer of yesterday requires an explanation. The haughty English return gun for gun to foreign officers of equal rank, and two less only to captains by flag officers. It is true, my command at present is not important, yet, as the senior American officer at present in Europe, it is my duty to claim an equal return of respect to the flag of the United States that would be shown to any other flag whatever.

"I therefore take the liberty of inclosing an appointment, perhaps as respectable as any which the French admiral can produce; besides which, I have others in my possession.

"If, however, he persists in refusing to return an equal salute, I will accept of two guns less, as I have not the rank of admiral.

"It is my opinion that he would return four less to a privateer or a merchant ship; therefore, as I have been honoured oftener than once with a chief command of ships of war, I can not in honour accept of the same terms of respect.

"You will singularly oblige me by waiting upon the admiral; and I ardently hope you will succeed in the application, else I shall be under a necessity of departing without coming into the bay.

"I have the honour to be, etc.

"To WILLIAM CARMICHAEL, ESQ.

"N. B.—Though thirteen guns is your greatest salute in America, yet if the French admiral should prefer a greater number he has his choice *on conditions.*"

A great stickler for his rights and for all the prerogatives of his station was John Paul Jones. In this instance he was maintaining the dignity of the United

States by insisting upon a proper recognition of his command.

However, having learned afterward that the contention of the French admiral was correct, Jones determined to accept the indicated return, realizing with his usual keenness that the gist of the matter lay in receiving any salute rather than in the number of guns which it comprised; so the Ranger got under way late in the evening of the 14th, and beat in toward the harbor. It was almost dark when she drew abreast the great French flagship. Backing his main-topsail, the 6-pounders on the main deck of the Ranger barked out their salute of thirteen guns, which was promptly returned by the French commander with nine heavy guns from the battle ship.

It was the first time the Stars and Stripes had been saluted on the high seas. It was, in fact, the first official recognition of the existence of this new power by the authorized military representatives of any civilized nation. A Dutch governor of St. Eustatius, a year before, had saluted an American ensign—not the Stars and Stripes, of course—on one of our cruisers, but the act had been disavowed and the governor promptly recalled for his presumption.

As this little transaction between Paul Jones and La Motte Piquet had occurred so late at night, the American sent word to the Frenchman that he proposed to sail through his line in broad daylight on the morrow, with the brig Independence, a privateer temporarily attached to his command, and salute him in the open light of day. With great good humor and complaisance, La Motte Piquet again expressed his intention of responding. Accordingly, the next morning, Jones repaired on board the Independence, which had been lying to during the night outside of signal distance, and, having made everything as smart and as shipshape as possible on the little vessel, with the newest and brightest of American ensigns flying from every masthead, the little brig sailed past the towering walls of the great ships of the line, saluting and receiving their reply. There were no doubts in any one's mind as to the reality of the salute to the flag after that!

It must have been a proud moment for the man who had hoisted the pine-tree flag for the first time on the Alfred; for the man who had been the first officer of the American navy to receive promotion; for the man who had first flung the Stars and Stripes to the breeze from the masthead of a ship; for the man who, in his little vessel, trifling and inconsiderable as she was, was yet about to maintain the honor of that flag with unexampled heroism in the home waters and in the presence of the proudest, most splendid, and most efficient navy of the world. That 15th of February, that bright, cold, clear winter morning, is one of the memorable anniversaries in the history of our nation.

Writing to the Marine Committee on the 22d of February, 1778, he says:

"I am happy in having it in my power to congratulate you on my having seen the American flag for the first time recognized in the fullest and completest manner by the flag of France. I was off their bay the 13th instant, and sent my boat in the next day, to know if the admiral would return my salute. He answered that he would return to me, as the senior American Continental officer in Europe, the same salute which he was authorized by his court to return to an admiral of Holland, or any other republic, which was four guns less than the salute given. I hesitated at this, for I demanded gun for gun. Therefore I anchored in the entrance of the bay, at a distance from the French fleet; but, after a very particular inquiry on the 14th, finding that he had really told the truth, I was induced to accept of his offer, the more so as it was, in fact, an acknowledgment of American independence. The wind being contrary and blowing hard, it was after sunset before the Ranger got near enough to salute La Motte Piquet with thirteen guns, which he returned with nine. However, to put the matter beyond a doubt, I did not suffer the Independence to salute till next morning, when I sent the admiral word that I would sail through his fleet in the brig, and would salute him in open day. He was exceedingly pleased, and he returned the compliment also with nine guns."

The much-talked-of treaty of alliance between France and the United States had been secretly signed six days before, but neither of the participants of this interchange of sea courtesies was then aware of this fact. Having discharged his duties by placing the merchant ships he had convoyed under La Motte Piquet's command, Jones left Quiberon Bay and went to Brest, where there was assembled a great French fleet under the famous Comte D'Orvilliers. Jones had the pleasure of again receiving, by the courtesy of that gallant officer, a reply to the Ranger's salute from the great guns of the flagship La Bretagne.

The Frenchman, whose acquaintance Jones promptly made, was much attracted by his daring and ingenuous personality, and, having been advised of the disappointment caused by the loss of the Indien, he offered to procure him a commission as a captain in the French navy and assign him to a heavy frigate instead of the petty sloop of war at present under his command—an unprecedented honor. Had Jones been the mere soldier of fortune which his enemies have endeavored to maintain he was, this brilliant offer would have met with a ready acceptance. The French marine, through the strenuous efforts of the king and his ministers, was then in a most flourishing condition. The terrific defeats at the close of the century and the beginning of the next were still in the womb of events and had not been brought forth, and the prospects of its success were exceedingly brilliant. With the backing of D'Orvilliers and his own capacity, speedy promotion and advancement might easily be predicted for the American. He refused decisively to accept the flattering offer, and remained with the Ranger.

On the 10th of April, having done what he could to put the ship in efficient trim, he sailed from Brest under the following orders:

"Paris, *January 16, 1778.*

"Sir: As it is not in our power to procure you such a ship as you expected, we advise you, after equipping the Ranger in the best manner for the cruise you propose, that you proceed with her in the manner you shall judge best for distressing the enemies of the United States, by sea or otherwise, consistent with the laws of war and the terms of your commission." (Directions here follow for sending prizes taken on the coasts of France and Spain into Bilboa or Corogne, unless the danger was too great, in which case they were to be sent to L'Orient or Bordeaux.) "If you make an attempt on the coast of Great Britain we advise you not to return immediately into the ports of France, unless forced by stress of weather or the pursuit of the enemy; and in such case you can make the proper representation to the officers of the port, and acquaint us with your situation. We rely on your ability, as well as your zeal, to serve the United States, and therefore do not give you particular instructions as to your operations. We must caution you against giving any cause of complaint to the subjects of France or Spain, or of other neutral powers, and recommend it to you to show them every proper mark of respect and real civility which may be in your power."

These orders had been dated and issued to him some months before, but were not modified or revoked in the interim. He was given an opportunity to carry out so much of his proposed plan for attacking the English coast as was possible with his single ship.

CHAPTER VII.

THE SECOND CRUISE OF THE RANGER—THE DESCENT ON WHITEHAVEN—THE ATTEMPT ON LORD SELKIRK—THE CAPTURE OF THE DRAKE.

The first few days of the cruise were uneventful. On the 14th of April, 1778, between the Scilly Isles and Cape Clear, the Ranger captured a brig bound for Ireland loaded with flaxseed. As the prize and her cargo were not worth sending in, the vessel was burned at sea. On the 17th, off St. George's Channel, they overhauled a large ship, the Lord Chatham, loaded with porter *en route* from London to Dublin. The ship and cargo being of great value— one likes to think how the porter must have appealed to the seamen, who, it is quite likely, were permitted to regale themselves to a limited extent from the cargo—she was manned and sent back to Brest as a prize. After this capture Jones proceeded up the Irish Channel, heading to the northeast, and on the 18th, finding himself off the northern extremity of the Isle of Man, and in line with Whitehaven, he attempted to carry out a preconceived project of destroying the shipping in the port; being determined, as he says, by one great burning of ships to put an end to the burnings and ravagings and maraudings of the British upon the undefended coasts of North America.

The wind was blowing from the east, and he beat up against it toward the town, where he hoped to find a large number of ships in the harbor. The adverse wind delayed him, however, and it was not until ten o'clock at night that the Ranger reached a point from which it was practicable to dispatch the boats. Preparations were hastily made, and the boats were called away and manned by volunteers. The boats were already in the water when the wind suddenly shifted and blew hard on shore, so that the Ranger was forced to beat out to sea promptly to avoid taking ground on the shoals under her lee. The expedition, therefore, for that time, was abandoned, the boats were swung up to the davits, and the Ranger filled away again.

The next morning, off the Mull of Galloway, they captured a schooner loaded with barley and sunk her. Learning from some prisoners that ten or twelve large ships, under the protection of a small tender, were anchored in Lochvyau, Scotland, Jones ran for that harbor, intending to destroy them, but the variable weather, as before, interfered with his plans, and a sudden squall drove the Ranger into the open once more and saved the ships. He captured and sunk a small Irish fishing sloop, making prisoners of the fishermen, that same afternoon. The sloop was of no value to Jones, and he would have let her go had it not been that he feared the alarm would be given. He treated the fishermen kindly, however, and, as we shall see, in the end they suffered no loss from his action.

On the 20th he captured a sloop loaded with grain, and on the 21st, off Carrickfergus, he took another small fishing boat. Learning from the fishermen that the British man-of-war Drake, twenty guns and a hundred and fifty men, was lying at anchor in Belfast Lough, he promptly determined upon a bold scheme to effect her capture. Beating to and fro off the mouth of the Lough until the evening, as soon as it was dark he ran for the harbor, proposing to lay his vessel athwart the hawse of the Drake, lying unsuspiciously at anchor, drop his own anchor over the cable of the English sloop of war, and capture her by boarding.

Every preparation was made to carry out this brilliant *coup de main*. The crew were mustered at quarters, armed for boarding with pike or cutlass and pistol, the best shots were told off to sweep the decks of the Drake with small-arm fire, guns were loaded and primed, and so on. It was blowing heavily as the Ranger under reduced canvas dashed gallantly into the harbor. With masterly seamanship Jones brought her to in exactly the right position, and gave the order to let go the anchor. His orders were not obeyed, through the negligence of a drunken boatswain, it was said, and the anchor was not dropped until the Ranger had drifted down past the lee quarter of the Drake, when she brought up. The position of the American was now one of extreme peril. The Ranger lay under the broadside of the Drake, subjected to her fire and unable to make reply.

The watch kept on the British ship, however, must have been very careless. In the darkness of the night, too, the guns of the Ranger being run in, it is probable that if they observed her they took her for a clumsy merchantman. Enjoining perfect silence on the part of his crew, with the greatest coolness Jones took the necessary steps to extricate the vessel from her dangerous position. The cable was cut, sail made, and under a heavy press of canvas the Ranger beat out of the harbor, barely clearing the entrance, and only escaping wreck by the consummate ability of her captain.

The plan was brilliantly conceived, and would have been successful but for the mischance, or delay, in dropping the anchor. The crew originally was only a fair one, as has been stated, and, owing to the fact that their wages had not been paid, they were in a more or less mutinous state by this time. Jones was covetous of glory only. A less mercenary man never lived. To fight and conquer was his aim, but in this he radically differed from the ideas of his officers and men. Where he wrote honor and fame they saw plunder and prize money, and it was sometimes difficult to get them to obey orders and properly to work the ship.

After leaving Belfast the Ranger ratched over to the southern coast of Scotland to ride out the sudden and furious gale under the lee of the land. The wind had abated by the morning of the 22d, and the sun rose bright and clear, discovering from the of the Ranger a beautiful prospect of the three kingdoms covered with snow as far as the eye could see. The wind now set fair for Whitehaven, and Jones squared away for that port to carry out his previous project. The breeze fell during the day, however, and it was not until midnight that the boats were called away.

The expedition comprised two boats, carrying thirty-one officers and men, all volunteers, Jones himself being in command of one boat, while Lieutenant Wallingford, one of the best officers of the ship, had the other. Simpson and the second lieutenant both pleaded indisposition and fatigue as excuse for not going on the expedition. The tide was ebbing, and it was not until nearly dawn, after a long, hard pull, that the two boats reached the harbor, which was divided into two parts at that time by a long stone pier. There were from seventy to one hundred ships on the north side of the pier, and about twice as many on the south side, ranging in size from two hundred to four hundred tons. As the tide was out, the ships were all aground, lying high and dry upon the beach, and in close touch with each other. Directing Wallingford to set fire to the ships on the north side of the pier, Jones and his party landed and advanced toward the fort which protected the harbor.

The weather was raw and cold, the fort was old and dilapidated, and manned by a few men. The sentry, ignorant of the presence of any foe, never dreaming of an enemy within a thousand miles of him, had calmly retired to the sentry box. Probably he was asleep. The little party approached the walls without being detected. Climbing upon the shoulder of one of his men, Jones sprang over the rampart, where he was followed by the rest of the party. The feeble garrison was captured without striking a blow. The guns were hastily spiked. Ordering the prisoners to be marched down to the wharf, and throwing out a few sentries, Jones, attended by a single midshipman, then made his way to the other fort or battery, a distance of about half a mile. Finding it untenanted, he spiked the few guns mounted there and returned to the landing place.

To his very great surprise and disappointment, no evidence of a conflagration was apparent. When he reached the wharf he was met by Wallingford, who explained his failure to fire the shipping by claiming that his lights had gone out. It was before the days of lucifer matches, and the party had carried candles in lanterns with which to kindle the fires. Wallingford excused himself by a remark which does more credit to his heart than to his head, to the effect that he could not see that anything was to be gained by burning poor people's property. Inasmuch as he was sent on the expedition to obey orders and not to philosophize, his statement gives the key to the disposition among the officers and crew. Whether his hesitation was dictated by charity to others or lack of possible profit to the officers and men it is not necessary to inquire particularly now, for Wallingford redeemed himself nobly later in the cruise. A hasty inspection revealed the fact that the candles had also burned out, or had been extinguished through carelessness, in Jones' own boat.

It was now broad daylight, and considerations of safety indicated an immediate return to the ship; but Jones was not willing to abandon his brilliantly conceived, carefully prepared, and coolly undertaken enterprise without some measure of success. Re-posting his sentries, therefore, he dispatched messengers who broke into a neighboring dwelling house and procured a light in the shape of a torch or glowing ember. With his own hand Jones kindled a fire on one of the largest ships in the midst of the huddle of vessels on the beach. In order to insure a thorough conflagration, a hasty search through the other vessels was made, and a barrel of tar was found which was poured upon the flames now burning fiercely.

One of the boat party, named David Freeman, happened to be an Englishman. In the confusion attendant upon these various maneuvers he made off, and, escaping observation, sought shelter in the town, which he quickly alarmed. The inhabitants came swarming out of their houses in the gray of the morning and hastened toward the wharf. Seeing that the fire on the ship was at last blazing furiously, and realizing that nothing more could be effected, Jones ordered his men to their boats. Then, in order that the fire already kindled might have sufficient time to develop, the undaunted captain stood alone on the wharf, pistol in hand, confronting the ever-increasing crowd. Impelled by pressure from behind, those in front finally made a movement toward him. He gave no ground whatever. Pointing his weapons at the front rank, he sternly bade them retire, which they did with precipitation. I should think so. Having remained a sufficient time, as he thought, he calmly entered the boat and was rowed to the Ranger.

Some of the inhabitants promptly made a dash for the burning ship, and succeeded by hard work in confining the fire to that one vessel. Others released the prisoners which Jones left bound on the wharf, taking, as he said, only two or three for a sample. The soldiers ran to the fort and managed to draw the hastily applied spikes from two or three of the guns, which they loaded and fired after the retreating boats. Answering the harmless fusillade with a few derisive musket shots, Jones returned to the Ranger; having had, he says, the pleasure of neither inflicting nor receiving any loss in killed or wounded.

The desertion and treachery of David Freeman undoubtedly saved the shipping. The enterprise was well conceived and carried out with the utmost coolness. Had the orders of Captain Jones been obeyed, the shipping would have been completely destroyed. As it was, the descent created the greatest consternation in England. No enemy had landed on those shores for generations, and the expedition by Jones was like slapping the face of the king on his throne. A burning wave of indignation swept over England, as the news was carried from town to town, from hall to hall, and from hamlet to hamlet. It was all very well to burn property in America, but the matter had a different aspect entirely when the burning took place in England. A universal demand arose for the capture of this audacious seaman, who was called many hard names by the infuriated British.

From Whitehaven the Ranger ran over to St. Mary's Isle, a beautifully wooded promontory at the mouth of the River Dee, which was the seat of the Earl of Selkirk. In furtherance of his usual desire to ameliorate the wretched condition of the Americans in British prisons, Jones determined to seize the earl. He cherished the hope that by securing the person of a peer of the realm, who could be either held as a hostage or exchanged for some prominent American captive, he could thus effect a recognition of the principle of exchange, which the British had refused to consider. It was a wild hope, to be sure, but not without a certain plausibility.

Two boat crews under the command of Lieutenants Simpson and Hall, with himself in charge of the expedition, landed on the shore. Before moving toward the hall, Jones learned that the earl was not at home. He proposed, therefore, to return to the ship, but the mutinous men demurred fiercely to this suggestion, and demanded that they be permitted to enjoy the opportunity for plunder presented. The situation was a precarious one, and Jones finally agreed, although very reluctantly, that they should demand the family silver from the Countess of Selkirk, who was at home. He did this with the full intention of purchasing the silver on his own account when the prizes were disposed of, and returning it to the earl. A party of the men, therefore, with

Simpson and Hall, went up to the house, leaving Jones pacing to and fro near the shore under the oaks and chestnuts of the estate. By Jones' orders the seamen did not enter the house. Simpson and Hall were ushered into the presence of the Lady Selkirk, made their demand upon her ladyship, received the silver, which the butler gathered up for them, and retired without molesting or harming any of the inmates or endeavoring to appropriate anything except what was given them. The men drank her ladyship's health in good Scots whisky, which was served them by the countess' orders. The party then embarked on the Ranger.

One of his biographers has said that the whole transaction was an evidence of the singular ability of Jones in creating difficulties which it afterward required greater labor to overcome; but the criticism is unfair. The only way in which he could satisfy the demands of his men and maintain even that precarious authority which the peculiar constitution of the crew and the character of his officers enabled him to have, was by permitting them to take something of value which could be turned into prize money. He could buy it from the prize court, or from the prize master, as well as any other man, and after it became his own property he could return it to its proper owners at his pleasure.

It was a perfectly legitimate transaction on his part, and he could only obviate the necessity by taking the proposed value of the silver out of his own pocket and handing it to his men, a proceeding which would have been subversive of the last remains of discipline, and therefore could not be considered for a moment. It would establish a precedent which could not be carried out in the future unless he were willing to abrogate his right of command; if he began that way he would have to buy their acquiescence to every command—bribe them to obey orders; so he said nothing whatever to them about his intentions with regard to the plate at present.

Standing away from St. Mary's Isle on the morning of the 24th, the Ranger came in sight once more of Carrickfergus. By this time her presence on the Irish coast had become well known, and expresses had been sent to the Drake with information of the propinquity of the enemy. In the afternoon the Ranger appeared in the offing easily visible from the Drake. The commander of the Drake, Captain George Burdon, with singular stupidity, sent a lieutenant and a boat off toward the Ranger to investigate and report what she was, meanwhile getting his ship under way and clearing for action. The boat foolishly came alongside the Ranger and was captured. As Burdon weighed anchor he was joined by Lieutenant William Dobbs, engaged on recruiting duty in the vicinity, and a band of volunteers ranging in number, according to different reports, from ten to forty.

The regular complement of the Drake was one hundred and fifty officers and men. This re-enforcement raised her crew to between one hundred and sixty and one hundred and ninety. It was developed at the court-martial, which was held upon the survivors some months after for the loss of the ship, that the Drake was poorly prepared for action; that she was short of commissioned and warrant officers and skilled men; that her powder charges were bad, matches poor, cartridges unfilled, and that her guns were badly mounted, so that they were easily "overset," and so on. In short, the whole catalogue of usual excuses for failure is given. It is true that although the Drake carried two more guns than the Ranger, they were of smaller caliber, being 4-pounders. Still, the two ships were well matched, and preparedness for action has always been considered a test of naval ability as much as capacity in maneuvering and courage in the actual fight.

The wind was now blowing toward the shore, and the Drake made but slow progress in ratching toward the sea. While the Ranger awaited her, the guns were run in and the English flag hoisted on the approach of the Drake's boat, and the character of the American disguised as much as possible. I presume that, save for her armament, she looked more like a merchant vessel than anything else, and, as Jones skillfully kept the sloop end on to the cutter, the British suspected, or at least discovered, nothing. Indeed, so well was the deception carried out that the Drake's officer actually boarded the Ranger and was made prisoner with his crew before he discovered her quality.

Meanwhile things were almost in a state of mutiny. Jones states in his journal that he was in peril of his life from his recalcitrant crew, who, under the leadership of Simpson, were apparently appalled at the prospect of encountering a regular man-of-war, and therefore manifested a great unwillingness to fight. Plunder without danger was the end of their ambition. However, after the capture of the Drake's boat, by putting a bold front on the situation, Jones succeeded in restoring comparative order and getting his men to their quarters. His power of persuasive and inspiring speech never stood him in better stead than on this occasion, and he actually seems to have succeeded in infusing some of his own spirit into the refractory men.

It was late in the evening before the Drake neared the Ranger. Jones had stood out to sea to draw his pursuer far away from the land to prevent his escape in case of defeat, and now awaited his advance. The Drake was accompanied by several pleasure yachts filled with people who were desirous of seeing the English victory, which was almost universally attendant upon single ship actions in which the British navy participated; but, not liking the look of things in this instance, they one by one dropped astern and returned to the land.

Between five and six o'clock, having come within easy distance, an officer of the Drake sprang on the rail and hailed, demanding to know the name of the stranger. Jones, still keeping the stern of his ship toward the bow of the enemy, seized the trumpet and replied:

"This is the American Continental ship Ranger. We are waiting for you. The sun is scarce an hour high. It is time to begin. Come on!"

While he was amusing the English captain with this rather lengthy rejoinder for the purpose of gaining time, the Stars and Stripes supplanted the red ensign of England, the helm of the Ranger, which was to windward of her antagonist, was suddenly put up, and by smart handling, in the twinkling of an eye she was rushed across the bow of the Drake, which was severely raked by a prompt broadside at short range. As Jones shifted his helm so as not to lose the weather gauge, the advantage of the first hard blow was clearly with the Americans. The English captain, after an attempt to cross her stern, which was frustrated by Jones' promptness, ran off by the side of the Ranger, and the combat resolved itself into a fair and square yardarm to yardarm fight, which was continued with the most determined persistence on both sides. The two ships under the gentle breeze sailed side by side, gradually nearing, and poured a furious fire upon each other. The lack of preparedness on the English ship was manifested in the slowness and inaccuracy of her gun practice. That of the Ranger, however, was very effective. An hour and five minutes after the first broadside the enemy called for quarter and hauled down the flag. The Drake was a wreck. Her fore and main topsail yards were cut adrift and lying on the caps; the fore topgallant yard and the spanker gaff were hanging up and down their respective masts; two ensigns had been shot away, and another one was hanging over the quarter galley and dragging in the water. The jib was dragging under her forefoot; her sails and rigging were entirely cut to pieces, most of the yards wounded, and her hull very much shattered. Many of her guns were dismounted, and she had lost, according to the statement of the Americans, forty-two[6] men in killed and wounded (or about twenty per cent of her force!), including her captain, who had been struck in the head by a musket ball at the close of the action, about a minute before the ship surrendered; the gallant first lieutenant, Dobbs, who had bravely volunteered for service, was so severely wounded that he survived the action only two days. Captain Burdon was still living when Jones boarded the prize, but died a few moments after. The Americans lost two killed, among them being poor Wallingford, whose death has somewhat redeemed him from his failure to obey orders in the raid on Whitehaven. There were six wounded on the Ranger, including the gunner and a midshipman who lost his arm; one of the wounded subsequently died.

The action was a sharp and brilliant one. Jones had maneuvered and fought his ship with his usual skill and courage, and had given fair evidence of what might be expected from him with a better vessel and better men under his command. The English captain had been outmaneuvered when he permitted the American to rake him, and he had been outfought in the action. Unpreparedness was the cause of the failure of the Drake to make a better showing in the fight. This lack must be laid at the captain's door. It is the business of a captain to see that things are ready. The deficiencies in the Drake's equipment were counterbalanced by equal deficiencies on the part of the Ranger. The apparent preponderance of the latter's gun power was, in fact, minimized by the shortening of her guns, of which Jones had previously complained. It is probable that the Drake had a better crew, and such officers as she had were probably better than those under Jones, with a few exceptions. It is always the custom of the defeated party to make excuses, and always will be; but the ships were as nearly matched in offensive qualities as two vessels in different navies are ever likely to be, and the difference between them, which determined the issue of the conflict, was purely a question of the personal equation. It was always hard to find anything to counterbalance Jones for the other side of the equality sign. Burdon was not the man.

The English captain was a brave but very stupid or very confident man. Jones was more than a match for him at best, and when the mistakes of Burdon are considered the comparison is painful. The English knew that the Ranger was on the coast; the Drake had picked up her anchor (it was, of course, recaptured), and an alert mind would have connected the recovered anchor with the attempt of the night of the 20th. The suspicious actions of the stranger—and there must have been some indication in her maneuvers and appearance at least to inspire caution—the failure of the boat crew either to return or to make any signal, should have made the English captain pause and consider the situation. But with the usual "uncircumspect gallantry" of his kind he charged down, bull-like, on his enemy, was promptly raked, hammered to pieces, killed, and his ship surrendered. He proved his courage in battle—which no one would question, bravery being usual and to be expected—and he died in the attempt to atone for his rashness; but professionally he was a failure, and his demise was fortunate for his reputation and future career. His death probably prevented some very inconvenient questions being asked him.

Jones treated his prisoners with a kindness and consideration the more remarkable from the fact that the contrary was the custom with the British toward American captives. During the night and the whole of the next day, the weather being moderate, the two ships were hove to while the Drake was refitted as well as their resources permitted. Late the next afternoon a large brigantine, actuated by an unfortunate curiosity, ran down so near the two ships that she was brought to by a shot from the Drake and taken possession of. Having repaired damages and put the Drake in as good trim as possible, Jones first determined to return to Brest by the South Channel, the way he had come, but the variable wind shifted and came strongly, and he decided to run northward before it and pass around the west coast of Ireland. In spite of his previous insubordination Simpson was placed in command of the Drake.

Before they left these waters, however, something still remained to be done. On the evening of the 25th the two ships sailed once more for Belfast Lough. There Jones hove the Ranger to, and, having given the poor Irish fishermen, whom he had captured on the 21st and held, one of the Drake's boats, and having charitably bestowed upon them all the guineas which he had left in his private purse (not many, I suppose) to remunerate them for the loss they had sustained, he sent them ashore. They took with them one of the Drake's sails, which would attest the truth of their story of what had happened. The grateful Irishmen were delighted and touched by such unusual treatment, and they signalized their gratitude to their generous and kindhearted captor by giving Jones three cheers from the boat as they passed the Ranger's quarter. The Americans then bore away to the northwestward.

The voyage around the coast of Ireland was uneventful. Lieutenant Dobbs, of the Drake, died on the cruise, and he and Captain Burdon were buried at sea with all possible honors, Jones himself reading the usual Church service. The cruise was continued without incident until the morning of the 5th of May, when the Ranger being off Ushant, and having the Drake in tow, Jones cut the towline and bore away in chase of a sail which had been sighted. Simpson, instead of continuing toward Brest, as he had been directed, hauled off to the south, so that when Jones had overtaken the chase and found her a neutral, the Drake was almost entirely out of sight to the southward.

The Ranger chased her and made various signals, to which no attention was paid. Simpson changed his course aimlessly several times. During the whole of the day the same eccentric maneuvers on the part of the Drake continued. To Jones' great annoyance, the inexplicable actions of the prize prevented him from chasing several large vessels which he saw standing into the Channel, among which he would probably have made many valuable captures. He was forced to abandon any attempt to take them and follow the Drake, which he only overhauled late in the evening. By Jones' orders Lieutenant Elijah Hall immediately replaced Simpson in command of the Drake, and the latter was placed under arrest. On the 8th of May both vessels arrived safely at Brest, from which point Jones promptly dispatched the following remarkable letter to the Countess of Selkirk:

"RANGER, BREST, *May 8, 1778.*

"*THE RIGHT HON. THE COUNTESS OF SELKIRK.*

"MADAM: It can not be too much lamented that, in the profession of arms, the officer of fine feelings and real sensibility should be under the necessity of winking at any action of persons under his command which his heart can not approve; but the reflection is doubly severe when he finds himself obliged, in appearance, to countenance such actions by his authority. This hard case was mine, when, on the 23d of April last, I landed on St. Mary's Isle. Knowing Lord Selkirk's interest with his king, and esteeming as I do his private character, I wished to make him the happy instrument of alleviating the horrors of hopeless captivity, when the brave are overpowered and made prisoners of war. It was perhaps fortunate for you, madam, that he was from home, for it was my intention to have taken him on board the Ranger and detained him until, through, his means, a general and fair exchange of prisoners, as well in Europe as in America, had been effected.

"When I was informed, by some men whom I met at landing that his lordship was absent, I walked back to my boat, determined to leave the island. By the way, however, some officers who were with me could not forbear expressing their discontent, observing that in America no delicacy was shown by the English, who took away all sorts of movable property, setting fire not only to towns and to the houses of the rich, without distinction, but not even sparing the wretched hamlets and milch cows of the poor and helpless, at the approach of an inclement winter. That party had been with me the same morning at Whitehaven; some complaisance, therefore, was their due. I had but a moment to think how I might gratify them, and at the same time do your ladyship the least injury. I charged the officers to permit none of the seamen to enter the house, or to hurt anything about it; to treat you, madam, with the utmost respect; to accept of the plate which was offered, and to come away without making a search or demanding anything else. I am induced to believe that I was punctually obeyed, since I am informed that the plate which they brought away is far short of the quantity expressed in the inventory which accompanied it. I have gratified my men, and when the plate is sold I shall become the purchaser, and will gratify my own feelings by restoring it to you by such conveyance as you shall please to direct.

"Had the earl been on board the Ranger the following evening he would have seen the awful pomp and dreadful carnage of a sea engagement, both affording ample subject for the pencil, as well as melancholy reflection for the contemplative mind. Humanity starts back from such scenes of horror, and can not sufficiently execrate the vile promoters of this detestable war.

"'For they, 'twas they unsheathed the ruthless blade, And Heaven shall ask the havoc it has made.'

"The British ship of war Drake, mounting twenty guns, with more than her full complement of officers and men, was our opponent. The ships met, and the advantage was disputed with great fortitude on each side for an hour and four minutes, when the gallant commander of the Drake fell, and victory declared in favor of the Ranger. The amiable lieutenant lay mortally wounded, besides near forty of the inferior officers and crew killed and wounded—a melancholy demonstration of the uncertainty of human prospects and of the sad reverses of fortune which an hour can produce. I buried them in a spacious grave, with the honors due to the memory of the brave.

"Though I have drawn my sword in the present generous struggle for the rights of men, yet I am not in arms as an American, nor am I in pursuit of riches. My fortune is liberal enough, having no wife and family, and having lived long enough to know that riches can not secure happiness. I profess myself a citizen of the world, totally unfettered by the little mean distinctions of climates or of country, which diminish the benevolence of the heart and set bounds to philanthropy. Before this war was begun, I had, at an early time in life, withdrawn from sea service in favor of 'calm contemplation and poetic ease.' I have sacrificed not only my favorite scheme of life, but the softer affections of the heart, and my prospects of domestic happiness, and I am ready to sacrifice my life also with cheerfulness, if that forfeiture could restore peace among mankind.

"As the feelings of your gentle bosom can not but be congenial with mine, let me entreat you, madam, to use your persuasive art with your husband, to endeavour to stop this cruel and destructive war, in which Britain can never succeed. Heaven can never countenance the barbarous and unmanly practice of the Britons in America, which savages would blush at, and which, if not discontinued, will soon be retaliated on Britain by a justly enraged people. Should you fail in this, and I am persuaded you will attempt it (and who can resist the power of such an advocate?), your endeavour to effect a general exchange of prisoners will be an act of humanity, which will afford you golden feelings on your deathbed.

"I hope this cruel contest will soon be closed; but, should it continue, I wage no war with the fair. I acknowledge their force, and bend before it with submission. Let not, therefore, the amiable Countess of Selkirk regard me as an enemy; I am ambitious of her esteem and friendship, and would do anything, consistent with my duty, to merit it. The honor of a line from your hand, in answer to this, will lay me under a singular obligation, and if I can render you any acceptable service in France or elsewhere I hope you see into my character so far as to command me, without the least grain of reserve. I wish to know the exact behaviour of my people, as I am determined to punish them if they have exceeded their liberty.

"I have the honor to be, with much esteem and with profound respect, madam, etc.,

"JOHN PAUL JONES."

The shrewd Franklin says of this extraordinary document: "It is a gallant letter, which must give her ladyship a high and just opinion of your generosity and nobleness of mind." But I seem to read a gentle laugh in the tactful words of the old philosopher. I like this epistle less than any of Jones' letters I have read, but it certainly does not merit the severe censures which have been passed upon it. No one would write such a letter to-day, certainly, but things were different then, and we need not too closely criticise the form and style of the document in view of its honest purpose and good intent.

As might have been expected, the Countess of Selkirk made no reply to this singular communication. To anticipate the course of events, and obviate the necessity of further discussion of this incident, it may be stated that more than a year after its capture Jones obtained possession of the plate through the prize court by strenuous effort, and by paying for it at an exorbitant valuation. The state of warfare then existing between France and England prevented the delivery of the silver for several years, though Jones made earnest efforts to get it into the hands of the Selkirks whenever apparent opportunity presented. It was not, however, until 1784, after peace had been declared, that the plate was restored to its original owners. It is stated that it was received by them in exactly the same condition as when it had been taken, even to the tea leaves which were still in the teapot! The receipt of the silver is thus acknowledged in a letter from Lord Selkirk:

"LONDON, *August 4, 1789.*

"*Monsieur le Chevalier Paul Jones, à Paris.*

"SIR: I received the letter you wrote to me at the time you sent off my plate, in order for restoring it. Had I known where to direct a letter to you at the time it arrived in Scotland I would then have wrote to you; but, not knowing it, nor finding that any of my acquaintance at Edinburgh knew it, I was obliged to delay writing till I came here, when, by means of a gentleman connected with America, I was told M. le Grand was your banker at Paris, and would take proper care of a letter for you; therefore, I inclose this to him.

"Notwithstanding all the precautions you took for the easy and uninterrupted conveyance of the plate, yet it met with considerable delays: first at Calais, next at Dover, then at London; however, it at last arrived at Dumfries, and I dare say quite safe, though as yet I have not seen it, being then at Edinburgh.

"I intended to have put an article in the newspapers about your having returned it; but before I was informed of its being arrived, some of your friends, I suppose, had put it in the Dumfries newspaper, whence it was immediately copied into the Edinburgh papers, and thence into the London ones. Since that time I have mentioned it to many people of fashion; and, on all occasions, sir, both now and formerly, I have done you the justice to tell that you made an offer of returning the plate very soon after your return to Brest; and, although you yourself was not at my house, but remained at the shore with your boat, that yet you had your officers and men in such extraordinary good discipline that your having given them the strictest orders to behave well, to do no injury of any kind, to make no search, but only to bring off what plate was given them; that in reality they did exactly as ordered, and that not one man offered to stir from his post on the outside of the house, nor entered the doors, nor said an uncivil word; that the two officers stayed not a quarter of an hour in the parlour and butler's pantry, while the butler got the plate together, behaved politely, and asked for nothing but the plate, and instantly marched their men off in regular order; and that both officers and men behaved in all respects so well that it would have done credit to the best disciplined troops whatever.

"Some of the English newspapers at that time having put in confused accounts of your expedition to Whitehaven and Scotland, I ordered a proper one of what had happened in Scotland to be put in the London newspapers, by a gentleman who was then at my house, by which the good conduct and civil behaviour of your officers and men was done justice to, and attributed to your order, and the good discipline you maintained over your people.

"I am, sir, your most humble servant,

"SELKIRK."

It is a handsome acknowledgment, but I note with great pleasure the sailor writes better than the peer!

CHAPTER VIII.

STANDING AND WAITING.

The Ranger and her prizes arrived at Brest at a propitious time, both for the fortunes of Jones and for those of his adopted country as well. The secret treaty of alliance between the confederated colonies and France had been signed on February 6th. The plenipotentiaries from the United States had been publicly received at Versailles on March 23d. On the same day the French ambassador left England, and the English ambassador, Lord Stormont, left France. The fleet of D'Estaing put to sea from Toulon a fortnight later. In two weeks the English fleet followed to American waters. The attempt was made on the part of the French to execute the brilliant strategic plan which Jones had devised, although, of course, the delay had rendered the effort fruitless.

The successful cruise of the Ranger, the rich captures she had made, the daring enterprises she had undertaken, the boldness and audacity of her commander in venturing with a little vessel of such trifling force into the very midst of the three kingdoms, and the brilliancy of his capture of a war vessel of nominally superior, and at least really equal, force, in a fair and open yardarm to yardarm fight, a thing to which the French navy was not accustomed, awakened the greatest admiration, and Paul Jones found himself in that most congenial of positions to him—and to almost any other man—of being the observed of all. On this expedition, his first real opportunity, he had demonstrated that he possessed an ability to plan, and a courage to carry out his conceptions, which put him in the front rank of the sea officers of his day. With one single vessel, laboring under every disadvantage conceivable, he had done what no European power or combination of powers had been able to accomplish in centuries, with all their resources at command. He had terrorized the whole English seaboard, and filled the United Kingdom with uneasiness and unrest.

The gallant men who had gone before him and accomplished so much with the Reprisal, the Revenge, and the others, had a worthy successor and superior in this little Scots-American, who, as a citizen of the world, in love with humanity, drew his sword for the cause of freedom. The French admired him, the English hated him. The American prisoners immediately felt the effect of his captures by the general amelioration of their unhappy condition, and Franklin at last realized that he had a man at hand upon whom he could depend to further his bold designs. When the news reached America, it was received with great joy, and the Naval Committee and the Congress generally knew they had made no mistake in sending Jones to Europe. The young navy looked to him with hope. His exploits were detailed and amplified in the cafés and on the boulevards of Paris, and were related with approbation even within the sacred confines of the court. He was the hero of the hour.

But there is a homely maxim exemplified by frequent experience that "Fine words butter no parsnips." It was true in this instance undoubtedly, and Jones learned that there was no necessary connection between glory and bread and butter. He was unable to procure actually necessary supplies for his crew. All the vessels of the Continental navy went to sea undermanned, ill-provided, and inadequately provisioned, and the ship's purser, as a rule, had no money. The seamen had not received their wages—no money at all, in fact, except that which Jones himself had advanced out of his own pocket. With the sanction of the Marine Committee he had made himself responsible for the regular payment of the wages of the men. His pocket was now empty, the last guineas having been given to the Irish fishermen aforementioned. His own resources were always drawn upon freely for the good of the service and his men; now they were entirely exhausted. His provisions had been consumed, he did not know where to get any more. In addition to his own people he had several prizes and over two hundred prisoners who had to be cared for, and who were a healthy and hungry lot.

When he arrived in France he had been authorized to draw upon the commissioners to the extent of twelve thousand livres, with the caution not to avail himself of the permission unless it were imperatively necessary. With great prudence, and by the exercise of rigid economy, he had avoided any inroad on the depleted and overtaxed fund of the commissioners. Something, however, had to be done in this instance, and without securing another authority, for which, indeed, time was wanting, so pressing were his needs, he made drafts upon the commissioners in the sum of twenty-four thousand livres, about five thousand dollars.

Meanwhile he subsisted his crew and prisoners through the generosity of the French naval authorities at Brest, which he secured by the pledge of his own private personal credit. The draft was dishonored. Certainly the commissioners were embarrassed almost beyond endurance by the demands

71

upon them from every side, but this was a matter to which they should have given attention if it were humanly possible, for they were the only resource that Jones had. His condition was simply desperate. He knew not what to do nor where to turn. The following extract of a letter to the commissioners on the 27th of May exhibits his painful position:

"Could I suppose that my letters of the 9th and 16th current (the first advising you of my arrival and giving reference to the events of my expedition; the last advising you of my draft in favour of Monsieur Bersolle, for twenty-four thousand livres, and assigning reasons for the demand) had not made due appearance, I would hereafter, as I do now, inclose copies. Three posts have already arrived here from Paris since Comte d'Orvilliers showed me the answer which he received from the minister, to the letter which inclosed mine to you. Yet you remain silent. M. Bersolle has this moment informed me of the fate of my bills; the more extraordinary as I have not yet made use of your letter of credit of the 10th of January last, whereby I then seemed entitled to call for half the amount of my last draft, and I did not expect to be thought extravagant when, on the 16th current, I doubled that demand. Could this indignity be kept secret I should disregard it; and, though it is already public in Brest and in the fleet, as it affects only my private credit I will not complain. I can not, however, be silent when I find the public credit involved in the same disgrace. I conceive this might have been prevented. To make me completely wretched, Monsieur Bersolle has now told me that he now stops his hand, not only of the necessary articles to refit the ship, but also of the *daily provisions*. I know not where to find to-morrow's dinner for the great number of mouths that depend on me for food. Are then the Continental ships of war to depend on the sale of their prizes for a daily dinner for their men? 'Publish it not in Gath.'

"My officers, as well as men, want clothes, and the prizes are precluded from being sold before farther orders arrive from the minister. I will ask you, gentlemen, if I have deserved all this. Whoever calls himself an American ought to be protected here. I am unwilling to think that you have intentionally involved me in this dilemma, at a time when I ought to expect some enjoyment.

"Therefore I have, as formerly, the honour to be, with due esteem and respect, gentlemen, yours, etc."

How he managed under such circumstances he relates in a journal which he prepared in later years for submission to the King of France.

"Yet during that time, by his [Jones'] personal credit with Comte

D'Orvilliers, the Duc de Chartres, and the Intendant of Brest, he fed his people and prisoners, cured his wounded, and refitted both the Ranger and the Drake for sea."

He could, of course, have relieved himself of some of his burden by turning over his prisoners to France, but, as that country was still nominally neutral, the people he had captured would have been set free at the demand of England. As long as he held possession of them it was possible that the circumstance would force an exchange for Americans—a thing the commissioners had been bent upon since their arrival in Europe. The English Government had long since sanctioned and carried out the exchange of soldiers, but for arbitrary and inadequate reasons seamen stood upon a different footing apparently. When Franklin previously wrote Lord Stormont, the British ambassador, offering to exchange one hundred men captured by the Reprisal for an equal number of American seamen held in English prisons, no answer was made to his letter; a second letter brought forth the following curt reply:

"The king's ambassador receives no applications from rebels, unless they come to implore his Majesty's mercy."

To this insulting and inexplicable message the following apt and dignified reply was made:

"In answer to a letter which concerns some of the material interests of humanity, and of the two nations, Great Britain and the United States of America, now at war, we received the inclosed indecent paper, as coming from your lordship, which we return for your lordship's more mature consideration."

Of course, the ostensible reason for refusing this exchange was that the captured seamen were traitors, and as such had no belligerent rights, yet how they differed from soldiers it is impossible to see. Indeed, the English authorities went so far as to call them pirates, and they could not have treated them worse—short of hanging them—if they had actually merited the opprobrious title. The real reason, however, lay in the hope that the Americans, having no place in France in which to confine their prisoners, would be compelled to set them free. This hope was frequently justified, and it was not until March, 1779, that the persistent determination of Franklin brought about a complete general recognition of the principle of exchange for which he had so valiantly contended, although he had been partially successful on particular occasions before that time. Jones knew the situation perfectly, and so with his usual grim determination he held on to his precious prisoners.

The prize agents were dilatory and incompetent. The seamen, lacking food, clothes, salary, and prize money, were naturally mutinous and discontented. But Jones repressed the crews, hurried up the sales, and managed at last to weather all his troubles.

The malcontent Simpson was a constant incentive to discord and mutiny, and he was finally removed to a French guardship, called the Admiral, where he was well treated and allowed the freedom of the deck. While there, he behaved in such a contumacious manner that D'Orvilliers, the French commander, sent him to the prison of the port. All his expenses during this interval were paid by Jones himself; indeed, when he did not pay personally, nobody did. There was nothing sordid or avaricious in Jones' character. He was greedy for glory and fame and reputation, but he cared nothing whatever for money. To dismiss a tiresome subject, Jones, with extraordinary complaisance, finally accepted Simpson's apologies and released him on his parole not to serve in the navy until he had been regularly tried by a court-martial. He even went further than this. He offered to relinquish the command of the Ranger to him in order that he might take her back to the United States and there take his trial.

While these efforts were pending, the commissioners, misunderstanding their tentative character, restored Simpson to the command of the Ranger, unconditionally, much to Jones' disgust. He was quite willing to relinquish the command of his little ship, because the King of France had requested the commissioners to allow France to avail herself of the services of Jones in a naval expedition which was projected. But that such contumacy and lack of subordination as had been exhibited by Simpson should go unpunished, and that he should receive the absolute command of the ship as a reward for his action, and should be allowed to return home without even an investigation, was not only harmful to the service, but an apparent reflection upon himself—though, of course, nothing was further from the commissioners' thoughts, as they specifically declared. In the end Jones acquiesced in the situation, and the matter was dropped. Simpson was never employed in the service after he returned home.

The famous action between the Arethusa and the Belle Poule, on June 17th, having made it clear to every observer that war between France and England was inevitable, though the formal declaration was not issued until the following September, the first enterprise which it was desired Jones should undertake under the auspices of France was proposed to him by Franklin as follows:

"The Jersey privateers," he says, "do us a great deal of mischief by intercepting our supplies. It has been mentioned to me that your small vessel, commanded by so brave an officer, might render great service by following them where greater ships dare not venture their bottoms; or, being accompanied and supported by some frigates from Brest, at a proper distance, might draw them out and then take them. I wish you to consider of this, as it comes from *high authority*."

It was not a particularly brilliant prospect; all the hard work and dangerous labor was to be performed by Jones, and the glory was to be reaped by the French frigates; but, with a noble disinterestedness in his desire to serve his country, he at once expressed his perfect willingness to co-operate. Before anything came of it, however, Franklin offered him the command of the Indien, in the following letter:

(Private.)

"DEAR SIR: I have the pleasure of informing you that it is proposed to give you the command of the great ship we have built at Amsterdam. By what you wrote to us formerly, I have ventured to say in your behalf, that this proposition would be agreeable to you. You will immediately let me know your resolution; which, that you may be more clear in taking, I must inform you of some circumstances. She is at present the property of the king; but, as there is no war yet declared, you will have the commission and flag of the States, and act under their orders and laws. The Prince de Nassau will make the cruise with you. She is to be brought here under cover as a French merchantman, to be equipped and manned in France. We hope to exchange your prisoners for as many American sailors; but, if that fails, you have your present crew to be made up here with other nations and French. The other commissioners are not acquainted with this proposition as yet, and you see by the nature of it that it is necessary to be kept a secret till we have got the vessel here, for fear of difficulties in Holland, and interception; you will therefore direct your answer to me alone. It being desired that the affair rest between you and me, perhaps it may be best for you to take a trip up here to concert matters, if in general you approve the idea.

"I was much pleased with reading your journal, which we received yesterday."

This is the first mention of the Prince of Nassau-Siegen, who will appear prominently hereafter, and be described in his proper place. Jones was naturally delighted with the flattering prospects, and at once wrote to the prince, acquainting him of the pleasure he anticipated in having him associated with him. A few days later Franklin wrote Jones again as follows:

"PASSY, *June 10, 1778.*

"DEAR SIR: I received yours of 1st instant, with the papers inclosed, which I have shown to the other commissioners, but have not yet had their opinion of them; only I know that they had before (in consideration of the disposition and uneasiness of your people) expressed an inclination to order your ship directly back to America. You will judge from what follows whether it will not be advisable for you to propose their sending her back with her people, and under some other command. In consequence of the high opinion the Minister of the Marine has of your conduct and bravery, it is now settled (observe, that it is to be a secret between us, I being expressly enjoined not to communicate it to any other person), that you are to have the frigate from Holland, which actually belongs to Government, and will be furnished with as many good French seamen as you shall require. But you are to act under Congress commission. As you may be likely to have a number of Americans, and your own are homesick, it is proposed to give you as many as you can engage out of two hundred prisoners, which the ministry of Britain have at length agreed to give us in exchange for those you have in your hands. They propose to make the exchange at Calais, where they are to bring the Americans. Nothing is wanting to this but a list of yours, containing their names and rank; immediately on the receipt of which an equal number are to be prepared, and sent in a ship to that port, where yours are to meet them.

"If by this means you can get a good new crew, I think it would be best that you are quite free of the old, for a mixture might introduce the infection of that sickness you complain of. But this may be left to your own discretion. Perhaps we shall join you with the Providence, Captain Whipple, a new Continental ship of thirty guns, which, in coming out of the river of Providence, gave the two frigates that were posted to intercept her each of them so heavy a dose of her 18- and 12-pounders that they had not the courage or were not able to pursue her. It seems to be desired that you will step up to Versailles (where one will meet you), in order to such a settlement of matters and plans with those who have the direction as can not well be done by letter. I wish it may be convenient to you to do it immediately.

"The project of giving you the command of this ship pleases me the more as it is a probable opening to the higher preferment you so justly merit."

In obedience to this request Jones went privately to Versailles, where he spent some time in consultation with the commissioners and the French ministry discussing the exchange of prisoners, and proposed several plans of attack by which his services could be utilized. These plans well indicate the fertility of imagination, the resourceful genius, and the daring hardihood of the man. One of them was for making another descent upon Whitehaven, another was to attack the Bank of Ayr and destroy or ransom that town; another was to burn the shipping on the Clyde. Expeditions on the coast of Ireland were suggested. London might be distressed, he thought, by cutting off the supplies of coal from Newcastle; but the most feasible projects were the capture or destruction of the West Indian or Baltic fleets of merchantmen or the Hudson Bay ships.

The Minister of Marine, M. de Sartine, lent an attentive ear to all of the plans which were proposed, and Jones returned to Brest with high hopes that he should be soon employed in an expedition to carry out one or the other of these plans with adequate means to do it well. It is quite likely that the minister was as earnest and honest in his intentions as the king in his desire to make use of Jones, but the formal declaration of war rendered it possible to prosecute the enterprises which had been suggested by Jones, if it were thought expedient to attempt them, under the French flag and with French officers. As France had only intended to use him under the cover of the American flag to harass England before war was declared, and as that could now be done openly under her own flag, they did not see the same necessity for his services as before.

The matter of finding employment for him was further complicated by the fact that since a state of actual war existed the ministry was besieged with applications from numbers of French officers for command, and the ships which had been proposed for Jones were naturally appropriated to the French themselves. Even if a command could have been found for the American, there would have been a natural disinclination, so great as to be nearly prohibitive of success, on the part of the French officers to serving under a foreigner. Time brought him nothing but disappointment, and the high hopes he had cherished gradually waned.

Always a persistent and voluminous letter writer, in his desperation he overwhelmed everybody with correspondence. Inaction was killing to him. Not to be employed was like death itself to a man of his intensely energetic temperament. His pride would not permit him to return to the United States and seek a command when he had specifically announced, in a letter to Congress by the returning Ranger, that the King of France asked that he might make use of his services, and therefore no command in America need be reserved for him; and yet he now found himself a hanger on the outskirts of a court and a ministry which had no further use for him.

The delicate situation of the commissioners, who had been themselves scarcely more than on sufferance, did not permit them, in the interests of expediency and diplomacy, to insist as strongly as they would have liked to do, that the king and the ministry should keep their engagement with Jones, which was, of course, an engagement with them and with the United States. Diplomacy and persuasion were the only weapons at their command. They certainly made good use of them. Franklin, pending something else, procured the minister's order that Jones should be received on the great French fleet of D'Orvilliers, which was about to put to sea to engage the English fleet under Keppel. He was very desirous of availing himself of this invitation, which he himself sought, for it would give him an opportunity he could not otherwise hope to enjoy, of perfecting himself in naval tactics and the fine art of maneuvering and governing a great fleet. He never allowed anything to interfere—so far as he was able to prevent it—with his advancement in professional study. The permission, however, to D'Orvilliers' great regret, arrived too late, for the fleet sailed without him. The French admiral seems to have appreciated the American captain, and to have highly esteemed him. It is stated that the delay in transmitting the permission was intentional, and was due to the jealousy of the French naval service.

Jones was exasperated by all these happenings almost to the breaking point. In one letter he says: "I think of going to L'Orient, being heartily sick of Brest." I should think he would be! As days passed without bringing him any nearer to the fruition of his hope, he became more modest in his demands and propositions. One significant phrase culled from one of his letters well indicates the bold, dashing character of the man: "I do not wish to have command of any ship that does not sail fast, *for I intend to go in harm's way*."[7] In the sentence which follows this statement, we get another touch of that entire consciousness of his own ability and high quality which, though warranted, it were better, perhaps, for his reputation if it were not so evident in his writing: "I know, I believe, that this is no other person's intention. Therefore, buy a frigate that sails fast and is sufficiently large to carry twenty-six or twenty-eight guns on one deck."

His state of mind may well be understood from this citation: "I have, to show my gratitude to France, lost so much time, and with it such opportunities as I can not regain. I have almost killed myself with grief."

Chafing, fretting, writing letters, the time dragged on. At last he addressed to the Minister of Marine, M. de Sartine, this emphatic protest and statement which he calls, and justly, an explicit letter. It is certainly sufficiently definite and clear, and shows that rank and position did not deter him from a free and somewhat sarcastic expression of his grievances and wrongs:

"BREST, *September 13, 1778.*

"HONOURED SIR: When his excellency Doctor Franklin informed me that you had condescended to think me worthy of your notice, I took such pleasure in reflecting on the happy alliance between France and America that I was really flattered, and entertained the most grateful sense of the honour which you proposed for me, as well as the favour which the king proposed for America, by putting so fine a ship as the Indien under my command, and under its flag, with unlimited orders.

"In obedience to your desire, I came to Versailles, and was taught to believe that my intended ship was in deep water, and ready for sea; but when the Prince [de Nassau] returned I received from him a different account; I was told that the Indien could not be got afloat within a shorter period than three months at the approaching equinox.

"To employ this interval usefully, I first offered to go from Brest with Count D'Orvilliers as a volunteer, which you thought fit to reject. I had then the satisfaction to find that you approved in general of a variety of hints for private enterprises which I had drawn up for your consideration, and I was flattered with assurances from Messieurs de Chaumont and Baudouin that three of the finest frigates in France, with two tenders and a number of troops, would be immediately put under my command; and that I should have unlimited orders, and be at free liberty to pursue such of my own projects as I thought proper. But this plan fell to nothing in the moment when I was taught to think that nothing was wanting but the king's signature.

"Another much inferior armament from L'Orient was proposed to be put under my command, which was by no means equal to the services that were expected from it; for speed and force, though both requisite, were both wanting. Happily for me, this also failed, and I was thereby saved from a dreadful prospect of ruin and dishonour.

"I had so entire a reliance that you would desire nothing of me inconsistent with my honour and rank, that the moment you required me to come down here, in order to proceed round to St. Malo, though I had received no written orders, and neither knew your intention respecting my destination or command, I obeyed with such haste, that although my curiosity led me to look at the armament at L'Orient, yet I was but three days from Passy till I reached Brest. Here, too, I drew a blank; but when I saw the Lively it was no disappointment, as that ship, both in sailing and equipment, is far inferior to the Ranger.

"My only disappointment here was my being precluded from embarking in pursuit of marine knowledge with Count D'Orvilliers, who did not sail till seven days after my return. He is my friend, and expressed his wishes for my company; I accompanied him out of the road when the fleet sailed, and he always lamented that neither himself nor any person in authority in Brest had received from you any order that mentioned my name. I am astonished therefore to be informed that you attribute my not being in the fleet to my stay at L'Orient.

"I am not a mere adventurer of fortune. Stimulated by principles of reason and philanthropy, I laid aside my enjoyments in private life, and embarked under the flag of America when it was first displayed. In that line my desire of fame is infinite, and I must not now so far forget my own honour, and what I owe to my friends and America, as to remain inactive.

"My rank knows no superior in the American marine. I have long since been appointed to command an expedition with five of its ships, and I can receive orders from no junior or inferior officer whatever.

"I have been here in the most tormenting suspense for more than a month since my return; and, agreeable to your desire, as mentioned to me by Monsieur Chaumont, a lieutenant has been appointed, and is with me, who speaks the French as well as the English. Circular letters have been written, and sent the 8th of last month from the English admiralty, because they expected me to pay another visit with four ships. Therefore I trust that, if the Indien is not to be got out, you will not, at the approaching season, substitute a force that is not at least equal both in strength and sailing to any of the enemy's cruising ships.

"I do not wish to interfere with the harmony of the French marine; but, if I am still thought worthy of your attention, I shall hope for a separate command, with liberal orders. If, on the contrary, you should now have no further occasion for my services, the only favour I can ask is that you will bestow on me the Alert, with a few seamen, and permit me to return, and carry with me your good opinion in that small vessel, before the winter, to America."

His intense, burning desire for action, however, did not permit him to degrade, as he thought, his Government and station by accepting the command of a privateer which was tendered to him. In the command of a speedy, smart privateer there is no limit to the plundering he might have done and the treasure he might have gained, if that had been what he wished. Many naval officers before and since his time have done this and thought it not derogatory to their dignity. It is therefore to Jones' credit that he was very jealous in this and many other instances on the point of honor of serving in no ship, under no flag, and with no commission save that of the United States. We shall see this spirit again and again. The citizen of the world was beginning to feel that the world as his country was hardly adequate to his needs; in theory it was a very pretty proposition, but in practice it was necessary to form and maintain a more definite and particular relationship. As a final effort to better his condition and secure that opportunity for which he thirsted, he prepared the following letter to the king:

"BREST, *October 19, 1778.*

"SIRE: After my return to Brest in the American ship of war the Ranger, from the Irish Channel, his excellency Doctor Franklin informed me by letter, dated June the 1st, that M. de Sartine, having a high opinion of my conduct and bravery, had determined, with your Majesty's consent and approbation, to give me the command of the ship of war the Indien, which was built at Amsterdam for America, but afterward, for political reasons, made the property of France.

"I was to act with unlimited orders under the commission and flag of America; and the Prince de Nassau proposed to accompany me on the ocean.

"I was deeply penetrated with the sense of the honour done me by this generous proposition, as well as of the favour your Majesty intended thereby to confer on America. And I accepted the offer with the greater pleasure as the Congress had sent me to Europe in the Ranger to command the Indien before the ownership of that vessel was changed.

"The minister desired to see me at Versailles to settle future plans of operation, and I attended him for that purpose. I was told that the Indien was at the Texel completely armed and fitted for sea; but the Prince de Nassau was sent express to Holland, and returned with a very different account. The ship was at Amsterdam, and could not be got afloat or armed before the September equinox. The American plenipotentiaries proposed that I should return to America; and, as I have repeatedly been appointed to the chief command of an American squadron to execute secret enterprises, it was not doubted but that Congress would again show me a preference. M. de Sartine, however, thought proper to prevent my departure, by writing to the plenipotentiaries (without my knowledge), requesting that I might be permitted to remain in Europe, and that the Ranger might be sent back to America under another commander, he having special services which he wished me to execute. This request they readily granted, and I was flattered by the prospect of being enabled to testify, by my services, my gratitude to your Majesty, as the first prince who has so generously acknowledged our independence.

"There was an interval of more than three months before the Indien could be gotten afloat. To employ that period usefully, when your Majesty's fleet was ordered to sail from Brest, I proposed to the minister to embark in it as a volunteer, in pursuit of marine knowledge. He objected to this, at the same time approved of a variety of hints for private enterprises, which I had drawn up for his consideration. Two gentlemen were appointed to settle with me the plans that were to be adopted, who gave me the assurance that three of the best frigates in France, with two tenders, and a number of troops, should be immediately put under my command, to pursue such of my own projects as I thought proper; but this fell to nothing, when I believed that your Majesty's signature only was wanting.

"Another armament, composed of cutters and small vessels, at L'Orient, was proposed to be put under my command, to alarm the coasts of England and check the Jersey privateers; but happily for me this also failed, and I was saved from ruin and dishonour, as I now find that all the vessels sailed slow, and their united force is very insignificant. The minister then thought fit that I should return to Brest to command the Lively, and join some frigates on an expedition from St. Malo to the North Sea. I returned in haste for that purpose, and found that the Lively had been bestowed at Brest before the minister had mentioned that ship to me at Versailles. This was, however, another fortunate disappointment, as the Lively proves, both in sailing and equipment, much inferior to the Ranger; but, more especially, if it be true, as I have since understood, that the minister intended to give the chief command of an expedition to a lieutenant, which would have occasioned a very disagreeable misunderstanding; for, as an officer of the first rank in the American marine, who has ever been honoured with the favour and friendship of Congress, I can receive orders from no inferior officer whatever. My plan was the destruction of the English Baltic fleet, of great consequence to the enemy's marine, and then only protected by a single frigate. I would have held myself responsible for its success had I commanded the expedition.

"M. de Sartine afterward sent orders to Count D'Orvilliers to receive me on board the fleet agreeably to my former proposal; but the order did not arrive until after the departure of the fleet the last time from Brest, nor was I made acquainted with the circumstance before the fleet returned here.

"Thus have I been chained down to shameful inactivity for nearly five months. I have lost the best season of the year, and such opportunities of serving my country and acquiring honour as I can not again expect this war; and, to my infinite mortification, having no command, I am considered everywhere an officer cast off and in disgrace for secret reasons.

"I have written respectful letters to the minister, none of which he has condescended to answer; I have written to the Prince de Nassau with as little effect; and I do not understand that any apology has been made to the great and venerable Dr. Franklin, whom the minister has made the instrument of bringing me into such unmerited trouble.

"Having written to Congress to reserve no command for me in America, my sensibility is the more affected by this unworthy situation in the sight of your Majesty's fleet. I, however, make no remark on the treatment I have received.

"Although I wish not to become my own panegyrist, I must beg your Majesty's permission to observe that I am not an adventurer in search of fortune, of which, thank God, I have a sufficiency.

"When the American banner was first displayed I drew my sword in support of the violated dignity and rights of human nature; and both honour and duty prompt me steadfastly to continue the righteous pursuit, and to sacrifice to it not only my own private enjoyments, but even life, if necessary. I must acknowledge that the generous praise which I have received from Congress and others exceeds the merit of my past services, therefore I the more ardently wish for future opportunities of testifying my gratitude by my activity.

"As your Majesty, by espousing the cause of America, hath become the protector of the rights of human nature, I am persuaded that you will not disregard my situation, nor suffer me to remain any longer in this unsupportable disgrace.

"I am, with perfect gratitude and profound respect, Sire, your Majesty's very obliged, very obedient, and very humble servant,

"J. PAUL JONES."

This letter, at once dignified, forceful, respectful, and modest, was inclosed to Dr. Franklin with the request that it should be delivered to the king. The deference paid to Franklin's opinion, the eager desire to please him, the respect in which he held him, is not the least pleasing feature of Jones' character, by the way. The letter in question was withheld by Franklin with Jones' knowledge and acquiescence, and the king, it is probable, never saw it. There was, in fact, no necessity for its delivery, for the appeals, prayers, and importunities had at last evoked a response. The minister, worn out by the persistence of Jones, determined, since none of the French naval vessels were available, to buy him a ship and assemble a squadron and send him forth.

The inquiry naturally arises why the French Government should care to go to the trouble and expense of doing this. Before the war was declared their action was understandable, but afterward the then operating cause disappeared. Yet there was another reason aside from the fact that M. de Sartine was willing to keep his promise if he could, and that was this:

It was not the custom to harry, plunder, and ravage the seacoasts in the wars between France and England. Military or naval forces were the sole objects of attack, and by a specific though unwritten law of custom, the efforts of the rival combatants were confined to ships of war, fortifications, and armies, and, of course, to merchant vessels belonging to the enemy. The peaceful seashore towns were generally let alone unless the inhabitants in exposed localities provoked retaliation by aggression—a thing they usually took good care not to do. To introduce the practice would be unfortunate and nothing would be gained, by France especially. The King of France, however, was more than willing to have the coasts of his neighbor ravaged, if no retaliation on his own unprotected shores were provoked thereby. No convention of any sort, expressed or understood, existed between Great Britain and the United States which would prevent such action on the part of the Americans. Great Britain was making a bloody ravaging warfare on the coasts of North America, and, never dreaming of reprisal, paid no attention whatever to this law of war, save when it suited her to do so, on our seaboard. Franklin and the commissioners wisely realized that the only way to stop this merciless and brutal burning and plundering was to let the enemy experience the thing himself. They were therefore in entire accord with the desire of the

French king. To produce the result he would furnish the squadron, they the flag. It was a charming arrangement from the king's point of view. Consequently the reason for the encouragement given Jones is apparent, and the determination of the minister is therefore explained and understood.

Jones received word early in November through the commissioners, with a solemn assurance from De Sartine, that a suitable ship would be purchased for him at the expense of France and a squadron assembled under his supreme command. Let those who would reproach Jones for his part in this plan remember that (as in his previous cruise) he only carried out the orders of Franklin. There was no sentimental nonsense about the old Quaker. He knew what was the best remedy for the deplorable conditions in America, and he grimly prepared to apply it. He had no illusions in the premises at all; it was a pure matter of business, and with sound policy he so treated it. Jones' appeals, be it understood, were only for a ship or ships and an opportunity to get into action with the enemy. His orders were outside of his control. All he had to do as a naval officer was to carry them out to the best of his ability when he received them. Therefore a censure of Jones is a censure of Franklin.

It was first designed to employ Jones and his proposed squadron for a descent upon Liverpool, for which purpose five hundred men from Fitzmaurice's Irish regiment were to be taken on the ships. Pending the assembling of the squadron, and while Jones was busily engaged in seeking for a proper vessel for himself in various French ports, Lafayette arrived from America, and sought the command of the land forces of the proposed expedition. His desire was a notable tribute to the sailor, by the way. The change was most agreeable to Jones, to whom, of course, the reputation and abilities of Lafayette were well known, and who would naturally prefer association with such a distinguished man in the undertaking, but, as usual, there were delays on the part of the minister.

Jones traveled about from port to port, looking at different ships which it was proposed to purchase for him. The minister offered him the Duc de Broglie, a large new ship lying at Nantes, capable of mounting sixty-four guns. He inspected her, and would have taken her gladly, but he felt utterly unable properly to man such a large ship, and he was reluctantly compelled to dismiss her from consideration. There was also at Nantes a smaller ship, the Ariel, of twenty guns, which had been captured from the English, which he was willing to accept if nothing better turned up. Another vessel that he looked at was a great old-fashioned merchant ship, lying dismantled at L'Orient, which had been some fourteen years in the India trade, and was very much out of repair. She was called the Duc de Duras. Jones thought she might do in default of anything else, and he so informed the minister.

However, in spite of the promises that had been made and reiterated to him, and the determination which had been arrived at, nothing was done. His visits of inspection were fruitless, his propositions were disregarded as before. Furthermore, the plan to send Lafayette with him fell through because France was at that time projecting a grand descent in force upon England, and Lafayette was designated to command a regiment in the proposed undertaking. Like other similar projects, the plan was never put in operation. Though France did enter the Channel with sixty-six French and Spanish ships of the line, she did not accomplish as much with this great armada as Paul Jones did with the little squadron he finally was enabled to assemble.

Meanwhile he was at his wits' end. The year had nearly passed and nothing had been done. He had been put off with promises until he was desperate. Chance, it is stated, threw in his way one day, as he sat idle at Nantes, gloomily ruminating on the prospect, or lack of it, and almost making up his mind to go back to the United States in the first vessel that offered and seek such opportunity for service as might arise there, a copy of Franklin's famous book of maxims, called Poor Richard's Almanac. As the harassed little captain sat listlessly turning its pages, his eyes fell upon this significant aphorism:

"If a man wishes to have any business faithfully and expeditiously performed, let him go on it himself; otherwise he may send."

The truth of the saying inspired him to one final effort before he abandoned European waters. He went to Versailles in November, 1778, for one last visit, and there settled the matter. His determination and persistence at last, as it had many times before, brought him success. De Sartine directed the purchase of the Duras, which Jones, from his love for Franklin and the circumstance just related, with the consent of the minister, renamed the Bon Homme Richard, that being the French equivalent for Poor Richard, or Good Man Richard, which was the caption of the almanac.

De Sartine appointed as the agent and commissary of the king for the purchase and refitting of the Duras and the other vessels of the squadron, and for the disposal of any prizes which might be taken, in short, as his representative with entire liberty of action, Monsieur le Ray de Chaumont. This gentleman, belonging, of course, to the nobility of the country, was a man of considerable influence at the court, where he had held the responsible dual position of Grand Master of the Forests and Waters of the King. Since the arrival of the American commissioners he had shown his devotion to the cause of liberty and to them personally by many and conspicuous acts of kindness.

It was his private residence at Passy that Franklin made his headquarters during his long tenure of office. De Chaumont had offered him the use of this house, and with generous and splendid hospitality had refused to accept of any remuneration by way of rental. Realizing the pressing necessity of the struggling colonists for every dollar they could scrape together, he positively declined to impair their limited resources by any charge whatsoever. Franklin endeavored to change his decision, and when John Adams replaced Deane he made the same effort, but the generous Frenchman refused to recede from his determination. He also placed his private purse at the disposal of Franklin, and in every way showed himself a worthy and disinterested friend of America.

He was one of those romantic Frenchmen who espoused the cause of the rights of man under the influence of the new philosophy of Rousseau and Voltaire; somewhat, it would seem, from motives similar to those proclaimed by Jones himself. He had nothing to gain by his action and much to lose should the effort of the colonists result in failure. He was a man of affairs and possessed an ample fortune. To anticipate events, it may be stated that he spent it all in the cause to which he had devoted himself, and eventually became bankrupt. He was not a military man; still less was he aware of the exigencies and demands of the naval service. For the present, however, he did his work efficiently and well.

The Duras was purchased immediately, as were two other merchant vessels, the Pallas and the Vengeance, all at the cost of the royal treasury. To these were added the Cerf, a king's cutter, a well-appointed and efficient vessel, and the United States ship Alliance, a new and very handsome frigate built at Salisbury, Massachusetts, in 1778, which had arrived in Europe with Lafayette as a passenger. Jones had specifically asked that the American frigate should be assigned to his squadron—a most unfortunate request, as it afterward turned out.

The Duras was an East Indiaman of obsolete type; a large, old-fashioned ship with a very high poop and topgallant forecastle. She had made, during many years of service, a number of round voyages to the East Indies. While stoutly built for a merchant ship, as compared to a man-of-war of her size she was of light and unsubstantial frame. In the absence of particular information I suppose her to have been of something under eight hundred tons burden. Neglect had allowed her to fall into such a bad condition that her efficiency as a proposed war vessel was further impaired by her inability to stand the necessary repairs.

Jones, however, surveyed her and determined to make her do. Indeed, there was no choice; it was that or nothing. He hoped to effect something with her which would warrant him in demanding a better ship; so, with a sigh of regret for the Indien, he set to work upon her, doing his best to make her efficient. By his orders she was pierced for twenty-eight guns on her main deck and six on the poop and forecastle. In order to further increase her force, Jones, after much deliberation, resorted to the hazardous experiment of cutting six ports in the gun room, on the deck below the gun deck, close to the water line; so close, in fact, that, with anything like a sea on, to open the ports would be to invite destruction by foundering.[8] Only under exceptionally favorable circumstances, therefore, could these guns be used. At best the gun-room battery could only be fought in the calmest weather and smoothest water. In this dangerous place he mounted six old and condemned 18-pounders, which were all that he could obtain from the French arsenals. On the main deck fourteen 12-pounders and fourteen 9-pounders were mounted.[9] Two 9-pounders were placed aft on the quarter-deck, two in each gangway, and two on the forecastle. All the guns were old and worn out; many of them had been condemned by the French Government as unfit for use. The six guns on the lower deck were mounted three on a side, but a sufficient number of ports had been cut to admit of shifting the guns and working the whole battery on either side. New guns had been ordered cast for the Richard at the French gun foundries; but the usual delays compelled Jones to take what he could, and finally sail with these old makeshifts. The guns intended for the Bon Homme Richard arrived after she had gone.

The Alliance was a frigate-built ship of thirty-two guns, 9- and 6-pounders, manned by two hundred and fifty men, and commanded by Pierre Landais. Landais was an ex-officer of the French navy, who had been dismissed for insubordination and incapacity. Ignorant of these facts, knowing only that he had been a navy officer, and wishing to please their royal ally, and perhaps pay a delicate compliment also to Lafayette, who was a passenger upon the ship on her first cruise, the marine commissioners had appointed him to the command of this fine and handsome little frigate. The Alliance was one of the fastest ships of her day; indeed, she may be regarded as the precursor of that long line of splendid frigates and sloops of war which have been the pride of American shipbuilders and the admiration of foreign navies. Properly re-armed and refitted, under the command of stout old John Barry she did splendid service on several occasions later in the war. Her swiftness and mobility, it was believed, would add greatly to the usefulness of Jones' squadron.

The Pallas was a fairly efficient merchant ship, frigate built, carrying thirty 6-pounders, commanded by Captain de Cottineau de Kloguene. The Vengeance was a twelve-gun brig of little force, and the Cerf a sixteen-gun cutter, under the command of Captains Ricot and de Varage respectively.

After many difficulties and disheartening delays, chiefly overcome by Jones' invincible determination and persistence, the squadron was at last made ready for use. The first duty assigned to the daring commodore was a cruise for the driving of the enemy's ships out of the Bay of Biscay, and convoying merchant ships bound from port to port along the coast. It was not a particularly congenial duty, but he entered upon it zealously and without complaint.

The squadron sailed on the 19th of June, 1779. During the night of the 20th the Alliance ran foul of the Richard, and as a result of the collision the mizzenmast of the Alliance was carried away, while the Richard lost her head, cutwater, jib boom, etc. The blame for the accident mainly rested on Landais, who, it was afterward developed, had behaved disgracefully on this occasion, showing such a lack of presence of mind and seamanly aptitude, coupled with such timidity and shrinking from duty, that, when the accident occurred, he not only gave no orders, but basely ran below to load his pistols, leaving the ship to be extricated from her critical situation by the junior officers. Perhaps he was afraid that the infuriated Jones would attack him for the mishandling of his ship. Jones, who had been below when the accident occurred, immediately assumed charge of the Richard, and by prompt action averted a more serious disaster. To do Landais justice, however, the officer of the watch on the Richard also must have been culpable, for he was subsequently court-martialed and broken for his lack of conduct on this occasion.

Refusing to return to port, and patching up the two ships as well as possible from their present resources, Jones performed the duties assigned to him, driving the enemy's ships out of those waters and safely delivering his convoy. On the return voyage, Captain de Varage, of the Cerf, had a spirited encounter with a heavily armed privateer of greater force than his own, which lasted for an hour and ten minutes and resulted in the privateer striking her flag. Before he could take possession, however, other ships of the enemy appeared, and he was forced to abandon his prize. The Richard chased several sail, two of which were thought to be frigates, and the officers and men manifested every disposition to get into action; but the ships sighted were all able to run away from the cumbrous and slow-sailing American ship.

On the last day of June the squadron put into L'Orient again to repair damages. During the cruise it is interesting to note that Jones dispatched thirty pounds, in the shape of a draft, through a friend in Dublin, to Scotland for the use of his family. He frequently made them remittances from his scanty supplies of money, and, in fact, he never forgot them, however busy with great undertakings he may have been.

Instructions were received at L'Orient from Franklin intended to govern the future movements of the squadron. They had, of course, been prepared after consultation with De Sartine. Jones was directed to cruise off the west coast of Ireland to intercept the West Indian ships and then to proceed to the northward, passing the Orkneys, and range down the coast of Scotland and endeavor to capture the Baltic fleet—which, by the way, had been one of his original projects. After carrying out these orders he was instructed to proceed to the Texel about August 15th, where he would find further directions awaiting him. Prizes were to be sent to Dunkirk or Ostend in France, or Bergen in Norway, consigned to such agents as De Chaumont should designate.

Jones was very much disappointed, naturally, with the Richard, and in acknowledging the receipt of these instructions he made a last effort to get the Indien. It was intimated that such might be the result of his cruise when he arrived at the Texel, if it were successful, but that no change could be made in his orders at present. Franklin refused to attempt to have them modified by consulting with the ministry, and, in a way gentle but sufficiently decided, he directed Jones to finish repairing the ships with all speed and proceed to carry out the orders he had received. The commodore, swallowing his disappointment and dissatisfaction with a rather ill grace, it must be confessed, hastened to get his ships in shape for the proposed expedition.

During the cruise in the Bay of Biscay a mutinous spirit had broken out among the English seamen, with whom in part Jones had been forced to man his ship in default of other men, which had become sufficiently developed to result in an organized conspiracy to take the Richard. The plot was discovered and the ringleaders were put in irons. When the Richard arrived at L'Orient, these men, two quartermasters, were court-martialed; but, instead of being sentenced to death, as they deserved, they were severely flogged with the cat-o'-nine-tails. Jones, who, if he erred, leaned to the side of mercy, seems to have been greatly relieved at this termination of the affair. At this time the lieutenant of the Richard, who had been in charge of the watch during the collision, was also court-martialed and dismissed the service.

These several unfortunate happenings had given De Sartine a very low idea of the efficiency and value of the Bon Homme Richard and the squadron, which galled Jones extremely. Indeed, I imagine De Sartine looked upon Jones in the light of a nuisance more than anything else. The repairs progressed very slowly, and it was not until August that the ships were ready to proceed. Meanwhile an event of the greatest importance had occurred in the arrival of a cartel at Nantes with one hundred and nineteen exchanged American prisoners. Many of them entered on the Richard, and Jones was thus enabled to weed out a large proportion of the mutinous and disorderly element in his crew. The fine qualities of some of these new recruits enabled him to replace many of his petty officers—invaluable adjuncts to an efficient crew—with experienced seamen who could be depended upon, not merely as sailors, but as men who, fresh from the horrors and brutalities of English prisons, were more than ready to fight against the red flag wherever it was planted. They leavened the whole mass.

The re-enforcement was of the greatest value; but Jones' good fortune did not end here, for before he sailed again he was joined by a young American naval officer of the highest capacity and courage, named Richard Dale, who had been captured in the Lexington and held a prisoner in England. He had effected a most daring and romantic escape from the Mill Prison by the assistance of an unknown woman, whose name and the circumstances of their acquaintance remained a mystery; Dale absolutely refused to divulge them to the day of his death.

Jones found in him a congenial spirit and an able subordinate. He promptly appointed him first lieutenant of the Richard, and between the two men there speedily developed a friendship as lasting as it was unaffected and disinterested. Next to Jones himself, in the early records, stands the name of this young man, then scarcely twenty-three years of age. Aside from the great commodore, it was he who contributed more to the subsequent success of the Richard than any other man. At the request of De Sartine, Jones also received on the Richard a battalion of royal marines, who were all French of course, and who had been augmented until they numbered one hundred and thirty-seven officers and men, under Lieutenant-Colonel de Chamillard de Warville. It was supposed by the minister that they could at least keep order on the ship! The time limited to the expiration of the cruise was extended to the end of the month of September.

The total complement of the Richard, therefore, according to Jones' statement, was about three hundred and eighty officers, men, and boys, including the one hundred and thirty-seven marines. A roll of officers and men is given by Sherburne in his Life of Jones.

On this list, which purports to contain the names of those who were on board on the date of the battle with the Serapis, are enumerated the names of but two hundred and twenty-seven officers and men. It omits the name of de Chamillard and another colonel of infantry, de Weibert, who were actually on board, and gives no names of the French marines. Adding the two hundred and twenty-seven to the one hundred and thirty-seven, we get three hundred and sixty-four, which is as near as we can come to Jones' figures. There may have been others whose names were added later on, but at any rate it is safe to take Jones' statement as practically correct.

Assuming that the known factors fairly represented the whole crew, we find that among the officers twenty-four were Americans, two were Frenchmen, and six British, including Jones and two surgeon's mates. Among the seamen fifty-five were American born, sixteen Irish, sixty-one British, twenty-eight Portuguese, twenty who are not described, of whom seven were probably Portuguese, and fifteen of other nationalities, including, according to Cooper, some Malays—possibly Filipinos learning thus early to fight for freedom under, not against, the Stars and Stripes! Thus, scarcely more than one fifth of the complement were native Americans. The marines, of course, were efficiently organized and commanded, and were of the usual character of the men in the French service. The rest of the crew, with the exception of the Americans, who were filling the posts of petty officers, were a hard-bitten, reckless crowd of adventurers, mercenaries, bravos, and what not, whom only a man like Jones could control and successfully direct. Under his iron hand they developed into as ready a crew as ever fought a ship, and in our estimation of his subsequent success the fact must not be lost sight of that he made out of such a motley assemblage so efficient an organization. The officers were fairly capable, though none of them reached the standard of Dale, and at least one of them left the cruise with a serious cloud upon his reputation.

Perhaps two thirds of the crew of the Alliance were English seamen who had been recruited from the men of the line of battle ship Somerset, which had been wrecked in America, and a large number of her crew captured. They enlisted on the Alliance in the hope of capturing her and making their escape, thus avoiding a sojourn in American prisons. On the way to France, owing to the presence of these men on the ship, a conspiracy had developed, the successful termination of which was only prevented by the resolution and courage of Lafayette and the passengers with the regular officers of the ship. There were but a small number of Americans on the Alliance, owing to the fact that she was commanded by a Frenchman, under whom Americans generally refused to sail. The officers, with few exceptions, were poor in quality. Her crew had been somewhat improved before the squadron sailed, by the enlistment of some of the prisoners from the cartel, but it was still far from being an efficient body of men, and under such a captain as Landais there was no hope of it ever becoming so.

The officers and crew of the Pallas, Vengeance, and Cerf were French *in toto*, the officers all holding French commissions. The squadron was entirely at the charges of the French Government, although each of the officers sailed with a supplementary American commission issued by Franklin and his *confrères*, and all the vessels were under the American flag.

De Chaumont had been indefatigable in fitting out the ships as best he could, and personally he had done everything in his power to further the success of the enterprise. If his labors had ceased there, the results would have been better; but, probably under the direction of the minister, and influenced by the natural reluctance of the French officers and men to serve under the command of an officer of another country, de Chaumont prepared a concordat, which he suppressed until just before the time of sailing, when it was exhibited to Jones and the other captains and their signatures demanded. By the terms of this singular document the officers and men and the several vessels of the squadron, instead of being under the absolute charge of Jones himself, as is the case with every properly organized expedition, were formed into a species of alliance offensive and defensive; and while, of course, the headship was necessarily under Jones while he lived, he was so hampered and restricted by the various articles of the agreement as to feel himself scarcely more than first among his equals. He was left with full responsibility for success, but so shorn of power and ability to compel obedience to his orders as to render it necessary for him to resort to persuasion to effect his end. Any ordinary commander would have withdrawn at the last moment, but Jones was determined upon effecting something; so, with great reluctance and unavailing protests, he signed the concordat, and the ill-assorted squadron proceeded on its way.[10]

Surely never before was such an expedition for warlike purposes put forth upon the narrow seas! It is difficult to see what result any sane man could have legitimately expected from it. That it accomplished anything was due to Jones himself—commodore by virtue of a paper agreement, just as binding and effective as any of the several signers wished it to be! The world had long known him as a man remarkable for audacity in conception, boldness in planning, hardihood in carrying out, and downright courage in the supreme moment. As a seaman and a fighter he had few equals and no masters. But the cruise developed that he possessed other qualities of leadership which are sometimes lost sight of in this brilliant galaxy, qualities which his previous experience had not led us to expect him to exhibit. He was shown to be considerate, tactful, forbearing, persuasive, holding himself under strong restraint. Naturally of a passionate, impetuous, uncontrollable nature, that he exhibited these qualities speaks well for the man. He had learned to control his feelings in the bitter school of procrastination, evasion, and disappointment of the past year.

CHAPTER IX.

THE CRUISE OF THE SQUADRON.

All things being as ready as it was possible to make them, on the 14th of August, 1779, amid the booming of cannon and the waving of flags, the expedition set sail. Very pretty it must have looked, dropping down the roads, as sail after sail was set on the broad yardarms extending above the little commander on the poop deck of the Indiaman, resolutely putting his difficulties and trials behind him, and glad to be at last at sea and headed for the enemy. And yet he might well have borne a heavy heart! Only a man of Jones' caliber could have faced the possibilities with a particle of equanimity. By any rule of chance or on any ground of probability the expedition was doomed to failure, capture, or destruction. But the personality of Jones, his serene and soon-to-be-justified confidence in himself, discounted chance and overthrew probability. I have noticed it is ever the man with the fewest resources and poorest backing who accomplishes most in the world's battles. The man who has things made easy for him usually "takes it easy," and accomplishes the easy thing or nothing.

The squadron was accompanied by two heavily armed privateers, the Monsieur and the Granvelle, raising the number of vessels to seven. The masters of the privateers did not sign the concordat, but they entered into voluntary association with the others and agreed to abide by the orders of Jones—an agreement they broke without hesitation in the face of the first prize, which was captured on the 18th of August. The prize was a full-rigged ship, called the Verwagting, mounting fourteen guns and loaded with brandy. The vessel, a Dutch ship, had been captured by the English, and was therefore a lawful prize to the squadron. The captain of the Monsieur, which was the boarding vessel, plundered the prize of several valuable articles for his own benefit, manned her, and attempted to dispatch her to Ostend. Jones, however, overhauled her, replaced the prize crew by some of his own men, and sent her in under his own orders. The Monsieur and her offended captain thereupon promptly deserted the squadron in the night.

On the 21st, off the southwest coast of Ireland, they captured a brig, the Mayflower, loaded with butter, which was also manned and sent in. On the 23d they rounded Cape Clear, the extreme southwestern point of Ireland. The day being calm, Jones manned his boats and sent them inshore to capture a brigantine. The ship, not having steerage way, began to drift in toward the dangerous shore after the departure of the boats, and it became necessary to haul her head offshore, for which purpose the captain's barge was sent ahead with a towline. As the shades of evening descended, the crew of the barge, who were apparently English, took advantage of the absence of the other boats and the opportunity presented, to cut the towline and desert. As they made for the shore, Mr. Cutting Lunt, third lieutenant, with four marines, jumped into a small boat remaining, and chased the fugitives without orders; but, pursuing them too far from the ship, a fog came down which caused him to lose his bearings, and prevented him from joining the Richard that night.

The crew of a commodore's barge, like the crew of a captain's gig, is usually made up of picked men, and the character of the Richard's crew is well indicated by this desertion. The other boats luckily managed to rejoin the Richard, after succeeding in cutting out the brigantine. The ships beat to and fro off the coast until the next day, when the captains assembled on the Richard. Landais behaved outrageously on this occasion. He reproached Jones in the most abusive manner, as if the desertion of the barge and the loss of the two boats was due to negligence on his part. One can imagine with what grim silence the irate little American listened to the absurd tirade, and in what strong control he held himself to keep from arresting Landais where he stood. It gives us a vivid picture of the situation of the fleet to find that Jones was actually compelled to consult with his captains and obtain the consent of de Varage before he could order the Cerf to reconnoiter the coast, if possible to find the two boats and their crews.

Thus, as Commodore Mackenzie, himself a naval officer, grimly remarks:

"Before giving orders of indispensable necessity, as a superior officer, we find him taking the advice of one captain and obtaining the consent and approbation of another."

But we may be sure that it was only dire necessity that required such a course of action. Evidently the situation was not to the liking of the commodore, but it was one that he could not remedy.

As the Cerf approached the shore to reconnoiter, she hoisted the English colors to disguise her nationality, and was seen by Mr. Lunt, who had evidently overtaken the deserters. Mistaking her character, he pulled in toward the shore to escape the fancied danger, and was easily captured by the English with the two boats and their crews. By this unfortunate mishap the Richard lost two of her boats, containing an officer and twenty-two men. The Cerf, losing sight of the squadron in the evening, turned tail and went back to France, instead of proceeding to the first of the various rendezvous which had been agreed upon. The Granvelle, having made a prize on her own account, took advantage of her entirely independent position and the fact that she was far away from the Richard to disregard signals and make off with her capture. This reduced the squadron to the Richard, Alliance, Pallas, and Vengeance. It was Jones' desire to cruise to and fro off the harbor of Limerick to intercept the West Indian ships, which, to the number of eight or ten, were daily expected. These vessels, richly laden, were of great value, and their capture could have easily been effected, but Landais protested vehemently against remaining in any one spot. Among other things, the Frenchman was undoubtedly a coward, and, of course, by remaining steadily in one place opportunities for being overhauled were greatly increased. Jones finally succumbed to Landais' entreaties and protestations, which were backed up by those of Captains Cottineau and Ricot.

Of course, it is impossible to say how far his authority would have lasted had he peremptorily refused to accede to their demands, as paper concordats are not very binding ties; but he might perhaps have made a more determined effort to induce them to carry out his plans and remain with him. To leave the position he had chosen, which presented such opportunities, was undoubtedly an error in judgment, and Jones tacitly admits it in the following words, written long afterward:

"Nothing prevented me from pursuing my design but the reproach that would have been cast upon my character as a man of prudence.[11] It would have been said: 'Was he not forewarned by Captain Cottineau and others?'"

The excuse is as bad as, if not worse than, the decision. But this is almost the only evidence of weakness and irresolution which appears in Jones' conduct in all the emergencies in which he was thrown. It is impossible to justify this action, but, in view of the circumstances, which we can only imagine and hardly adequately comprehend, we need not censure him too greatly for his indecision. In fact, the decision itself was a mistake which the ablest of men might naturally make. The weakness lay in the excuse which he himself offers, and which it pains one to read. In this connection the noble comment of Captain Mahan is interesting:

"The subordination of public enterprises to considerations of personal consequences, even to reputation, is a declension from the noblest in a public man. Not life only, but personal credit, is to be fairly risked for the attainment of public ends."

It can not be said that Jones was altogether disinterested in his actions. The mere common, vulgar, mercenary motives were absent from his undertakings, but it must be admitted that he never lost sight of the results, not only to his country and its success, but to his own reputation as well. If Jones had proceeded in his intention, and Landais had finally deserted him, the results would have been very much better for the cruise—always provided that the Pallas at least remained with the Richard. We shall see later on that all the ships deserted him on one occasion.

On the 26th of August a heavy gale blew up from the southwest, and Jones scudded before it to the northward along the Irish coast. Landais deliberately changed the course of the Alliance in the darkness, and, the tiller of the Pallas having been carried away during the night, Jones found himself alone with the Vengeance the next morning. The gale having abated, these two remaining vessels continued their course in a leisurely manner along the Irish coast. On the 31st the Alliance hove in sight, followed by a valuable West Indiaman called the Betsy, mounting twenty-two guns, which she had captured—a sample of what might have resulted if the squadron had stayed off Limerick.

The Pallas having also joined company again, on the 1st of September the Richard brought to the Union, a government armed ship of twenty-two guns, bound for Halifax with valuable naval stores. Before boats were called away and the prize taken possession of, with unparalleled insolence Landais sent a messenger to Jones asking whether the Alliance should man the prize, in which case he should allow no man from the Richard to board her! With incredible complaisance the long-suffering Jones allowed Landais to man this capture also, while he himself received the prisoners on the Richard. These two vessels, in violation of Jones' explicit orders, were sent in to Bergen, Norway, where they were promptly released by the Danish Government and returned to England on the demand of the British minister. Their value was estimated at forty thousand pounds sterling. The unwarranted return of the vessels was the foundation of a claim for indemnity against Denmark, of which we shall hear later. On the day of the capture Landais disregarded another specific signal from the flagship to chase; instead of doing which, he wore ship and headed directly opposite the direction in which he should have gone. The next morning he again disregarded a signal to come within hail of the Richard, on which occasion he did not even set an answering pennant.

On September 3d and 4th the squadron captured a brig and two sloops off the Shetland Islands. On the evening of this day Jones summoned the captains to the flagship. Landais refused to go, and when de Cottineau tried to persuade him to do so he became violently abusive, and declared that the matters at issue between the commodore and himself were so grave that they could only be settled by a personal meeting on shore, at which one or the other should forfeit his life. Fortunately for the peace of mind of the commodore, whose patience had reached the breaking point, the Alliance immediately after parted company, and did not rejoin the command until the 23d of September. If Landais had stayed away altogether, or succeeded in getting himself lost or captured, it would have been a great advantage to the country.

Another gale blew up on the 5th, and heavy weather continued for several days. The little squadron of three vessels labored along through the heavy seas to the northward, passed the dangerous Orkneys, doubled the wild Hebrides, rounded the northern extremity of Scotland, and on the evening of the 13th approached the east coast near the Cheviot Hills. On the 14th they arrived off the Firth of Forth, where they were lucky enough to capture one ship and one brigantine loaded with coal. From them they learned that the naval force in the harbor of Leith was inconsiderable, consisting of one twenty-gun sloop of war and three or four cutters. Jones immediately conceived the idea of destroying this force, holding the town under his batteries, landing a force of marines, and exacting a heavy ransom under threat of destruction.

Map showing the cruises of the Ranger and the Bon Homme Richard, and the dash of the Alliance from the Texel.

Although weakened in force by the desertion of the ships, by the number of prizes he had manned, and the large number of prisoners on board the Richard, he still hoped, as he says, to teach English cruisers the value of humanity on the other side of the water, and by this bold attack to demonstrate the vulnerability of their own coasts. He also counted upon this diversion in the north to call attention from the expected grand invasion in the south of England by the French and Spanish fleets. The wind was favorable for his design, but unfortunately the Pallas and the Vengeance, which had lagged as usual, were some distance in the offing. Jones therefore ran back to meet them in order to advise them of his plan and concert measures for the attack. He found that the French had but little stomach for the enterprise; they positively refused to join him in the undertaking, a decision which, by the terms of the concordat, they had a right to make. After a night spent in fruitless argument between the three captains—think of it, arguments in the place of orders!—Jones appealed to their cupidity, probably the last thing that would have moved him. By painting the possibilities of plunder he wrung a reluctant consent from these two gentlemen, and proceeded rapidly to develop the plan.

As usual, not being able to embrace the opportunity when it was presented, a change in the wind rendered it impossible for the present. The design and opportunity were too good, however, to be lost, and the squadron beat to and fro off the harbor, waiting for a shift of wind to make practicable the effort. On the 15th they captured another collier, a schooner, the master of which, named Andrew Robertson, was bribed by the promised return of his vessel to pilot them into the harbor of Leith. Robertson, a dastardly traitor, promised to do so, and saved his collier thereby. On the morning of the 16th an amusing little incident occurred off the coast of Fife. The ships were, of course, sailing under English colors, and one of the seaboard gentry, taking them for English ships in pursuit of Paul Jones, who was believed to be on the coast, sent a shore boat off to the Richard asking the gift of some powder and shot with which to defend himself in case he received a visit from the dreaded pirate. Jones, who was much amused by the situation, made a courteous reply to the petition, and sent a barrel of powder, expressing his regret that he had no suitable shot. He detained one of the boatmen, however, as a pilot for one of the other ships. During the interim the following proclamation was prepared for issuance when the town had been captured. The document is somewhat diffuse in its wording, but the purport of it is unmistakable:

"The Honorable J. Paul Jones, Commander-in-chief of the American Squadron, now in Europe, to the Worshipful Provost of Leith, or, in his absence, to the Chief Magistrate, who is now actually present, and in authority there.

"SIR: The British marine force that has been stationed here for the protection of your city and commerce, being now taken by the American arms under my command, I have the honour to send you this summons by my officer, Lieutenant-Colonel de Chamillard, who commands the vanguard of my troops. I do not wish to distress the poor inhabitants; my intention is only to demand your contribution toward the reimbursement which Britain owes to the much-injured citizens of the United States; for savages would blush at the unmanly violation and rapacity that have marked the tracks of British tyranny in America, from which neither virgin innocence nor helpless age has been a plea of protection or pity.

"Leith and its port now lie at our mercy; and, did not our humanity stay the hand of just retaliation, I should, without advertisement, lay it in ashes. Before I proceed to that stern duty as an officer, my duty as a man induces me to propose to you, by means of a reasonable ransom, to prevent such a scene of horror and distress. For this reason I have authorized Lieutenant-Colonel de Chamillard to conclude and agree with you on the terms of ransom, allowing you exactly half an hour's reflection before you finally accept or reject the terms which he shall propose. If you accept the terms offered within the time limited, you may rest assured that no further debarkation of troops will be made, but the re-embarkation of the vanguard will immediately follow, and the property of the citizens shall remain unmolested."

On the afternoon of the 16th, the squadron was sighted from Edinburgh Castle, slowly running in toward the Firth. The country had now been fully alarmed. It is related that the audacity and boldness of this cruise and his previous successes had caused Jones to be regarded with a terror far beyond that which his force justified, and which well-nigh paralyzed resistance. Arms were hastily distributed, however, to the various guilds, and batteries were improvised at Leith. On the 17th, the Richard, putting about, ran down to within a mile of the town of Kirkaldy. As it appeared to the inhabitants that she was about to descend upon their coast, they were filled with consternation. There is a story told that the minister of the place, a quaint oddity named Shirra, who was remarkable for his eccentricities, joined his people congregated on the beach, surveying the approaching ship in terrified apprehension, and there made the following prayer:

"Now, deer Lord, dinna ye think it a shame for ye to send this vile piret to rob our folk o' Kirkaldy? for ye ken they're puir enow already, and hae naething to spaire. The wa the ween blaws, he'll be here in a jiffie, and wha kens what he may do? He's nae too guid for onything. Meickle's the mischief he has dune already. He'll burn thir hooses, tak their very claes and tirl them to the sark; and wae's me! wha kens but the bluidy villain might take their lives! The puir weemen are maist frightened out o' their wits, and the bairns skirling after them. I canna thol't it! I canna thol't it! I hae been lang a faithfu' servant to ye, Laird; but gin ye dinna turn the ween about, and blaw the scoundrel out of our gate, I'll na staur a fit, but will just sit here till the tide comes. Sae tak yere will o't."

This extraordinary petition has probably lost nothing by being handed down. At any rate, just as that moment, a squall which had been brewing broke violently over the ship, and Jones was compelled to bear up and run before it. The honest people of Kirkaldy always attributed their relief to the direct interposition of Providence as the result of the prayer of their minister. He accepted the honors for his Lord and himself by remarking, whenever the subject was mentioned to him, that he had prayed but the Lord had sent the wind!

It is an interesting tale, but its effect is somewhat marred when we consider that Jones had no intention of ever landing at Kirkaldy or of doing the town any harm. He was after bigger game, and in his official account he states that he finally succeeded in getting nearly within gunshot distance of Leith, and had made every preparation to land there, when a gale which had been threatening blew so strongly offshore that, after making a desperate attempt to reach an anchorage and wait until it blew itself out, he was obliged to run before it and get to sea. When the gale abated in the evening he was far from the port, which had now become thoroughly alarmed. Heavy batteries were thrown up and troops concentrated for its protection, so that he concluded to abandon the attempt. His conception had been bold and brilliant, and his success would have been commensurate if, when the opportunity had presented itself, he had been seconded by men on the other ships with but a tithe of his own resolution.

The squadron continued its cruise to the southward and captured several coasting brigs, schooners, and sloops, mostly laden with coal and lumber. Baffled in the Forth, Jones next determined upon a similar project in the Tyne or the Humber, and on the 19th of the month endeavored to enlist the support of his captains for a descent on Newcastle-upon-Tyne, as it was one of his favorite ideas to cut off the London coal supply by destroying the shipping there; but Cottineau, of the Pallas, refused to consent. The ships had been on the coast now for nearly a week, and there was no telling when a pursuing

English squadron would make its appearance. Cottineau told de Chamillard that unless Jones left the coast the next day the Richard would be abandoned by the two remaining ships. Jones, therefore, swallowing his disappointment as best be might, made sail for the Humber and the important shipping town of Hull.

It was growing late in September, and the time set for the return to the Texel was approaching. As a matter of fact, however, though Jones remained on the coast cruising up and down and capturing everything he came in sight of, in spite of his anxiety Cottineau did not actually desert his commodore. Cottineau was the best of the French officers. Without the contagion of the others he might have shown himself a faithful subordinate at all times. Having learned the English private signals from a captured vessel, Jones, leaving the Pallas, boldly sailed into the mouth of the Humber, just as a heavy convoy under the protection of a frigate and a small sloop of war was getting under way to come out of it. Though he set the English flag and the private signals in the hope of decoying the whole force out to sea and under his guns, to his great disappointment the ships, including the war vessels, put back into the harbor. The Richard thereupon turned to the northward and slowly sailed along the coast, followed by the Vengeance.

Early in the morning of September 23d, while it was yet dark, the Richard chased two ships, which the daylight revealed to be the Pallas and the long-missing Alliance, which at last rejoined. The wind was blowing fresh from the southwest, and the two ships under easy canvas slowly rolled along toward Flamborough Head. Late in the morning the Richard discovered a large brigantine inshore and to windward. Jones immediately gave chase to her, when the brigantine changed her course and headed for Bridlington Bay, where she came to anchor.

Bridlington Bay lies just south of Flamborough Head, which is a bold promontory bearing a lighthouse and jutting far out into the North Sea. Vessels from the north bound for Hull or London generally pass close to the shore at that point, in order to make as little of a detour as possible. For this reason Jones had selected it as a particularly good cruising ground. Sheltered from observation from one side or the other, he waited for opportunities, naturally abundant, to pounce upon unsuspecting merchant ships. The Baltic fleet had not yet appeared off the coast, though it was about due. Unless warned of his presence, it would inevitably pass the bold headland and afford brilliant opportunity for attack. If his unruly consorts would only remain with him a little longer something might yet be effected. To go back now would be to confess to a partial failure, and Jones was determined to continue the cruise even alone, until he had demonstrated his fitness for higher things. Fate had his opportunity ready for him, and he made good use of it.

CHAPTER X.

THE BATTLE WITH THE SERAPIS.

About noon on the 23d of September, 1779, the lookouts on the Richard became aware of the sails of a large ship which suddenly shot into view around the headland. Before any action could be taken the first vessel was followed by a second, a third, and others to the number of six, all close hauled on the starboard tack, evidently intent upon weathering the point. The English flags fluttering from their gaff ends proclaimed a nationality, of which, indeed, there could be no doubt. The course of the Richard was instantly changed. Dispatching a boat under the command of Lieutenant Henry Lunt to capture the brigantine, Jones, in high anticipation, headed the Richard for the strangers, at the same time signaling the Alliance, the Pallas, and the Vengeance to form line ahead on his ship—that is, get into the wake of the Richard and follow in single file. The Alliance seems to have been ahead and to windward of the Richard, the Pallas to windward and abreast, and the Vengeance in the rear of the flagship.

It had not yet been developed whether the six ships, which, even as they gazed upon them, were followed by others until forty sail were counted, were vessels of war or a merchant fleet under convoy; but with characteristic audacity Jones determined to approach them sufficiently near to settle the question. He had expressed his intention of going in harm's way, and for that purpose had asked a swift ship. He could hardly have had a slower, more unwieldy, unmanageable vessel under him than the Richard, but the fact had not altered his intention in the slightest degree, so the course of the Richard was laid for the ships sighted.

Captain Landais, however, was not actuated by the same motives as his commander. He paid no attention, as usual, to the signal, but instead ran off to the Pallas, to whose commander he communicated in a measure some of his own indecision. In the hearing of the crews of both vessels Landais called out to his fellow captain that if the fleet in view were convoyed by a vessel of more than fifty guns they would have nothing to do but run away, well knowing that in such a case the Pallas, being the slowest sailer of the lot—slower even than the Richard—would inevitably be taken. Therefore, with his two other large vessels beating to and fro in a state of frightened uncertainty, Jones with the Richard bore down alone upon the enemy. The Vengeance remained far enough in the rear of the Richard to be safe out of harm's way, and may be dismissed from our further consideration, as she took no part whatever in the subsequent events.

Closer scrutiny had satisfied the American that the vessels in sight were the longed-for Baltic merchant fleet which was convoyed by two vessels of war, one of which appeared to be a small ship of the line or a heavy frigate. In spite, therefore, of the suspicious maneuvers of his consorts, Jones flung out a signal for a general chase, crossed his light yards and swept toward the enemy. Meanwhile all was consternation in the English fleet off the headland. A shore boat which had been noticed pulling hard toward the English convoying frigate now dashed alongside, and a man ascended to her deck. Immediately thereafter signals were broken out at the masthead of the frigate, attention being called to them by a gun fired to windward. All the ships but one responded by tacking or wearing in different directions in great apparent confusion, but all finally headed for the harbor of Scarborough, where, under the guns of the castle, they hoped to find a secure refuge. As they put about they let fly their topgallant sheets and fired guns to spread the alarm.

Meanwhile the English ship, which proved to be the frigate Serapis, also tacked and headed westward, taking a position between her convoy and the approaching ships. Some distance to leeward of the frigate, and farther out to sea, to the eastward, a smaller war vessel, in obedience to orders, also assumed a similar position, and both waited for the advancing foe. Early that morning Richard Pearson, the captain of the Serapis, had been informed that Paul Jones was off the coast, and he had been instructed to look out for him. The information had been at once communicated to the convoy, to which cautionary orders had been given, which had been in the main disregarded, as was the invariable custom with convoys. The shore boat which the men on the Richard had just observed speaking the Serapis contained the bailiff of Scarborough Castle, who confirmed the previous rumors and undoubtedly pointed out the approaching ships as Jones' squadron.

Pearson, as we have seen, had signaled his convoy, and the latter, now apprised of their danger beyond all reasonable doubt by the sight of the approaching ships, had at last obeyed his orders. Then he had cleverly placed his two ships between the oncoming American squadron to cover the retreat of his charges and to prevent the enemy from swooping down upon them. His position was not only proper and seamanlike, but it was in effect a bold challenge to his approaching antagonist—a challenge he had no wish to disregard, which he eagerly welcomed, in fact. In obedience to Jones' signal for a general chase, the Richard and the Pallas were headed for their two enemies. As they drew nearer the Pallas changed her course in accordance with Jones' directions, and headed for the smaller English ship, the Countess of Scarborough, a twenty-four gun, 6-pounder sloop of war, by no means an equal match for the Pallas. The Vengeance followed at a safe distance in the rear of the commodore, while Landais disregarded all signals and pursued an erratic course of his own devising. Sometimes it appeared that he was about to follow the Richard, sometimes the Pallas, sometimes the flying merchantmen attracted his attention. It was evident that the one thing he would not do would be to fight.

In utter disgust, Jones withdrew his attention from him and concentrated his mind upon the task before him. He was about to engage with his worn-out old hulk, filled with condemned guns, a splendid English frigate of the first class. A comparison of force is interesting. Counting the main battery of the Richard as composed of twelves and the spar-deck guns as nines, and including the six 18-pounders in the gun room as being all fought on one side, we get a total of forty guns throwing three hundred and three pounds of shot to the broadside; this is the extreme estimate. Counting one half of the main battery as 9-pounders, we get two hundred and eighty-two pounds to the broadside, and, considering the 18-pounders as being fought only three on a side, we reduce the weight of the broadside to two hundred and twenty-eight pounds. As it happened, as we shall see, the 18-pounders were abandoned after the first fire, so that the effective weight of broadside during the action amounted to either one hundred and ninety-five or one hundred and seventy-four pounds, depending on the composition of the main battery. Even the maximum amount is small enough by comparison.

The crew of the Richard had been reduced to about three hundred officers and men, as near as can be ascertained. The desertion of the barge, the loss of the boat under Cutting Lunt off the Irish coast, the various details by which the several prizes had been manned, and the absence of the boat sent that morning under the charge of Henry Lunt, which had not, and did not come back until after the action, had reduced the original number to these figures. A most serious feature of the situation was the lack of capable sea officers. There were so few of the latter on board the Richard originally that the absence of the two mentioned seriously hampered her work. Dale himself was a host. Those that remained, who, with the exception of the purser, sailing master, and the officers of the French contingent, were young and inexperienced, mostly midshipmen—boys, in fact—made up for their deficiencies by their zeal and courage. The officers of the French contingent proved themselves to be men of a high class, who could be depended upon in desperate emergencies.

The Serapis was a brand-new, double-banked frigate, of about eight hundred tons burden—that is, she carried guns on two covered and one uncovered decks. This was an unusual arrangement, not subsequently considered advantageous or desirable, but it certainly enabled her to present a formidable battery within a rather short length; her shortness, it was believed, would greatly enhance her handiness and mobility, qualities highly desirable in a war vessel, especially in the narrow seas. On the lower or main deck twenty 18-pounders were mounted; on the gun deck proper, twenty 9-pounders; and on the spar deck, ten 6-pounders, making a total of fifty guns, twenty-five in broadside, throwing three hundred pounds' weight of shot at each discharge as against the Richard's one hundred and seventy-four. She was manned by about three hundred trained and disciplined English seamen, forming a homogeneous, efficient crew, and well they proved their quality. Richard Pearson, her captain, was a brave, competent, and successful officer, who had enjoyed a distinguished career, winning his rank by gallant and daring enterprises; no ordinary man, indeed, but one from whom much was to be expected.

In making this comparison between the two ships it must not be forgotten that while the difference in the number of guns—ten—was not great, yet in their caliber and the consequent weight of broadside the Richard was completely outclassed. Then, too, the penetrative power of an 18-pound gun is vastly greater than that of a 12-pound gun, a thing well understood by naval men, though scarcely appearing of much moment on paper. Indeed, it was a maxim that a 12-pound frigate could not successfully engage an 18-pounder, or an 18-pound frigate cope with a 24-pound ship.[12]

In addition to this vast preponderance in actual fighting force, there was another great advantage to the Serapis in the original composition of her crew as compared with the heterogeneous crowd which Jones had been compelled to hammer into shape. Worthily, indeed, did both bodies of men demonstrate their courage and show the effect of their training. There was a further superiority in the English ship in that she was built for warlike purposes, and was not a converted and hastily adapted merchant vessel. She was of much heavier construction, with more massive frames, stouter sides, and heavier scantling. The last advantage Pearson's ship possessed was in her superior mobility and speed. She should have been able to choose and maintain her distance, so that with her longer and heavier guns she could batter the Richard to pieces at pleasure, herself being immune from the latter's feebler attack.

In but one consideration was the Richard superior to the Serapis, and that was in the personality of the man behind the men behind the guns! Pearson was a very gallant officer. There was no blemish upon his record, no question as to his capacity. In personal bravery he was not inferior to any one. As a seaman he worthily upheld the high reputation of the great navy to which he belonged; but as a man, as a personality, he was not to be mentioned in the same breath with Jones.

This is no discredit to that particular Englishman, for the same disadvantageous comparison to Jones would have to be made in the case of almost any other man that sailed the sea. There was about the little American such Homeric audacity, such cool-headed heroism, such unbreakable determination, such unshakable resolution, that so long as he lived it was impossible to conquer him. They might knock mast after mast out of the Richard; they might silence gun after gun in her batteries; man after man might be killed upon her decks; they might smash the ship to pieces and sink her beneath his feet, but there was no power on earth which could compel him to strike her flag.

Jones was the very incarnation of the indomitable *Ego*: a soul that laughed at odds, that despised opposition, that knew but one thing after the battle was joined—to strike and strike hard, until opposition was battered down or the soul of the striker had fled. In action he would be master—or dead. But his fighting was no baresark fury; no blind, wild rage of struggle; no ungovernable lust for battle; it was the apotheosis of cool-blooded calculation. He fought with his head as well as with his heart, and he knew perfectly well what he was about all the time. Pearson was highly trained matter of first-rate composition; Jones was mind, and his superiority over matter was inevitable. The hot-tempered spirit of the man which involved him in so many difficulties, which made him quarrelsome, contrary, and captious, gave place to a coolness and calmness as great as his courage in the presence of danger, in the moment of action. By his skill, his ability, his address, his persistence, his staying power, his hardihood, Jones deserved that victory which his determination absolutely wrested from overwhelming odds, disaster, and defeat. The chief players in the grim game, therefore, were but ill matched, and not all the superiority in the pawns upon the chessboard could overcome the fearful odds under which the unconscious Pearson labored. We pity Pearson; in Jones' hands he was as helpless as PontiusPilate.

The crew of the Richard, having had supper and grog, had long since gone to their stations to the music of the same grim call of the beat to quarters which had rolled upon the decks of every warship of every nation which had joined battle for perhaps two hundred years. Jones was a great believer in drill and gun practice. His experience on his first cruise in the Alfred, if nothing else, had taught him that, and upon this ill-found ship with its motley crew probably a more thorough regimen of control and discipline existed than could be found in any other ship afloat. Frequent target practice was had, too, and the result proved the value of the exercise. Had this not been the case the approaching battle might have had a different termination.

The great guns had been cast loose and provided; having been run in and loaded, they were run out and a turn taken with the training tackles to hold them steady. The magazines had been opened, and the gunner and his mates stationed inside the wetted woolen screen, which minimized the danger of fire, to hand out charges of powder to the lads called powder boys, or powder "monkeys," who, with their canvas carrying boxes, were clustered about the hatches. The gun captains saw that the guns were properly primed, and they looked carefully after the slow matches used to discharge the pieces, keeping them lighted and freely burning. In the iron racks provided were laid rows of round shot, with here and there a stand of grape. Arm chests were opened and cutlasses and pistols distributed, and the racks filled with boarding pikes. Many of the officers discarded their hats and put on round steel boarding caps with dropped cheek pieces. Swords were buckled on and the priming of pistols carefully looked to. The men in many cases stripped off their shirts and jackets, laid aside caps and shoes, and slipped into their stations half naked, with only a pair of trousers and their arms upon them. Division tubs filled with water were placed conveniently at hand, and the decks were well sanded to prevent them from becoming slippery with blood when the action began. The pumps were overhauled and put in good condition, and hose led along the decks in case of fire. The carpenter and his mates, well provided with shot plugs to stop up possible holes, were stationed in the more vulnerable parts of the ship. The boats were wrapped with canvas to prevent splintering under heavy shot, and heavy nettings triced up fore and aft as a protection against boarders. Preventer braces were rove from the more important yardarms, the heavier yards were slung with chains, and the principal rigging, including the backstays, stoppered to minimize the danger in case they should be carried away by shot. Grapnels, strong iron hooks securely fastened to the ends of stout ropes or slender iron chains, were swung from every yardarm, and laid along the bulwarks in case it became possible or desirable to lash the ships together. Everything which would impede the working of the guns or hinder the fighting of the men was either stowed below or thrown overboard. Around the masts and at the braces the sail trimmers were clustered, some of them armed with boarding axes or hatchets, handy for cutting away wreckage. Aft on the quarter-deck and forward on the forecastle large bodies of French marines were drawn up, musket in hand.

The broad, old-fashioned tops of the Richard were filled with seamen and marines, armed with muskets and having buckets full of small grenades close at hand. Among these seamen were many of the more agile and daring among the topmen—who from their stations in making and taking in sail were designated as "light yardmen"—while the marines stationed in the tops were selected for their skill as marksmen. The main body of the crew was distributed at the battery of great guns on the main deck, which were in charge of Richard Dale and a French lieutenant colonel of infantry, named de Weibert. In the gloomy recesses of the gun room, close to the water line, a little group of men was told off to fight the heavy 18-pounders. Around the hatches leading to the hold was stationed another body of seamen and marines with the master at arms, all armed to the teeth, to guard the English prisoners, whose number is variously stated from two to three hundred. The relieving tackles to use in steering the ship in case the wheel was carried away occupied the attention of another group.

Far below the water line in the dark depths of the ship—a bloody place familiarly known as the cockpit—the surgeon and his mates unconcernedly spread out the foreboding array of ghastly instruments and appliances of the rude surgery of the rude period, in anticipation of the demands certain to be made upon them. At the break of the poop a veteran quartermaster and several assistants stood grasping the great wheel of the ship with sturdy fingers. Little groups of men were congregated on the quarter-deck and forecastle and in the gangways to man the 9-pounders, which were to play so important a part in the action. Jones himself, a quiet, composed little figure of slender proportions, paced steadily to and fro athwart the ship, now eagerly peering ahead as the shades of night descended, now casting a solemn glance aloft at the swelling canvas softly rounded out into huge curves in the gentle breeze. Ever and anon he threw a keen glance back toward the Alliance. When his gaze fell upon her, the compression of his lips and the fierceness of his look boded ill for Landais when he had time to deal with him.

What must have been his thoughts in this momentous hour! One likes to dwell upon him there and then; so alone and so undaunted on that old deck in that gray twilight, resolutely proceeding to battle with a ship which, now that it was in plain view, his practised eye easily determined surpassed his own in every particular. At such a moment, when every faculty of his mind naturally would be needed to fight his own vessel, suggestions of treachery and disobedience and an utter inability to tell what his cowardly and soon-to-be-proved traitorous subordinate would do, made his situation indeed unbearable. But he dismissed all these things from his mind. Confident in the justice of his cause—in the approval of Heaven for that cause—and full of trust in his own ability and personality, he put these things out of his head and swept on. He was a figure to inspire confidence on the deck of any ship. The men, who had perhaps as vivid an appreciation of their situation and all its dangers as he had himself, looked to their captain and took confidence in the quiet poise of the lithe figure at the break of the poop, balancing itself so easily to the lumbering roll of the great ship. The young midshipmen, his personal aides, slightly withdrawn from close contact with him, respected his silence as he paced to and fro.

Presently another graceful active figure, belonging to the first lieutenant of the ship, came running from below, walked rapidly along the deck, sprang up the ladder, and stopped before the little captain, whom he overtowered to a degree. He saluted gravely, and announced that the Richard was clear, the men at quarters, and the ship was ready for action. After a few moments of conversation Jones and Dale descended to the lower deck and walked through the ship. A hearty word of appreciation and encouragement here and there, as occasion suggested, heartened and stimulated the reckless crew, until they had almost risen to the captain's level. Presently he returned to the deck alone. A few final directions, one last glance of approval at the Pallas closing in on the Scarborough, one last regret, one last flush of indignation as he looked toward the Alliance—a moment, and the battle would be joined.

It was about seven o'clock in the evening. The harvest moon had long since risen in the eastern sky, and was flooding the pallid sea with its glorious radiance. On the western horizon the broad, bright beacon of Flamborough Head was sending out its bright ray of yellow light over the trembling water. With a night glass, clusters of people could be seen upon the shore and upon the ships anchored under the guns of Scarborough Castle, towering grim and black against the horizon. Ahead was the white Serapis, calmly confident, lying broadside on, port shutters triced up, lights streaming from every opening. She lay with her topsails to the mast, gallantly waiting. Upon her, too, like preparations for combat had been made. Along her decks the same beating call to battle had rolled. Men who spake the same language, who read the same Bible, who but a few years since had loved the same flag, who had vied with each other in loyalty to a common king, now made ready to hurl death and destruction at each other. Presently sharp words of command rang out; there was a sudden bustle on the deck of the English ship. The braces were manned, the yards swung, and the Serapis slowly gathered way and gently forged ahead. Then all was still once more on the serene English ship.

As the Richard drew nearer to the Serapis a deep silence settled over the American ship. Even over the roughest and rudest among her crew crept a feeling of awe at the terrible possibilities of the next few moments. The magnitude of their task as they came nearer became more apparent. Forced laughter died away; coarse words remained unspoken; lips foreign to prayer formed words of belated and broken petition. Thoughts went back to home: to sunny fields and vine-clad cottages in France; to frontier huts in verdant clearings in America; to rude houses in seaboard towns where the surf of the western ocean broke in wild thunder upon the rocky shore. Pictures of wives, of children, of mothers, of sweethearts, rose before the misted vision. Here and there a younger man choked down a sob. The rude jests with which men sometimes strive to disguise emotion fell unnoticed, or were sternly reprehended by the older and more thoughtful. The fitful conversation died away, and the silence was broken only by the soft sigh of the wind through the top hamper, the gentle flap of the lighter sails as the pitch of the ship threw the canvas back and forth, the soft splash of the bluff bows through the water, the straining of the timbers, the creak of the cordage through the blocks. Candle-filled battle lanterns in long rows throughout the ship shed a dim radiance over the bodies of the stalwart, half-naked, barefooted men. Here and there a brighter flash told of moonlight reflected from some gleaming sword.

And the ships drew nearer—nearer. In a moment the dogs of war would be loose. Presently a sound broke the silence, a hail from the English ship. A man leaped up on her rail and a cry came faintly up through a hollowed hand against the gentle breeze:

"What ship is that?"

The Richard had been kept skillfully end on to the Serapis, and the commander of the latter ship had still some lingering doubts as to her nationality. Measuring the distance between the two ships, Jones quickly motioned to the watchful quartermaster beneath him. With eager hands the men began, spoke by spoke, to shift the helm to starboard. As the American ship began to swing to port it would be but a moment before her broadside would be revealed and concealment at an end. That precious moment, however, Jones would have. He sprang on the taffrail to starboard, and, catching hold of the backstay, leaned far out and called loudly:

"I do not understand you."

The Richard was swinging still more now. The English caught a glimpse of a lighted port forward. From it a huge gun thrust its muzzle out into the night.

Quick and sharp came the hail once more:

"What ship is that? Answer at once or I fire!"

With what breathless silence the two ships listened for the reply!

The helm was hard over now, the quartermasters holding it down with grim determination, sweat pouring from their foreheads, the ship swinging broadside in to, and a little forward of, the Englishman. Bending over toward the quarter-deck, in a clear voice heard throughout his ship, Jones called out a sharp word of command. Even as he spoke a line of fire lanced out into the night, followed by the roar of one of the 12-pounders. It was an answer not to be mistaken. Immediately the whole broadside of the Richard was let go. Simultaneously the iron throats on the Serapis belched forth their rain of hell and destruction, and the great battle was on! It was perhaps a quarter after seven. Side by side the two ships, covered with blinding smoke, sailed in the still night, broadside answering broadside, the roar of the great guns sounding in one horrible continuous note vibrating over the ocean. The thunderous diapason was punctuated by the sharp staccato rattle of the small arms.

The Richard, having more way on her, forged slightly ahead of the Serapis, which had so lately filled away that she had scarcely yet begun to move. Jones, watchful of his opportunity, swung the head of his ship in toward the English frigate, hoping to cross her bows and rake her; but the careful Pearson, presently feeling the wind, gathered way and with his superior speed easily regained his distance. The game was being played as he would have it, and the bolts from his long eighteens were making havoc of the Richard. Jones now determined to back his topsails, check the speed of his own ship, allow the Serapis to forge ahead, and then fill away again, and rush the Richard alongside the English frigate so that he could board and make use of his preponderant force of soldiery. Accordingly, the way of his frigate was checked and the Serapis drew slightly ahead, receiving the fire of the Richard's battery as she passed, and maintaining her own fire in the smoke and darkness for some moments, until Pearson discovered that he had passed ahead of the Richard. The way of his ship was immediately checked. The conflict had been maintained with incredible fierceness for more than three quarters of an hour.

As soon as Jones had gained sufficient distance, he smartly filled away again and headed the clumsy Richard at the Serapis; but the slow old vessel was not equal to the demands of her commander. The Richard only succeeded in striking the Serapis on the port quarter very far aft. To have attempted boarding from such a position would have been madness. There are only two positions from which a ship can be boarded advantageously. In one case, when two ships are laid side by side, by massing the crew at some point of the long line of defense necessitated by the relative position of the vessels, it may be possible to break through and effect a lodgment on the enemy's deck. The other case is when the ship desirous of boarding succeeds in crossing the bows of her enemy so that the latter vessel is subjected to a raking fire from the battery of the attacking ship, which beats down opposition and sweeps everything before it, thus affording a chance for favorable attack. Neither of these opportunities was presented at this time.

Jones, nevertheless, mustered his boarders on the forecastle at this moment, heading them himself, but the English appeared in such force at the point of contact that the attempt was of necessity abandoned. The two ships hung together a moment, then separated, and, the Serapis going ahead, the Richard backing off, they formed a line ahead, the bow of the Richard following the stern of the Serapis. There was not a single great gun which bore on either ship. The roar of the battle died away, and even the crackle of the small arms ceased for a space. At this moment Pearson hailed the Richard. Having been subjected to the battering of his superior force for so long a time, Pearson concluded that it was time for the Richard to surrender. He was right in theory—in practice it was different. His own ship had suffered severely in the yardarm to yardarm fight, and he realized that the loss upon the Richard must have been proportionately greater. Even the most unskilled seaman had learned by this time the difference in the power of the two vessels. Therefore, taking advantage of the momentary cessation of the battle, he sprang up on the rail of the Serapis in the moonlight and called out:

"Have you struck?"

And to this interrogation Paul Jones returned that heroic answer, which since his day has been the watchword of the American sailor:

"*I have not yet begun to fight!*" he cried with gay audacity.

The ringing tones of his voice carried his answer not only to the ears of the English captain, but threw it far up into the high tops where the eager seamen had so busily plied their small arms. The men on the gun deck heard it with joy. It even penetrated to the gloomy recesses of the gun room, which had been the scene of such misfortune and disaster as would have determined the career of any other ship. The wounded caught the splendid inspiration which was back of the glorious declaration, and under the influence of it stifled their groans, forgot their wounds, and strove to fight on. It told the dying that their lives were not to be given in vain. Nay, those mighty words had a carrying power which lifted them above the noise of the conflict, which sent them ringing over the narrow seas, until they reverberated in the Houses of Parliament on the one side and the Court of Versailles on the other. They had a force which threw them across the thousand leagues of ocean until they were heard in every patriot camp, and repeated from the deck of every American ship, until they became a part of the common heritage of the nation as eternal as are its Stripes and Stars! The dauntless phrase of that dauntless man:

"I have not yet begun to fight!"

It was no new message. The British had heard it as they tramped again and again up the bullet-swept slopes of Bunker Hill; Washington rang it in the ears of the Hessians on the snowy Christmas morning at Trenton; the hoof beats of Arnold's horse kept time to it in the wild charge at Saratoga; it cracked with the whip of the old wagoner Morgan at the Cowpens; the Maryland troops drove it home in the hearts of their enemies with Greene at Guilford Courthouse, and the drums of France and England beat it into Cornwallis' ears when the end came at Yorktown. There, that night in that darkness, in that still moment of battle, Paul Jones declared the determination of a great people. His was the expression of an inspiration on the part of a new nation. From this man came a statement of an unshakable determination at whatever cost to be free! A new Declaration of Independence, this famous word of warning to the British king. Give up the contest now, O monarch! A greater majesty than thine is there!

I imagine a roar of wild exultation quivering from truck to keelson, a gigantic Homeric laugh rising from the dry throats of the rough men as yet unharmed on the Richard as they caught the significance of their captain's reply. "It was a joke, the character of which those blood-stained ruffians could well appreciate; but the captain was in no mood for joking. He was serious, and in the simplicity of the answer lay its greatness. Strike! Not now, nor never! Beaten! The fighting is but just begun! The preposterous possibility of surrender can not even be considered. What manner of man this, with whom you battle in the moonlight, brave Pearson! An unfamiliar kind to you and to most; such as hath not been before, nor shall be again. Yet all the world shall see and understand at this time.

"'I have not yet begun to fight!'

"Surprising answer! On a ship shattered beyond repair, her best guns exploded and useless, her crew decimated, ringed about with dead and dying, the captain had not yet begun to fight! But there was no delay after the answer, no philosophizing, no heroics. The man of action was there. He meant business. Every moment when the guns were silent wasted one."[113]

The Richard was in a dreadful condition, especially below. At the first fire two of the 18-pounders in the gun room had exploded, killing most of the officers and men of their crews, blowing out the side of the ship, shattering the stanchions, blowing up the deck above them, and inflicting injuries of so serious a character that they virtually settled the fate of the ship. The other guns there were immediately abandoned, and the men left alive in the division, who were not required to guard the prisoners, were sent to the gun deck to report to Dale and de Weibert. The battery which had been the main dependence of Jones had proved worse than useless. Indeed, it had done more harm than had the guns of the Serapis. I know of no action between two ships in which a similar, or even a less frightful, happening did not cause the ship suffering it to surrender at once.

The two ships hung in line for a moment, then Jones put his helm hard a-starboard again and swung off to port, perhaps hoping to rake the Serapis; but the English captain, anticipating his maneuver, backed his own topsails, and the two ships passed by each other once more, the batteries reopening their fire at close range. The combat at once recommenced with the most heroic determination. Fortunately, however, the captain of the Serapis miscalculated either the speed at which his own ship backed or the speed with which the Richard drew ahead, for, before Pearson filled away again, Jones had drawn so far ahead that by consummate seamanship and quick, desperate work he managed to swing the Richard across the path of the Serapis, an astonishing feat for the slower and more unwieldy American frigate. It was his one opportunity and he embraced it—one was enough for Jones. Pearson had just succeeded in checking the stern board of his own ship, and was going ahead slowly, when the bow of his frigate ran aboard the starboard quarter of the American, thrusting her jib boom through the mizzen rigging far across the quarter-deck of the Richard. Pouring a raking fire upon the English frigate from his starboard battery, Jones, with his own hand, sprang to lash the two ships together. The sailing master, Mr. Stacy, leaped to assist him. As the officer strove to overhaul the gear lying in a tangled mass upon the deck, he broke into the natural oath of a sailor at the delay.

"Don't swear, Mr. Stacy," Jones is reported to have said quietly, although he was working with feverish energy to the same end—"in another moment we may all be in the presence of our Maker—but let us do our duty."

The lashing was soon passed, and passed well. The American boarders were called away again, but they could do nothing in the face of the sharp fire of the English repelling force. Meanwhile, the pressure of the wind upon the after-sails of the Serapis had broken off her bowsprit and forced her stern around until she lay broadside to the American ship. A spare anchor on the Serapis caught in the mizzen chains of the Richard, and with it and the grapnels which were hastily flung the two ships were firmly bound together, the bow of one ship by the stern of the other, heading in different ways, their starboard sides touching. Pearson at once dropped his port anchor, hoping that, his ship being anchored and the Richard under way, the American would drag clear, when his superiority in gun power would enable him to continue the process of knocking her to pieces at long range; but, fortunately for the Richard, the wind had gradually decreased until it was now nearly killed, or so light that it did not prevent the ships from swinging to the Serapis' anchor with the tidal current then setting strongly to the northward.

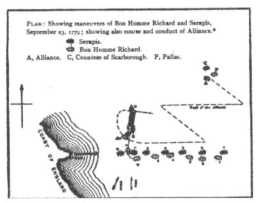

Plan: Showing maneuvers of Bon Homme Richard and Serapis, September 23, 1779; showing also course and conduct of Alliance. After a drawing by Captain A. T. Mahan, U. S. N., by permission of Charles Scribner's Sons.

It was some time after eight o'clock now, and the battle at once recommenced with the utmost fury. As the Serapis had not hitherto been engaged on the starboard side,[14] it was necessary for her men to blow off the port lids of their own ship at the first discharge of her battery. They were so close together that the conflict resolved itself into a hand-to-hand encounter with great guns. As Dale said, the sponges and rammers had to be extended through the ports of the enemy in order to serve the guns. Though the American batteries were fought with the utmost resolution, they were, of course, no match whatever for those of the English ship, which had two tiers of heavier guns to oppose to one of the American. Below decks, therefore, the Americans were at a fearful disadvantage. Above, however, the number of soldiers and marines, constantly re-enforced by a stream of men sent from below as their guns were put out of action, gave them a compensating factor, and by degrees the concentrated fire of the Americans cleared the deck of the Serapis. The two ships lying side by side, slowly grinding together in the gentle sea, the yardarms were interlaced and the American topmen, again outnumbering their English antagonists, ran along the yards, and a dizzy fight in midair ensued, as the result of which, after suffering severe loss, the

Americans gained possession of the British maintop. Turning their fire forward and aft, aided by attacking parties from the fore and crossjack yards, they finally cleared the English entirely out of the upper works of their ship. From this lofty point of vantage they poured such a rain of fire upon the Serapis that Pearson was left practically alone on the quarter-deck. To a chivalrous admiration for his courage he is said to owe his immunity. He, too, should have his meed of praise for the undaunted heroism with which he stood alone on the bullet-swept, blood-stained planks, maintained his position, and fought his ship.

Now, to go back a little. Shortly after the two ships were lashed together, the Alliance, apparently having recovered from her hesitation, came sweeping toward the combatants, and deliberately poured a broadside into the Richard, which did not a little damage and killed several men. In spite of all signals, Landais repeated his treacherous performance, but before the Richard's men could fairly realize the astonishing situation he sailed away from them and ran over before the wind toward the Pallas, which had been for some time hotly engaged with the Countess of Scarborough, where he is said to have done the same thing.[15] This strange action of the Alliance had but little effect upon the battle at this time, which was continued with unremitting fury.

One by one the small guns on the main deck of the Richard were silenced. The crews were swept away, guns were dismounted, carriages broken and shattered, and finally the whole side of the Richard from the mainmast aft was beaten in; so much so, that during the latter part of the action the shot of the Serapis passed completely through the Richard, and, meeting no opposition, fell harmlessly into the sea far on the other side. In the excitement the English never thought of depressing their guns and tearing the bottom out of the Richard. As it was, transoms were beaten out, stern frames were cut to pieces, and a few stanchions alone supported the decks above. Why they did not collapse and fall into the hull beneath it, with the guns and men on them, is a mystery. In addition to all this, the ship was on fire repeatedly, and men were continually called away from their stations to fight the flames.

Dale and de Weibert had just fired their last shots from the remaining guns of the main battery which were serviceable when a new complication was added to the scene. The men guarding the prisoners had been gradually picked off by the shot of the enemy. The Richard was leaking rapidly, and when the carpenter sounded the well a little after nine o'clock, late in the action, he discovered several feet of water in it. In great alarm he shrieked out that they were sinking. The few remaining men in the gun room ran for the hatchways. The master at arms, thinking that all was over, unlocked the hatches and released the prisoners, crying out at the same time, "On deck, everybody; the ship is sinking!" The Englishmen in panic terror scrambled up through the narrow hatchways, and fought desperately with each other in their wild hurry to reach the deck, where the carpenter had preceded them, still shouting that the ship was sinking, and now crying loudly, "Quarter! Quarter!"

As the carpenter ran aft, shouting his message of fear and alarm, he was followed by some of the forward officers, who, catching the contagion of his terror, repeated his words. Reaching the poop deck, the carpenter fumbled in the darkness for the halliards to haul down the flag, calling out to Jones that all was lost, the ship sinking, and that he must surrender. Other officers and men joined in the cry. It was another critical moment. Pearson, hearing the commotion, again hailed, asking if the Richard had struck. Jones, unable to stop the outcry of the terrified carpenter, smashed his skull with the butt of his pistol, and answered the second request of Pearson with, as he says, a most determined negative. We can imagine it. By his presence of mind in silencing the carpenter, and a supreme exertion of his indomitable will power, Jones soon succeeded in checking the incipient panic on the spar deck. At this period of the fight some accounts say that Pearson called his boarders from below and attempted to board. The advance was met by Jones at the head of a few men, pike in hand, with such firmness that it was not pressed home, and the men returned to their stations at the guns and resumed the fight.

Meanwhile, Richard Dale, seconded by his midshipmen, with rare and never-to-be-undervalued presence of mind, had stopped the oncoming rush of frightened English prisoners, who now greatly outnumbered the broken crew of the Richard. He sprang among them, beating them down, driving them back, menacing them with the point of the sword, at the same time telling them that the English ship was sinking, and that they were in the same condition, and unless they went to the pumps immediately all hands would be inevitably lost. The audacity of this statement was worthy of Jones himself. It was a rare action on the part of a boy of twenty-three years of age. Such a young man under present conditions in the United States Navy probably would be filling the responsible station of a naval cadet afloat![16] Instantly divining this new peril, the commodore himself sprang to the hatchway and seconded Dale's effort. Incredible as it seems, the two men actually forced the panic-stricken, bewildered, and terrified English prisoners to man the pumps, thus relieving a number of the crew of the Richard; and the singular spectacle was presented of an American ship kept afloat by the efforts of Englishmen, and thus enabled to continue an almost hopeless combat. Dale, with imperturbable audacity, remained below in command of them.

The Richard was a wreck. She had been fought to a standstill. Her battery was silenced, her decks were filled with released prisoners, she was making water fast, she was on fire in two or three places; numbers of her crew had been killed and wounded, the water had overflowed the cockpit, and the frightened surgeon had been driven to the deck, where, in conjunction with some of the French officers, he counseled surrender.

"What!" cried Paul Jones, smiling at the surgeon, "What, doctor! Would you have me strike to a drop of water? Help me to get this gun over!"

But the doctor, liking the looks of things on deck even less than below, ran down the hatchway, and, his station untenable, wandered to and fro and ministered to the wounded on every side as best he could. Meanwhile Jones had taken the place of the purser, Mr. Mease, commanding the upper battery, who had been severely wounded and forced to leave his station. The commodore was personally directing the fire of the upper deck guns left serviceable on the Richard, the two 9-pounders on the quarter-deck. With great exertion another gun was dragged over from the port side, Jones lending a hand with the rest, and the fire of the three was concentrated upon the mainmast of the Serapis.

About this time, between half after nine and ten o'clock, a huge black shadow came darting between the moonlight and the two frigates grinding against each other. It was the Alliance once more entering the fray. After running away from the Richard toward the Scarborough and the Pallas, she hovered about until she found that the former had capitulated after a gallant defense against the overwhelming superiority of the French ship. Then Landais headed once more for the Richard and the Serapis. To reach them, he was forced to make two tacks. As he approached, a burning anxiety filled the minds of Jones and the officers who were left on deck with him, as to what Landais would do. They were soon enlightened.

Sailing across the bow of the Serapis, the Alliance drew past the stern of the Richard, and when she had reached a position slightly on the quarter of the latter ship, she poured in a broadside. There could be no misapprehension on the part of Landais as to which ship he was firing into. The Richard was a black ship with a high poop, and the Serapis was painted a creamy white with much lower stern. The moon was filling the sky with brilliant light. Things were as plain as if it were daytime. In addition to all this, Jones had caused the private night signals to be hung upon the port side of the Richard. Shouts and cries warned the Alliance that she was firing upon her own people. These were disregarded. It was the opinion of the Americans that the English had taken the ship and were endeavoring to compass the destruction of the Richard. They could not otherwise explain the astonishing action. Sailing slowly along the starboard side of the Richard, the Alliance poured in another broadside. Then she circled the bows of the American ship, and from some distance away raked her with a discharge of grape which killed and wounded many, including Midshipman Caswell, in charge of the forecastle. It was just before ten o'clock when this happened. Some of the shot from these several broadsides may have reached the Serapis and possibly have done some damage, but the brunt of the severe attack fell upon the Richard. Her men, in the face of this awful stab in the back from a friend, naturally flinched from their guns and ran from their stations.

All seemed hopeless; but Jones was still left, and while he was alive he would fight. He and his officers drove the men back to their guns, and as the Alliance sailed away, for the time being, they forgot her. The fight went on!

It is greatly to the credit of the men that under such circumstances they could be induced to continue the contest. But the men had actually grown reckless of consequences: filled with the lust of battle, the brute in them was uppermost. They fought where they stood, with what they had. When the American guns were silenced, the seamen struck at their British foes over their silent muzzles with ramrods and sponges. Some endeavored to subdue the flames which broke out on every side. Others joined the English prisoners at the pumps. Many ran to the upper deck to replace the decimated crews of the 9-pounders. Some seized the muskets of the dead French soldiers and poured in a small-arm fire. They had grown careless of the fire, indifferent to the progress of the battle, ignorant of the results of the action. There was but one spirit among them, one idea possessed them—to fight and to fight on. Both crews had done their best; both had fought as men rarely had fought before; the battle was still undecided. The issue lay between Jones and Pearson. What was it to be?

Things on the Richard were hopeless, but things on the Serapis had not gone much better. She, too, was on fire—in no less than twelve places at once. The fearful musketry fire from the quarter-deck and forecastle of the Richard, and from the tops, had practically cleared her decks of all but Pearson. By Jones' orders the men in the American tops had made a free use of their hand grenades. A daring sailor, sent by Midshipman Fanning from the maintop, ran out upon the main yardarm, which hung over the after hatch of the Serapis, and began to throw grenades down the hatchway. On the lower deck of that ship a large pile of powder cartridges had been allowed to accumulate, for which, on account of the silencing of a large number of guns, there had been no demand. With reckless improvidence, in their haste, the powder boys continued to pile up these unused charges on the deck of the ship between the batteries. Nobody cautioned them, perhaps nobody noticed them in the heat of the action. At last a hand grenade struck the hatch combing, bounded aft, and fell into the midst of the pile of cartridges. There was a detonating crash, a terrific explosion, which absolutely silenced the roar of the battle for a moment. The two ships rolled and rocked from the shock of it. When the smoke cleared away, the decks were filled with dead and dying. Some twenty-eight men were killed or desperately wounded by the discharge; many others on the decks were stunned, blinded, and thrown in every direction by the concussion. Clothes were ripped from them, and many of them were severely burned. Lieutenant Stanhope, in charge of that gun division, his clothing on fire, actually leaped into the sea to get relief from his agony. Afterward, though frightfully burned, he regained his station and fought on.

It was this last shock that determined Pearson to surrender. He had beaten his antagonist a half dozen times, but his antagonist did not seem to realize it. In the face of such implacable determination his own nerve gave way. He was surrounded by dead and dying, no human soul apparently fit for duty on his decks but himself, the roar of his own guns silenced by this terrific explosion. He had fought through many desperate battles—never one like this. The other American frigate might come back. His consort had been captured. His nerve was broken. He turned and walked aft to the flagstaff raking from the taffrail. To this staff, with his own hand before the action, he had nailed the English flag.[17] With the same hand he seized the drooping folds of bunting, and with a breaking heart tore it from the staff.

CHAPTER XI.

AFTER THE BATTLE REMARKS ON THE ACTION.

"They have struck their flag!" cried Jones, who had witnessed the action. "Cease firing!" His powerful voice rang through the two ships with such a note of triumph as has rarely been heard in the fought-over confines of the narrow seas.

As the little scene transpired above, from the decks beneath them came the roar of the Serapis' guns. She had resumed her fire. Her men, too, were of heroic breed! A British ship captain among the English prisoners, recovering from his panic and noting the desperate condition of the Richard, had slipped away from the pumps, and, eluding the observation of Dale and his men, had crawled through the gaping openings in the sides of the Richard and the Serapis at the risk of his life—for the first Englishman who saw him moved to cut him down—and had announced the dreadful plight of the Richard to the first lieutenant of the Serapis, who had succeeded in rallying his men and forcing them once more back to the guns.

But the cry of the American was taken up by the men on the different ships until Dale came bounding up the hatchway, when Jones ordered him to board the English frigate and take possession. Followed by Midshipman Mayrant and a party of boarders with drawn swords, Dale leaped up on the rail of the Richard, seized the end of the main brace pennant, swung himself to the lower Serapis, and jumped down upon her quarter-deck. As Mayrant followed he was met by an English seaman coming from the waist, pike in hand. The sailor, ignorant of or disbelieving the surrender, thrust violently at Mayrant, inflicting a serious wound in the thigh before he could be stopped.

Aft upon the lee side of the deck, Pearson was standing alone with bowed head, leaning against the rail, the flag in one hand, his face being covered by the other. As the Americans clambered over the rail he raised his head—his hand fell to the breast of his coat. There was the look of defeat, the saddest aspect humanity can bear, upon his face. As Dale approached him, the English first lieutenant, not believing that the ship had struck, also came bounding from below.

"Have you struck?" cried Dale, stepping before the English captain.

"Yes, sir," was the reply. The anguish of the broken-hearted sailor was apparent in his face and in his voice.

"Sir, I have orders to send you on board the ship alongside," replied the American.

"Very good, sir," answered Pearson, reaching for his sword and dropping the flag. Just at this moment his subordinate interrupted them.

"Has the enemy struck to you, sir?" he asked.

"No, sir; on the contrary, he has struck to us," interposed Dale. But the English lieutenant refused to believe him.

"A few more broadsides, sir, and they are ours," he persisted. "Their prisoners have escaped. They are sinking!"

"The ship has struck, sir," Dale burst out hurriedly, scarcely giving the miserable Pearson an opportunity of replying, "and you are my prisoner!" Very properly, however, the English officer would take such news from no one but his own captain.

"Sir!" he cried in astonishment to Pearson, "have you struck?"

"Yes, sir," at last answered Pearson reluctantly.

There was a deadly little pause.

"I have nothing more to say, sir," replied the officer at last, turning to go below. As Dale interposed, he added, "If you will permit me to go below I will silence the firing of the lower deck guns."

"No, sir," answered Dale, "you will accompany your captain on board our ship at once, by the orders of Commodore Jones. Pass the word to cease firing. Your ship has surrendered!"

Dale was fearful lest the lieutenant should go below and, refusing to accept the captain's decision, attempt to resume the conflict. So, with his usual presence of mind, he sternly insisted upon both officers proceeding on board the Richard at once. In the face of the swarming crowd of the Richard's men on the Serapis' quarter-deck they had, of course, no option but to obey. By the aid of the dangling ropes they climbed up to the rail of the Indiaman and thence dropped to the quarter-deck of the American ship. They found themselves in the presence of a little man in a blue uniform which was rent and torn from the labors he had undergone during the action. He was hatless, and his dark face was grimed with the smoke and soil of battle. Blood spattering from a slight wound upon his forehead was coagulated upon his cheek. In the lurid illumination of the fire roaring fiercely forward, which, with the moon's pallid irradiation, threw a ghastly light over the scene of horror, he looked a hideous spectacle—a picture of demoniac war. Nothing but the fierce black eyes still burning with the awful passions of the past few hours and gleaming out of the darkness, with the exultant light of the present conquest proclaimed the high humanity of the man. In his hand he held a drawn sword. As the English officers stepped upon the deck he advanced toward them and bowed gracefully.

"You are—" began Pearson interrogatively.

"Commodore John Paul Jones, of the American Continental squadron, and the ship Bon Homme Richard, at your service, gentlemen; and you are—"

"Captain Richard Pearson, of His Britannic Majesty's ship Serapis," responded the other, bowing haughtily, as he tendered his sword.

Pearson is reputed to have said on this occasion, "I regret at being compelled to strike to a man who has fought with a halter around his neck," or words to that effect. He did not utter the remark at that time, according to

123

Jones' specific statement made long afterward. The substance of the statement was used, however, in Pearson's testimony before a court martial subsequently for the loss of his ship. And the story probably arose from that circumstance. Jones retained the sword, which was customary at that period, though different customs obtained later.

As he received the proffered sword the American replied, with a magnanimity as great as his valor:

"Sir, you have fought like a hero, and I make no doubt that your sovereign will reward you in the most ample manner."

His countrymen have ever loved Paul Jones for the chivalrous nobility of this gracious answer. But he wasted no further time in discussion. There was too much to be done; not a moment could be lost. It was half after ten o'clock at night; the battle was over, but their tasks were not yet completed. Both ships were burning furiously. Their decks were filled with desperately wounded men, whose agonies demanded immediate attention. Their screams and groans rose above the sound of the crackling, roaring flames. With but half a single crew Jones had to man both ships, put out the fires, force the escaped English prisoners back into the hold, secure the additional prisoners, and care for the wounded on the Serapis. From the actions of the Alliance, too, there was no telling what Landais might take it into his head to do. He had fired twice upon them; he might do it again, and possibly it might be necessary for Jones to defend the flagship and her prize from a more determined attack by Landais than any to which they had yet been subjected.

He turned over the command of the Serapis to Dale, sending him, as usual, a generous contingent for a prize crew, and then, as a preliminary to further work, the lashings which had held the two vessels in their death grapple were cut asunder. The Richard slowly began to draw past her beaten antagonist. Dale immediately filled his head sail and shifted his helm to wear ship and carry out his orders. He was much surprised to find that the Serapis lay still and did not obey the helm. Fearing that the wheel ropes had been shot away, he sent a quartermaster to examine them, who reported that they were intact. At this moment the master of the Serapis, coming aft and observing Dale's surprise, informed him that the English ship was anchored, which was the first intimation of that fact the Americans had received. Dale ordered the cable cut, whereupon the ship paid off and began to shove through the water, which fortunately still continued calm. As he spoke, he rose from the binnacle upon which he had been seated, and immediately fell prone to the deck. He discovered at that moment, by his inability to stand, that he had been severely wounded in the leg by a splinter, a thing which he had not noticed in the heat of the action. As he lay upon the deck, Mr. Henry Lunt, the second lieutenant of the Richard, came on board the Serapis at this juncture. This officer had been dispatched in the afternoon to pursue the brigantine, and had caused his boat's crew to lay on their oars at a safe distance from the two ships during the whole of the desperate battle, because, as he states, he "thought it not prudent to go alongside in time of action." Mr. Lunt no doubt lived to regret the pusillanimous "prudence" of his conduct on this occasion, although, if that conduct be an index to his character, his services would not be of great value in the battle. Dale turned over the command of the Serapis to Lunt, and was assisted on board the Richard.

As the Richard cleared the Serapis, the tottering mainmast of that ship, which had been subjected to a continual battering from the 9-pounders and which had only been sustained by the interlocking yards, came crashing down, just above the deck, carrying with it the mizzen topmast, doing much damage as it fell, and adding an element of shipwreck to the other evidence of disaster. The frigate was also on fire, and the flames, unchecked in the confusion of the surrender, were gaining great headway. Moved by a sense of their common peril and necessity, the English crew joined with the Americans in clearing away the wreck and subduing the fire. They did not effect this without a hard struggle, but they finally succeeded in saving the ship and following the Richard.

The situation on that ship was precarious in the extreme. She was very low in the water and leaking like a sieve. She was still on fire in several places, and the flames were blazing more furiously than ever. There was not a minute's respite allowed her crew. Having conquered the English, they turned to fight the fire and water. The prisoners were forced to continue their exhausting toil at the pumps. Pressing every man of the crew into service, including the English officers, except those so badly wounded as to be incapable of anything, Jones and his men turned their attention to the fire. They had a hard struggle to get it under control. At one time the flames approached so near to the magazine that, fearful lest they should be blown up, Jones caused the powder to be removed and stowed upon the deck preparatory to throwing it overboard. For some time they despaired of saving the ship. Toward daybreak, however, they managed to extinguish the flames and were saved that danger. In the morning a careful inspection of the ship was made. A fearful situation was revealed. She had been torn to pieces. It was hardly safe for the officers and men to remain on the after part of the ship. Everything that supported the upper deck except a few stanchions had been torn away. Her rotten timbers had offered no resistance to the Serapis' searching shot. Jones writes:

"With respect to the situation of the Bon Homme Richard, the rudder was cut entirely off, the stern frame and the transoms were almost entirely cut away; the timbers, by the lower deck especially, from the mainmast to the stern, being greatly decayed with age, were mangled beyond my power of description, and a person must have been an Eyewitness to form a just idea of the tremendous scene of carnage, wreck, and ruin that everywhere appeared. Humanity can not but recoil from the prospect of such finished horror, and lament that war should produce such fatal consequences."

It was evident that nothing less than a miracle could keep her afloat even in the calmest weather. With a perfectly natural feeling Jones determined to try it.

A large detail from the Pallas was set to work pumping her out. Every effort, meanwhile, was made to patch her up so that she could be brought into the harbor. The efforts were in vain. Owing to the decayed condition of her timbers, even the poor remnants of her frames that were left standing aft could not bear the slightest repairing. She settled lower and lower in the water, until, having been surveyed by the carpenters and various men of experience, including Captain de Cottineau, about five o'clock in the evening it was determined to abandon her. It was time. She threatened to sink at any moment—would surely have sunk, indeed, if the pumps had stopped. She was filled with helpless wounded and prisoners. They had to be taken off before she went down.

During the night everybody worked desperately transferring the wounded to the other ships, further details of men from the Pallas being told off to man the frigate and keep her afloat. Such was the haste with which they worked that they barely succeeded in trans-shipping the last of the wounded just before daybreak on the 25th. Although the sea fortunately continued smooth, the poor wounded suffered frightfully from the rough handling necessitated by the rapid transfer.

The removal of the prisoners from the Richard was now begun; naturally, these men, expecting the ship to sink at any moment, were frantic with terror. They had only been kept down by the most rigorous measures. As day broke, the light revealed to them the nearness of the approaching end of the ship. They also realized that they greatly outnumbered the Americans remaining on the Richard. There was a hurried consultation among them: a quick rush, and they made a desperate attempt to take the ship. Some endeavored to overpower the Americans, others ran to the braces and wheel and got the head of the ship toward the land. A brief struggle ensued. The Americans were all heavily armed, the English had few weapons, and after two of them had been shot dead, many wounded, and others thrown overboard, they were subdued once more and the ship regained. In the confusion some thirteen of them got possession of a boat and escaped in the gray of the morning to the shore. By close, quick work during the early morning all the men alive, prisoners and crew, were embarked in the boats of the squadron before the Richard finally disappeared.[18] At ten o'clock in the morning of the 25th she plunged forward and went down bow foremost. The great battle flag under which she had been fought, which had been shot away during the action, had been picked up and reset. It fluttered above her as she slowly sank beneath the sea. [19]

So filled had been the busy hours, and so many had been the demands made upon him in every direction, that Jones, ever careless of himself in others' needs, lost all of his personal wardrobe, papers, and other property. They went down with the ship. From the deck of the Serapis, Jones, with longing eyes and mingled feelings, watched the great old Indiaman, which had earned everlasting immortality because for three brief hours he and his men had battled upon her worn-out decks, sink beneath the sea. Most of those who had given their lives in defense of her in the battle lay still and silent upon her decks. There had been no time to spare to the dead. Like the Vikings of old, they found their coffin in her riven sides, and sleep to-day in the quiet of the great deep on the scene of their glory. During the interval after the action, a jury rig had been improvised on the Serapis, which had not been severely cut up below by the light guns of the Richard, and was therefore entirely seaworthy, and the squadron bore away by Jones' orders for Dunkirk, France.

Before we pass to a consideration of the subsequent movements of the squadron, a further comparison between the Richard and the Serapis, with some statement of the losses sustained and the various factors which were calculated to bring about the end, will be in order, and will reveal much that is interesting. The accounts of the losses upon the two ships widely differ. Jones reported for the Richard forty-nine killed and sixty-seven wounded; total, one hundred and sixteen out of three hundred; but the number is confessedly incomplete. Pearson, for the Serapis, reported the same number of killed and sixty-eight wounded, out of a crew of three hundred and twenty; but it is highly probable that the loss in both cases was much greater. The records, as we have seen, were badly kept on the Richard, and most of them were lost when the ship went down. The books of the Serapis seemed to have fared equally ill in the confusion. The crews of both ships were scattered throughout the several ships of the American squadron, and accurate information was practically unobtainable. Jones, who was in a better position than Pearson for ascertaining the facts, reports the loss of the Serapis as over two hundred men, which is probably nearly correct, and the loss of the Richard was probably not far from one hundred and fifty men. The Countess of Scarborough lost four killed and twenty wounded. The loss of the Pallas was slight, and that of the Alliance and Vengeance nothing.

However this may be, the battle was one of the most sanguinary and desperate ever fought upon the sea. It was unique in that the beaten ship, which was finally sunk by the guns of her antagonist, actually compelled that antagonist to surrender. It was remarkable for the heroism manifested by both crews. It is invidious, perhaps, to make a comparison on that score, yet, if the contrast can be legitimately drawn, the result is decidedly in favor of the Richard's men, for they had not only the enemy to occupy their attention, but they sustained and did not succumb to the treacherous attack of the Alliance in the rear. The men of the Serapis were, of course, disheartened and their nerves shattered by the explosion which occurred at the close of the action, but a similar and equally dreadful misfortune had occurred at the commencement of the engagement on the Richard, in the blowing up of the two 18-pounders. In ninety-nine cases out of a hundred either of these two terrible incidents would have caused a prompt surrender of the ship on which they occurred; but the Richard's men rallied from the former, and it must not be forgotten that the Serapis' men did the like from the latter, for they had recommenced the fire of their guns just as Pearson hauled down his flag.

The officers on the two ships appear to have done their whole duty, and the difference, as I have said, lay in the relative qualities of the two captains. Jones could not be beaten, Pearson could. When humanity enters into a conflict with a man like Jones, it must make up its mind to eventually discontinue the fight or else remove the man. Fortunately, Jones, though slightly wounded, was not removed; therefore Pearson had to surrender. Next to Jones, the most unique personality which was produced by the action was Richard Dale. I do not refer to his personal courage—he was no braver than Pearson; neither was Jones, for that matter; in fact, the bravery of all three was of the highest order—but to his astonishing presence of mind and resource at that crucial moment which was the third principal incident of the battle, when the English prisoners were released. The more one thinks of the prompt, ready way in which he cajoled, commanded, and coerced these prisoners into manning the pumps so that his own men could continue the battle, the result of which, if they succeeded would be to retain the English still as prisoners, the more one marvels at it. The fame of Dale has been somewhat obscured in the greater fame of Jones, but he deserves the very highest praise for his astonishing action. And in every possible public way Jones freely accorded the greatest credit to him.

There is one other fact in connection with the battle which must be mentioned. The English have always claimed that the presence of the Alliance decided Pearson to surrender. In justice, I have no doubt that it did exercise a moral influence upon the English captain. In the confusion of the fight, what damage, whether little or great, had been done to the Serapis by the fire of the Alliance could not be definitely ascertained. Again, it would never enter the head of an ordinary commander that the Alliance was deliberately firing into her consort. So far as can be determined now, no damage worthy of account had been done to the English ship by the Alliance; but Pearson knew she was there, and he had a right to believe that she would return at any time. When she returned, if she should take position on the starboard side of the Serapis, the unengaged side, he would have to strike at once.

Something of this sort may have been in his mind, and it would undoubtedly contribute to decide him to surrender; but, admitting all this, he should have delayed the formal surrender until the possible contingency had developed into a reality, until he actually saw the Alliance alongside of him again. As a matter of fact, he did not strike until about thirty minutes after the Alliance had fired the last broadside and sailed away. The American frigate was out of gunshot when he surrendered, and going farther from him with every minute.

Imagine what Jones would have done under similar circumstances! Indeed, we do not have to imagine what he would have done, for as it happened the Alliance had on two occasions fired full upon him, and he was actually in the dilemma which Pearson imagined he might fall into, and yet it only re-enforced his already resolute determination to continue the fight more fiercely than ever. A nice point this: with Pearson the Alliance was an imaginary danger, with Jones a real one! While the presence of the Alliance, therefore, explains in a measure Pearson's surrender, it does not enhance his reputation for dogged determination. The unheard-of resistance which he had met from the Richard, the persistence with which the attack was carried on, the apparently utterly unconquerable nature of his antagonist—of whose difficulties on the Richard he was not aware, for there was no evidence of faltering in the battle—the frightful attack he had received, and his isolation upon the deck filled with dead and dying men, broke his own power of resistance. There were two things beaten on that day—the Richard and Pearson; one might almost say three things: both ships and the captain of one. It is generally admitted, even by the English, that the result would have been the same if the Alliance had never appeared on the scene. No, it was a fair and square stand-up fight, and a fair and square defeat.[20]

The conduct of Landais has presented a problem difficult of solution. It has been surmised, and upon the warrant of his own statement, that he would have thought it no harm if the Richard had struck to the Serapis, and he could have had the glory of recapturing her and then forcing the surrender of the English frigate; but whether he really meant by his dastardly conduct to compel this situation from which he trusted he could reap so much honor, is another story. Most of the historians have been unable to see anything in his actions but jealousy and treachery. The most eminent critic, however, who has treated of the battle[21] has thought his actions arose from an incapacity, coupled with a timidity amounting to cowardice, which utterly blinded his judgment; that he was desirous of doing something, and felt it incumbent upon him to take some part in the action and that his firing into the Richard was due to incompetency rather than to anything else. With all deference, it is difficult to agree with this proposition. The officers of the squadron, in a paper which was prepared less than a month after the action, bore conclusive testimony that while it is true that he was an incapable coward, he was, in addition, either a jealous traitor, or—and this is the only other supposition which will account for his action—that he was irresponsible, in short, insane. This is a conclusion to which his own officers afterward arrived, and which his subsequent career seems to bear out. At any rate, this is the most charitable explanation of his conduct which can be adopted. If he had been simply cowardly, he could have done some service by attacking the unprotected convoy, which was entirely at his mercy, and among which he could have easily taken some valuable prizes. It is stated to their credit that some of the officers of the Alliance remonstrated with Landais, and pointed out to him that he was attacking the wrong ship, and that some of his men refused to obey his orders to fire.

There is but one other circumstance to which it is necessary to refer. All the plans of the battle which are extant, and all the descriptions which have been made, from Cooper to Maclay and Spears, show that the Richard passed ahead of the Serapis and was raked; and that the Serapis then ranged alongside to windward of the American and presently succeeded in crossing the Richard's bow and raking her a second time. Richard Dale's account, in Sherburne's Life of Paul Jones, written some forty-six years after the action, seems to bear out this idea. Jones himself, whose report is condensed and unfortunately wanting in detail, says: "Every method was practiced on both sides to gain an advantage and rake each other, and I must confess that the enemy's ship, being much more manageable than the Bon Homme Richard, gained thereby several times an advantageous situation, in spite of my best endeavors to prevent it." Nathaniel Fanning, midshipman of the maintop in the action, stated in his narrative, published in 1806, twenty-seven years later, that the Serapis raked the Richard several times.

Notwithstanding this weight of apparent testimony, I must agree with

Captain Mahan in his conclusion that the Serapis, until the ships were lashed together, engaged the Richard with her port battery only, and that the plan as given above is correct. In the first place, Jones' statement is too indefinite to base a conclusion upon unless clearly corroborated by other evidence. Dale, being in the batteries, where he could hardly see the maneuvers, and writing from memory after a lapse of many years, may well have been mistaken. Fanning's narrative is contradicted by the articles which he signed concerning the conduct of Landais, in October, 1779, in the Texel, so that his earliest statement is at variance with his final recollection, and Fanning is not very reliable at best.

However, we might accept the statements of these men as decisive were it not for the fact that Pearson, whose report is very explicit indeed, makes no claim whatever to having succeeded in raking the Richard, though it would be so greatly to his credit if he had done so that it is hardly probable he would fail to state it. His account of the battle accords with the plan of the present work. Again, when the Serapis engaged the Richard in the final grapple, she had to blow off her starboard port shutters, which were therefore tightly closed. If she had been engaged to starboard (which would necessarily follow if she had been on the port side of the Richard at any time), the ports would have been opened.[22] This is not absolutely conclusive, because, of course, it would be possible that the ports might have been closed when the men were shifted to the other battery, but in the heat of the action such a measure would be so improbable as to be worthy of little consideration. But the most conclusive testimony to the fact that the Serapis was not on the port side of the Richard at any time is found in the charges which were signed by the officers concerning the conduct of Landais. Article 19 reads: "As the most dangerous shot which the Bon Homme Richard received under the water were under the larboard bow and quarter, they must have come from the Alliance, *for the Serapis was on the other side.*"[23]

Captain Mahan well sums it up: "As Landais' honor, if not his life, was at stake in these charges, it is not to be supposed that six officers (besides two French marine officers), four of whom were specially well situated for seeing, would have made this statement if the Serapis had at any time been in position to fire those shots."

This consideration, therefore, seems to settle the question. Again, the maneuvers as they have been described in this volume are the simple and natural evolutions which, under the existing conditions of wind and weather and the relative positions of the two ships, would have been in all human probability carried out. The attempt to put the ships in the different positions of the commonly accepted plans involves a series of highly complicated and unnecessary evolutions (scarcely possible, in fact, in the very light breeze), which no commander would be apt to attempt in the heat of action unless most serious contingencies rendered them inevitable.

CHAPTER XII.

UPHOLDING AMERICAN HONOR IN THE TEXEL.

After the sinking of the Richard, Jones turned his attention to the squadron. Those ships which had been in action were now ready for sea, so far, at least, as it was possible to make them, and it was necessary to make a safe port as soon as possible. He had now some five hundred English prisoners, including Captains Pearson and Piercy and their officers, in his possession. These equaled all the American seamen held captive by the English, and, with one of the main objects of his expedition in view, Jones earnestly desired to make a French port, in which case his prizes would be secure and he would be able to effect a proper exchange of prisoners. But the original destination of the squadron had been the Texel. It is evident that in sending the squadron into the Zuyder Zee Franklin shrewdly contemplated the possibility of so compromising Holland by the presence of the ships as to force a recognition from that important maritime and commercial power of the belligerency of the United States. This was the real purport of the orders. There was an ostensible reason, however, in the presence of a large fleet of merchant vessels in the Texel, which would be ready for sailing for France in October, and Jones' squadron could give them a safe convoy.

The events of the cruise had brought about a somewhat different situation from that contemplated in the original orders, and Jones was undoubtedly within his rights in determining to enter Dunkirk, the most available French port; in which event the difficulties which afterward arose concerning the exchange of prisoners and the disposition of the prizes would never have presented themselves. In the latter case, however, the hand of Holland might not have been so promptly forced, and the recognition accorded this country would probably have been much longer delayed, although in the end it would have come. But the balance of advantage lay with Jones' choice of Dunkirk.

For a week the ships beat up against contrary winds, endeavoring to make that port. Their position was most precarious. Sixteen sail, including several ships of the line, were seeking the audacious invaders, and they were likely to overhaul them at any time. The Frenchmen naturally grew nervous over the prospect. Finally, the captains, who had been remonstrating daily with Jones, refused to obey his orders any longer; and, the wind continuing unfavorable for France, they actually deserted the Serapis, running off to leeward in a mass and heading for the Texel.

The officers of the American squadron were fully aware of the assigned destination, although the deep reasons for Franklin's subtle policy had probably not been communicated to them. In view of this unprecedented situation, which may be traced distinctly to the concordat, there was nothing left to Jones but to swallow the affront as best he might, and follow his unruly squadron.

Landais had not yet been deposed from the command of the Alliance, because it would have probably required force to arrest him on the deck of his own ship, and an internecine conflict might have been precipitated in his command. On the 3d of October, having made a quick run of it, the squadron entered the Texel.

From the mainland of the Dutch Republic, now the Kingdom of the Netherlands, the state of North Holland thrusts a bold wedge of land far to the northward, between the foaming surges of the German Ocean on the one hand, and the tempest-tossed waters of the Zuyder Zee on the other. Opposite the present mighty fortifications of Helder, justly considered the Gibraltar of the North, which terminate the peninsula, lies a deep and splendid channel, bounded on the north side by the island of Texel, from which the famous passage gets its name. Through this ocean gateway, from time immemorial, a splendid procession of gallant ships and hardy men have gone forth to discover new worlds, to found new countries, to open up new avenues of trade with distant empires, and to uphold the honor of the Orange flag in desperate battles on the sea. Through the pass sailed the first great Christian foreign missionary expedition of modern times, when in 1624 the Dutchmen carried the Gospel to the distant island of Formosa, the beautiful.

Brederode and the wild beggars of the sea; Tromp, De Ruyter, van Heemskerk, De Winter, leading their fleets to battles which made their names famous, had plowed through the deep channel with their lumbering keels. Of smaller ships from these familiar shores, the little Half Moon, of Henry Hudson, and the pilgrim-laden Mayflower had taken their departure. But no bolder officer nor better seaman had ever made the passage than the little man on the deck of the battered Serapis on that raw October morning. It is a rather interesting coincidence that among the prizes of this cruise was one which bore the name of the Mayflower.

As the cables of the ships tore through the hawse pipes when they dropped anchor, Jones may have imagined that his troubles were over. As a matter of fact, they had just begun, and his stay in the Texel was not the least arduous nor the least brilliant period in his life. His conduct in the trying circumstances in which he found himself was beyond reproach. The instant that he appeared, Sir Joseph Yorke, the able and influential Minister of England at The Hague, demanded that the States-General deliver the Serapis and the Scarborough to him and compel the return of the English prisoners held by Jones, and that the American "Pirate" should be ordered to leave the Texel immediately, which would, of course, result in the certain capture of his ships, for the English pursuing squadron appeared off the mouth of the channel almost immediately after Jones' entrance.

Sir Joseph made the point—and it was a pretty one—that by the terms of past treaties prizes taken by ships whose commanders bore the commission of no recognized power or sovereign were to be returned to the English whenever they fell into the hands of Holland. This placed the States-General in a dilemma. Paul Jones would show no commission except that of America; indeed, he had no other. In Sir Joseph's mind the situation was this: The States-General would comply with the terms of the treaty or it would not. If it did, he would get possession of the ships and of Jones as well. If it did not, the logic of events would indicate that the States-General considered the commission which Paul Jones bore as being valid, in that it was issued by a sovereign power. This would be in effect a recognition of belligerency. In other words, the shrewd British diplomatist was endeavoring to force the hand of the States-General. To determine the position of Holland with regard to the revolted colonies of Great Britain was a matter of greater moment than to secure Paul Jones or to receive the two ships, the loss of which, except so far as it affronted the pride of England, was of no consequence whatever. The States-General, however, endeavored to evade the issue and postpone the decision, for, while their "High Mightinesses" refused to cause the ships to be given up, they ordered Jones to leave the harbor at once, and they earnestly disclaimed any intention of recognizing the revolted colonies.

As a matter of fact, since there were two parties in the government of Holland, and two opinions on the subject, they could come to no more definite conclusion. Jones was intensely popular with the people, and the democratic opinion favored the immediate recognition of American independence, and protested against any arbitrary action toward him and his ships. The Prince of Orange and the aristocratic party took the contrary view, and they pressed it upon him as far as they dared. Realizing the precarious nature of his stay in Holland, Jones immediately set to work with his usual energy to refit the ships, especially the Serapis. Dispatching a full account of his cruise and his expedition to Franklin, he went in person to Amsterdam to facilitate his desire. A contemporary account states that he was dressed in an American naval uniform,[24] wearing on his head, instead of the usual cocked hat, a Scotch bonnet edged with gold lace.

When he appeared in the exchange he received a popular ovation, which naturally greatly pleased him. However, he modestly strove to escape the overwhelming demonstrations of admiration and approval with which he was greeted, by retiring to a coffee room, but he was compelled to show himself again and again at the window in response to repeated demands from crowds of people assembled in the street who desired a sight of him. He was made the hero of song and story, and one of the ballads of the time, a rude, rollicking, drinking song, very popular among sailors, which celebrates his exploits, is sung to this day in the streets of Amsterdam.[25] So delighted were the Dutch with the humiliation he had inflicted upon their ancient enemy that some of the principal men of the nation, including the celebrated Baron van der Capellen, subsequently noted for his friendship for America (evidently not in harmony with the aristocratic party), entered into a correspondence with him, which must have been highly flattering to him, from the expressions of admiration and approval with which every letter of the baron's abounds. They desired to receive at first hand an account of his exploits. In response to this request Jones had his report to Dr. Franklin copied and sent to van der Capellen, together with other documents illustrative of his career, accompanied by the following letter:

"ON BOARD THE SERAPIS AT THE TEXEL,

"*October 19, 1779.*

"MY LORD: Human nature and America are under a very singular obligation to you for your patriotism and friendship, and I feel every grateful sentiment for your generous and polite letter.

"Agreeable to your request I have the honour to inclose a copy of my letter to his Excellency Doctor Franklin, containing a particular account of my late expedition on the coasts of Britain and Ireland, by which you will see that I have already been praised far more than I have deserved; but I must at the same time beg leave to observe that by the other papers which I take the liberty to inclose (particularly the copy of my letter to the Countess of Selkirk, dated the day of my arrival at Brest from the Irish Sea), I hope you will be convinced that in the British prints I have been censured unjustly. I was, indeed, born in Britain, but I do not inherit the degenerate spirit of that fallen nation, which I at once lament and despise. It is far beneath me to reply to their hireling invectives. They are strangers to the inward approbation that greatly animates and rewards the man who draws his sword only in support of the dignity of freedom.

"America has been the country of my fond election from the age of thirteen, when I first saw it.[26] I had the honour to hoist, with my own hands, the flag of freedom, the first time that it was displayed on the Delaware, and I have attended it with veneration ever since on the Ocean; I see it respected even here, in spite of the pitiful Sir Joseph, and I ardently wish and hope very soon to exchange a salute with the flag of this Republick. Let but the two Republicks join hands, and they will give Peace to the World."

Among the documents transmitted was the famous letter to Lady Selkirk, of which sententious epistle he evidently remained inordinately proud. In acknowledging this courtesy van der Capellen wrote as follows:

"The perusal of the letters with which you have favoured me has done the very same effect upon me that his Excell. Dr. Franklin expected they would do on the Countess of Selkirk, as you are represented in some of our Newspapers as a rough, unpolished sailor, not only, but even as a man of little understanding and no morals and sensibility, and as I think the 4 papers extremely fit to destroy these malicious aspersions, I must take the liberty of asking your permission to publish them in our gazettes. The public will soon make this very just conclusion that the man honoured by the friendship and intimacy of a Franklin can not be such as you have been represented.[27] There are three points on which you will oblige me by giving some elucidation, 1st. whether you have any obligations to Lord Selkirk? 2d. whether Lady Selkirk has accepted your generous offer? 3d. whether you have a commission of France besides that of the Congress? 'Tis not a vain curiosity that incites me to be so importunate; no, sir, the two first questions are often repeated to me by your enemies, or, at least, by prejudiced people; and as to the last, a relative of mine, a known friend of America, has addressed himself to me for information on that subject, which he will be glad to have before the States of his province, of which he is a member (but not yet, as I am, expelled the house), be assembled.

"You will greatly oblige me by sending me as soon as possible such information as you will think proper to grant.

"You may rely on our discretion; we can keep a secret, too. I am in a great hurry, with the most perfect esteem ..."

The baron's statement gives us a contemporary opinion—one of entire approbation, by the way—of the letter to Lady Selkirk, and it shows us that our great-grandfathers looked at things with different eyes from ours.

In reply, Jones dispatched the following letter a month later:

"ALLIANCE, TEXEL, *November 29, 1779.*

"MY LORD: Since I had the honour to receive your second esteemed letter I have unexpectedly had occasion to revisit Amsterdam; and, having changed ships since my return to the Texel, I have by some accident or neglect lost or mislaid your letter. I remember, however, the questions it contained: 1st, whether I ever had any obligation to Lord Selkirk? 2dly, whether he accepted my offer? and 3dly, whether I have a French commission? I answer: I have never had any obligation to Lord Selkirk, except for his good opinion, nor does know me nor mine except by character. Lord Selkirk wrote me an answer to my letter to the Countess, but the Ministry detained it in the general post office in London for a long time, and then returned it to the author, who afterward wrote to a friend of his (M. Alexander), an acquaintance of Doctor Franklin's then at Paris, giving him an account of the fate of his letter to me & desiring him to acquaint his Excellency and myself that if the plate was restored by Congress or by any public Body he would accept it, but that he would not think of accepting it from my private generosity. The plate has, however, been bought, agreeable to my letter to the Countess, and now lays in France at her disposal. As to the 3rd article, *I never bore nor acted under any other commission than what I have received from the Congress of the United States of America.*[28]

"I am much obliged to you, my Lord, for the honour you do me by proposing to publish the papers I sent you in my last, but it is an honour which I must decline, because I can not publish my letter to a lady without asking and obtaining the lady's consent, and because I have a very modest opinion of my writings, being conscious that they are not of sufficient value to claim the notice of the public. I assure you, my Lord, it has given me much concern to see an extract of my rough journal in print, and that, too, under the disadvantage of a translation. That mistaken kindness of a friend will make me cautious how I communicate my papers.

"I have the honour to be, my Lord, with great esteem and respect,

"Your most obliged,

"And very humble servant."

The nice delicacy of his conduct in refusing to permit the publication of a letter to a lady without her consent goes very far toward redeeming the absurdity of the letter itself. While this interesting correspondence was going on, events of great moment were transpiring. In the first place, Captain Pearson was protesting against his detention as a prisoner in the most vehement way, and otherwise behaving in a very ill-bred manner. When the commodore offered to return him his plate, linen, and other property, which had been taken from the Serapis, he refused to accept it from Jones; but he intimated that he would receive it from the hand of Captain de Cottineau! Jones had the magnanimity to overlook this petty quibbling, and returned the property through the desired channel. Pearson, like Jones, was of humble origin; but, unlike Jones, he never seems to have risen above it. On October 19th he addressed the following note to Jones:

"PALLAS, TUESDAY EVENING, *October 19, 1779.*

"*Captain Jones, Serapis.*

"Captain Pearson presents his compliments to Captain Jones, and is sorry to find himself so little attended to in his present situation as not to have been favoured with either a *Call* or a line from Captain Jones since his return from Amsterdam. Captain P ... is sorry to say that he can not look upon such behaviour in any other light than as a breach of that *Civility*, which his Rank, as well as behaviour on all occasions entitles to, he at the same time wishes to be informed by Captain Jones whether any *Steps has* been taken toward the enlargement or exchange of him, his officers and people, or what is intended to be done with them. As he can not help thinking it a very unprecedented circumstance their being *keeped* here as prisoners on board of ship, being so long in a neutral port."

He received in return this decided and definite reply:

"Serapis, Wednesday, *October 20, 1779.*

"*Captain Pearson.*

"Sir: As you have not been prevented from corresponding with your friends, and particularly with the English ambassador at The Hague, I could not suppose you to be unacquainted with his memorial, of the 8th, to the States-General, and therefore I thought it fruitless to pursue the negotiation for the exchange of the prisoners of war now in our hands.

"I wished to avoid any painful altercation with you on that subject; I was persuaded that you had been in the highest degree sensible that my behaviour 'toward you had been far from a breach of civility.' This charge is not, Sir, a civil return for the polite hospitality and disinterested attentions which you have hitherto experienced.

"I know not what difference of respect is due to 'Rank,' between your service and ours; I suppose, however, the difference must be thought *very great* in England, since I am informed that Captain Cunningham, of equal denomination, and who bears a senior rank in the service of America, than yours in the service of England, is now confined at Plymouth *in a dungeon, and in fetters.*

"Humanity, which hath hitherto superseded the plea of retaliation in American breasts, has induced me (notwithstanding the procedure of Sir Joseph Yorke) to seek after permission to land the dangerously wounded, as well prisoners as Americans, to be supported and cured at the expense of our Continent. The permission of the Government has been obtained, but the magistrates continue to make objections. I shall not discontinue my application. I am ready to adopt any means that you may propose for their preservation and recovery, and in the meantime we shall continue to treat them with the utmost care and attention, equally, as you know, to the treatment of our people of the same rank.

"As it is possible that you have not yet seen the memorial of your ambassador to the States-General, I enclose a paper which contains a copy, and I believe he has since written what, in the opinion of good men, will do still less honour to his pen.

"I can not conclude without informing you that unless Captain Cunningham is immediately better treated in England, I expect orders in consequence from His Excellency Dr. Franklin; therefore, I beseech you, Sir, to interfere."

The States-General having refused to consent to the restoration of the ships and the surrender of the prisoners, Paul Jones went to The Hague for the purpose of pleading his own cause; and there, through the representations of the French ambassador, the Duc de la Vauguyon, received permission from their High Mightinesses to land the more dangerously wounded among his prisoners and crew as well, numbering over one hundred, in order that he might better care for them and establish them in more comfortable quarters than the crowded ships permitted.

From motives of humanity, in view of the condition of the prisoners, Sir Joseph Yorke acquiesced in this arrangement. It was first proposed that Jones should land them and establish a hospital at Helder; but the magistrates of that town objecting to the proposition, a fort on the Texel was assigned to him, of which the entire charge was committed to him. Colonel de Weibert, with a sufficient force to garrison the works, was placed in command of the fort.

Meanwhile, the charges against Landais, having been formulated and signed, were dispatched to Franklin, who, with the consent of the French Government, ordered him to resign the command of the Alliance and repair immediately to Paris. Before he left the Texel the erratic Frenchman compelled Captain de Cottineau to accord him the honor of a duel. As Landais was an expert swordsman, he succeeded in severely wounding his less skillful but far more worthy antagonist. Elated by this exploit, the mad Frenchman sent Jones a challenge also. In reply to Landais' note, the commodore, Marius-like, promptly dispatched men to arrest him; but Landais got wind of the attempt and hastened to escape, taking up his departure for Paris. During the stay in the Texel Jones succeeded in effecting the exchange of Captain Pearson for Captain Gustavus Cunningham, whom he had at last the pleasure of receiving upon his own ship.[29] Meanwhile, with true British persistence, Sir Joseph kept at the States-General, and it in turn pressed upon Jones, who imperturbably passed the matter on to the French ambassador and Dr. Franklin.

On the 12th of November, to relieve a situation which had become well-nigh insupportable, the French Government, with the consent of Franklin, directed that the command of the Serapis should be given to Captain de Cottineau, and that all the other vessels, except the Alliance, to which the French had no claim, should hoist the French flag, and that the Americans should be sent on board the Alliance, which should be turned over to Paul Jones. To his everlasting regret, Jones had to obey the heartbreaking order, and in one moment found himself deprived of his command and his prizes taken from him. It was a crushing blow, but he had no option save to bear it as best he could. The exchange was effected at night, and the next morning, when the Dutch admiral sent his flag captain on board the Serapis to attempt his usual bullying, he was surprised to see the French flag flying from her gaff end, and to be informed that she was now the property of France, as were all the other ships except the Alliance. Proceedings at once, therefore, fell to the ground as regarded all the ships but the American frigate. There was no possible reason for giving up the ships of the French king to the British Government, so Sir Joseph Yorke necessarily, although with a very bad grace, dropped the matter, and a short time after the French ships and the prizes sailed with the merchant fleet under a strong Dutch convoy for France, where they all arrived safely. Yorke persisted, however, in attempting to secure the person of Jones, it is gravely alleged, through the efforts of private individuals, kidnappers or bravos. At any rate, he redoubled his representations regarding the Alliance, and his efforts to force the departure of the ship that she might fall into the hands of the waiting English.

The Serapis had been thoroughly overhauled and refitted, and the other ships, with the exception of the Alliance, were in good shape. By his unsailorly antics and foolish arrangements Landais had almost destroyed the qualities of that noble frigate. She was in a dreadful condition. Thirteen Dutch men-of-war, all of them two-deckers, or line of battle ships, had assembled in the Texel to enforce the orders of the States-General, which, on the 17th of November, by a specific resolution directed the Admiralty Board at Amsterdam to command Jones to let no opportunity escape to put to sea, as the approach of winter might make his departure inconvenient or impossible if he delayed longer. Vice-Admiral Rhynst, who had succeeded Captain Rimersina (like van der Capellen, another friend of the United States) in the command of the Dutch fleet, was peremptorily ordered to permit no delay which was not unavoidable in the carrying out of these orders. He was instructed and empowered to use force if necessary. Outside the harbor there was a constantly increasing number of English ships, so that Jones found himself "between the devil and the deep sea." He was not to be intimidated, however, and he absolutely refused to go out at all until he was ready, sending Admiral Rhynst a rather boastful letter to the effect that he could not engage more than three times his force with any hope of success, but were the odds any less he should go out at once. M. Dumas, the French commissary and the agent of the United States at The Hague, had been directed to proceed to the Texel and do what he could for Jones, and an interesting correspondence was carried on between them and the French ambassador on the subject of Jones' departure. With clear-eyed diplomacy and stubborn resolution the American held on; go he would not until he was ready! It was, no doubt, very exasperating to the Dutch, and they did everything possible save using force to get rid of their unwelcome visitor.

The Alliance, as has been stated, was in an unseaworthy condition. An old-fashioned sailing vessel was as complex and delicate a thing as a woman; rude, brutal, and unskillful handling had the same effect on both of them—it spoiled them. Jones at once began the weary work of refitting her so far as his limited resources provided. The powder which had been saved from the wreck of the Richard replaced the spoiled ammunition of the Alliance. Two cables had been borrowed from the Serapis, and such other steps taken as were possible. When the squadron was turned over to France the prisoners, except those already exchanged by agreement between Jones and Pearson, also were directed to be surrendered to the French Government, who immediately exchanged them with the English for an equal number of French prisoners, promising Franklin that they would presently exchange a corresponding number of French prisoners for the Americans. But Jones resolutely refused to give up all of his prisoners. In spite of protests and orders he re-embarked the hundred men who had been recovering from their wounds in the fort on the Texel, and taking all the Americans of the squadron, so that the Alliance was heavily overmanned, he made his preparations to get away.

At this time the Duc de la Vauguyon, by the direction of De Sartine, made Jones the offer of a French naval letter of marque, which might have protected the captain of the Alliance on her proposed homeward passage, and have removed all legal cause of objection as to her stay in the Texel. To this proposition, which he considered insulting, Jones made the following characteristic answer:

"My Lord: Perhaps there are many men in the world who would esteem as an honour the commission that I have this day refused. My rank from the beginning knew no superior in the marine of America; how then must I be humbled were I to accept a letter of marque! I should, my lord, esteem myself inexcusable were I to accept even a commission of equal or superior denomination to that I bear, unless I were previously authorised by Congress, or some other competent authority in Europe. And I must tell you that, on my arrival at Brest from the Irish Channel, Count D'Orvilliers offered to procure for me from court a commission of '*Capitaine de Vaisseau*,' which I did not then accept for the same reason, although the war between France and England was not then begun, and of course the commission of France would have protected me from an enemy of superior force.

"It is a matter of the highest astonishment to me that, after so many compliments and fair professions, the court should offer the present insult to my understanding, and suppose me capable of disgracing my present commission. I confess that I never merited all the praise bestowed on my past conduct, but I also feel that I have far less merited such a reward. Where profession and practice are so opposite I am no longer weak enough to form a wrong conclusion. *They may think as they please of me; for where I can not continue my esteem, praise or censure from any man is to me a matter of indifference.*[30]

"I am much obliged to them, however, for having at last fairly opened my eyes, and enabled me to discover truth from falsehood.

"The prisoners shall be delivered agreeable to the orders which you have done me the honour to send me from his excellency the American ambassador in France.

"I will also with great pleasure not only permit a part of my seamen to go on board the ships under your excellency's orders, but I will also do my utmost to prevail with them to embark freely; and if I can now or hereafter, by any other honourable means, facilitate the success or the honour of his Majesty's arms, I pledge myself to you as his ambassador, that none of his own subjects would bleed in his cause with greater freedom than myself, an American.

"It gives me the more pain, my lord, to write this letter, because the court has enjoined you to prepare what would destroy my peace of mind, and my future veracity in the opinion of the world.

"When, *with the consent of the court*, and by order of the American ambassador, I gave American commissions to French officers, I did not fill up those commissions to command privateers, nor even for a rank *equal* to that of their commissions in the marine of France. They were promoted to rank *far superior*. And why? Not from personal friendship, nor from my knowledge of their services and abilities (the men and their characters being entire strangers to me), but from the respect which I believed America would wish to show for the service of France.

"While I remained eight months seemingly forgot by the court at Brest, many commissions, such as that in question, were offered to me; and I believe (when I am in pursuit of *plunder*) I can still obtain such an one without application to court.

"I hope, my lord, that my behaviour through life will ever entitle me to the continuance of your good wishes and opinion, and that you will take occasion to make mention of the warm and personal affection with which my heart is impressed toward his Majesty."

In no other letter among the many which I have examined does Jones appear in so brilliant and successful a light. His high-souled decision, and his dignified but explicit way of conveying it, alike do him the greatest credit. In the hands of such a man, not only his own honor but that of his country would be perfectly safe always. As usual, on the 16th of December, he inclosed a copy of his letter to Franklin with the following original comment:

"I hope," he said, "that the within copy of my letter to the Duc de la Vauguyon will meet your approbation, for I am persuaded that it never could be your intention or wish that I should be made the tool of any great r— whatever; or that the commission of America should be overlaid by the dirty piece of parchment which I have thus rejected! They have played upon my good humour too long already, but the spell is at last dissolved. They would play me off with assurance of the personal and particular esteem of the king, to induce me to do what would render me contemptible even in the eyes of my own servants! Accustomed to speak untruths themselves, they would also have me to give under my hand that I am a liar and a scoundrel. They are mistaken, and I would tell them what you did to your naughty servant. 'We have too contemptible an opinion of one another's understanding to live together.' I could tell them, too, that if M— de C— had not taken such safe precautions to keep me honest by means of his famous *concordat*, and to support me by so many able colleagues, these great men would not have been reduced to such mean shifts; for the prisoners could have been landed at Dunkirk the day that I entered the Texel, and I could have brought in double the numbers."

After annoying him with daily injunctions and commands, on the 16th of December Vice Admiral Rhynst finally commanded Jones to come on board his flagship and report his intentions. Jones promptly refused to obey this astonishing order, telling the Dutchman that he had no right to order him anywhere. Whereupon the vice admiral wrote to him as follows:

"I desire you by this present letter to inform me how I must consider the Alliance which you are on board of: whether as a French or American vessel. If the first, I expect you to cause his Majesty's commission to be shown to me, and that you display the French flag and pendant, announcing it by discharging a gun. If the second, I expect you to omit no occasion of departing, according to the orders of their High Mightinesses."

Jones had passed beyond the arguing point, and treated this communication with contempt. He rightly judged that the Dutch would not resort to force in the end, and he refused to go out to certain capture; indeed, he would not move until he was ready and a fair chance of escape presented itself.

When the French Commissary of Marine at Amsterdam, the Chevalier de Lironcourt, saw Rhynst's communication, which Jones sent to him, he suggested that Jones might waive the point and display French colors on his ship, disclaiming, at the same time, any ulterior motive not in consonance with the dignity of the commander, on the part of himself or his government, in this proposition. But Jones was not to be moved from the stand he had taken. The man of the world was becoming the dauntless citizen of the United States at last. He curtly told the Dutch admiral that he had no orders to hoist any other flag than the American, and that it only should fly from the gaff of his ship. He also told him that as soon as a pilot would undertake to carry out his ship he would leave. But his most significant action was to state emphatically to the vice admiral's flag captain, who came aboard the Alliance for an answer to his note of the 16th, that he was tired of the annoyances, insults, and threats which had been directed at him daily, and that they must be stopped in future, as he would receive no more communications from the vice admiral. He also requested the flag captain to say to his superior officer that, although the Dutch flagship mounted sixty-four guns, if she and the Alliance were at sea together the vice admiral's conduct toward him would not have been tolerated for a moment. I have no doubt that Jones meant exactly what he said, and I think the vice admiral was lucky in not being required to test the declaration. From this time until his departure no communications of any sort were received by Jones from his baffled and silenced tormentor.

He had done all that mortal man could do to retain his prizes, to protract his stay in Dutch waters, to commit Holland to the side of the United States, to effect an exchange of prisoners, and to maintain the honor of the American flag. In doing this, on all sides he had been harassed and insulted beyond measure. It was therefore some consolation to him to receive on the 21st the following note of explanation and apology from De la Vauguyon:

"December 21, 1779.

"I perceive with pain, my dear commodore, that you do not view your situation in the right light; and I can assure you that the ministers of the king have no intention to cause you the least disagreeable feeling, as the honourable testimonials of the esteem of his majesty, which I send you, ought to convince you. I hope you will not doubt the sincere desire with which you have inspired me to procure you every satisfaction you may merit. It can not fail to incite you to give new proofs of your zeal for the common cause of France and America. I flatter myself to renew, before long, the occasion and to procure you the means to increase still more the glory you have already acquired. I am already occupied with all the interest I promised you; and if my views are realized, as I have every reason to believe, you will be at all events perfectly content; but I must pray you not to hinder any project by delivering yourself to the expressions of those strong sensations to which you appear to give way, and for which there is really no foundation. You appear to possess full confidence in the justice and kindness of the king; rely also upon the same sentiments on the part of his ministers."

To this letter Jones sent the following reply; he was a generous man, who bore no malice:

"ALLIANCE, TEXEL, *December 25, 1779.*

"The Duke de Vauguyon.

"MY LORD: I have not a heart of stone, but I am duly sensible of the obligations conferred on me by the very kind and affectionate letter that you have done me the honour to write me the 21st current.

"Were I to form my opinion of the ministry from the treatment that I experienced while at Brest, or from their want of confidence in me afterward, exclusive of what has taken place since I had the misfortune to enter this port, I will appeal to your Excellency as a man of candour and ingenuousness, whether I ought to desire to prolong a connection that has made me so unhappy, and wherein I have given so little satisfaction? M. de Chev. de Lironcourt has lately made me reproaches on account of the expense that he says France has been at *to give me reputation,* in preference to twenty captains of the royal navy, better qualified than myself, and who, each of them, solicited for the command that was lately given to me! This, I confess, is quite new and indeed surprising to me, and had I known it before I left France I certainly should have resigned in favour of the twenty men of superior merit. I do not, however, think that his first assertion is true, for the ministry must be unworthy of their places were they capable of squandering the public money merely to give an individual reputation! and as to the second, I fancy the court will not thank him for having given me this information, whether true or false. I may add here that, with a force so ill-composed, and with powers so limited, I ran ten chances of ruin and dishonour for one of gaining reputation; and had not the plea of humanity in favour of the unfortunate Americans in English dungeons superseded all considerations of self, I faithfully assure you, my lord, that I would not have proceeded under such circumstances from Groix. I do not imbibe hasty prejudices against any individual, but when many and repeated circumstances, conspiring in one point, have inspired me with disesteem toward any person, I must see very convincing proofs of reformation in such person before my heart can beat again with affection in his favour; for the mind is free, and can be bound only by kind treatment.

"You do me great honour, as well as justice, my lord, by observing that no satisfaction can be more precious to me than by giving new proofs of my zeal for the common cause of France and America; and the interest that you take to facilitate the means of my giving such proofs by essential services, claims my best thanks. *I hope I shall not, through any imprudence of mine, render ineffectual any noble design that may be in contemplation for the general good.*[31] Whenever that object is mentioned, my private concerns are out of the question, and where I can not speak exactly what I could wish with respect to my private satisfaction, I promise you in the meantime to observe a prudent silence.

"With a deep sense of your generous sentiments of personal regard toward me, and with the most sincere wishes to merit that regard by my conduct through life."

The following extract from a letter to Robert Morris well indicates how his treatment by the French ambassador rankled:

"By the within despatches for Congress I am persuaded you will observe with pleasure that my connection with a court is at an end, and that my prospect of returning to America approaches. The great seem to wish only to be concerned with tools, who dare not speak or write truth. I am not sorry that my connection with them is at an end. In the course of that connection I ran ten chances of ruin and dishonour for one of reputation; and all the honours or profit that France could bestow should not tempt me again to undertake the same service with an armament, equally ill composed, and with powers equally limited. It affords me the most exalted pleasure to reflect that, when I return to America, I can say that *I have served in Europe at my own expense, and without the fee or reward of a court,*[32] When the prisoners we have taken are safely lodged in France I shall have no further business in Europe, as the liberty of our fellow citizens who now suffer in English prisons will then be secured; and I shall hope hereafter to be usefully employed under the immediate direction of the Congress."

It is a remarkable thing that, during the perplexities and harassing incidents of his stay in the Texel, with the constant demands made upon him in every direction, the difficulties with which he had to cope, the responsibilities he assumed, the problems he had to solve, and the dangers grappled with, he found time to carry on such a voluminous and extraordinary correspondence as has been preserved. Among other documents he drew up a long memorial to Congress recounting his career and public services to date, which is of much service to those who strive to solve the enigma of his complex life and character. The tendency to lionize a hero was as prevalent then as now, and Jones was compelled by the exigencies of his situation to refuse many invitations of a social nature at Amsterdam and The Hague. "Duty," he says, "must take precedence of pleasure. I must wait a more favourable opportunity to kiss the hands of the fair." Certain young impressionable misses, after the custom of the day, indited poetical effusions to him. In the hurry and rush of business he could only find time in his replies to deplore the fact that so much was expected from him that he could not respond in rhyme to these metrical communications.

CHAPTER XIII.

THE ESCAPE OF THE ALLIANCE.

Christmas day passed gloomily enough, I imagine, for the Americans on the Alliance. There had been opportunities, of course, when it would have been possible for Jones to have made the mouth of the harbor, but his capture would have been inevitable. So, on one pretext or another, he delayed until the night of the 27th of December, when he weighed anchor and dropped down to the mouth of the Texel. Early the next morning in a howling gale he dashed for the sea. On the same day he sent the following note back to Dumas, and merrily proceeded on his way:

"I am here, my dear sir, with a good wind at east, and under my best American colours; so far you have your wish. What may be the event of this critical moment I know not; I am not, however, without good hopes. Through the ignorance or drunkenness of the old pilot the Alliance last night got foul of a Dutch merchant ship, and I believe the Dutchmen cut our cable. We lost the best bower anchor, and the ship was brought up with the sheet anchor so near the shore that this morning I have been obliged to cut the cable in order to get clear of the shore, and that I might not lose this opportunity of escaping from purgatory."

Though he had escaped from the Texel, his situation was one of extreme peril. It is claimed that no less than forty sail were on the lookout for him in the English Channel; and, besides those specifically detailed for the purpose, there were a number of ships and at least two great fleets at anchor in these narrow waters, which he would have to pass. I suppose that never before had so many vessels been on the lookout for a single ship as in this instance. It never seems to have occurred to the blockading ships that Jones would attempt to pass down the Channel; his safest course from the point of view of the ordinary man would have been through the North Sea and around Scotland and Ireland. But Jones was not an ordinary man, though the English refused to see the fact. Consequently, his bold course took them by surprise, and, as usual, by choosing apparently the most dangerous way he escaped. And the way of it was this: By the exercise of his usual seamanship Jones managed to hug the Flemish banks so closely that he passed to windward of the British blockading ships, which were driven to the northward by the same gale of which he had taken advantage.

The wind came strongly from the east, and under a great press of canvas the Alliance staggered away toward the south, keeping as close as possible to the weather shore until all danger from the immediate blockading fleet was avoided. Then Jones ran for the middle of the Channel, and the next day the Alliance passed through the straits of Dover and ran close to the Goodwin Sands, passing in full view of a large English fleet anchored in the Downs only three miles to leeward. On the day after, the 29th, the Alliance flew by the Isle of Wight, running near enough to take a good look at another fleet at Spithead.

On the 1st of January Jones was out of the Channel, having passed in sight of, and almost in range, at different times in this bold dash for freedom, of several British ships of the line, just out of gunshot to leeward. During all this time he had not ceased to fly the American flag. I do not know of a more splendid piece of sea bravado than this dash of the Alliance from the Texel. The daring and gallantry of the man at first seemed to have led him into injudicious and dangerous situations when he took the Alliance so close to the English coast and the British fleets; but his effrontery was governed by that sound and practical sense which ever distinguished his conduct from mere unthinking recklessness, for no one would ever imagine that the escaping ship would take such a course, and those vessels on the lookout for him would probably be found where a less subtle commander would have endeavored to pass—off the Flemish coast and near the French shore, for instance. Be that as it may, the little Alliance, with her Stars and Stripes flapping defiantly in the great breeze in the face of the overmastering English ships, running the gantlet of her enemies, is a picture we love to think upon.

The ship was in a critical condition. Damages which she had incurred in her voyage from Boston to France were still unrepaired. Her trim had been altered for the worse by Landais' blunders, and the improper stowage of the ballast had dangerously strained her and greatly diminished her speed, which had originally been very high. There was no way these things could have been temporarily repaired in the Texel; in fact, but little could be done until the vessel reached France. Owing to the unsanitary regimen of Landais, disease had broken out at different times, and the ship had become so dirty that nothing short of a thorough disinfection would render her safe for her crew. She was much overcrowded with men, all actually or professedly American, and carried a hundred prisoners as well. There were two sets of officers on board—those originally attached to her and the officers of the Richard. Jealousy and bickerings between the two crews were prevalent. Naturally, they had no love for each other. The officers and men of the Richard could not forget the conduct of those on the Alliance, and they looked upon them with hatred and contempt. Sailorlike, the men of the Alliance reciprocated that feeling. It was the desire of every one, except Jones and a few others, to get to France at once, but the commodore wished to return with more prizes; so he bore away to the south and west, seeking for ships, impressing upon his discontented men that the Alliance was equal to anything under a fifty-gun ship! He was not fortunate on this occasion, however, and finally, to avoid a threatened gale, he ran into the port of Corunna in Spain, on the 16th of January, 1780, where he was kindly received and hospitably entertained. During this cruise, in spite of the responsibilities of his position, he found time to compose the following verses in reply to a similar communication which he had received from the daughter of M. Dumas (it will be remembered that he deplored his inability in the Texel to find time for his present occupation):

"Were I, Paul Jones, dear maid, 'the king of sea,' I find such merit in thy virgin song,
A coral crown with bays I'd give to thee,
 A car which on the waves should smoothly glide along;
The Nereides all about thy side should wait,
And gladly sing in triumph of thy state,
'Vivat! vivat! the happy virgin Muse!
Of liberty the friend, who tyrant power pursues!'

"Or, happier lot! Were fair Columbia free
From British tyranny, and youth still mine,
I'd tell a tender tale to one like thee
 With artless looks and breast as pure as thine.
If she approved my flame, distrust apart,
Like faithful turtles, we'd have but one heart;
Together, then, we'd tune the silver lyre,
As love or sacred freedom should our lays inspire.

"But since, alas! the rage of war prevails,
 And cruel Britons desolate our land,
For freedom still I spread my willing sails,
 My unsheath'd sword my injured country shall command.
Go on, bright maid! the Muses all attend
Genius like thine, and wish to be its friend.
Trust me, although conveyed through this poor shift,
My New Year's thoughts are grateful for thy gift."

I have read worse poetry than this, also better, but it is very creditable to the sailor. If the reader has a low opinion of it, let him essay some verse-writing himself.[33]

While at Corunna, the ship was careened and her bottom scraped as far as possible without docking her, and, having procured an anchor to take the place of the two lost in the Texel, Jones prepared to set forth once more. The 28th of January was fixed for his departure, but the discontent among the crew reached such a pitch that they positively refused to weigh anchor unless they received at least a portion of their pay or prize money. Nothing had been paid them from the time the ships had been put in commission until they reached the Texel. There Jones had received from Amsterdam a small sum of money, from which he advanced five ducats to each of the officers and one to each of the men. The amount, compared to their dues and needs, was so insignificant that many of the men threw the money into the sea in disgust—a very foolish but extremely sailorlike action.

There were many patriotic men on these ships who merit the approbation and deserve the gratitude of their country. They had shown, especially those belonging to the Richard, a most desperate courage in most trying scenes. They had performed services upon which no monetary value could be placed, and had subjected themselves to dangers which no mere pecuniary consideration could have tempted them to face. It may at first, therefore, seem surprising that they should have so resolutely demanded their pay and prize money, even to the extent of mutinying for it; but it is a common experience that men who will freely offer themselves for the most dangerous undertakings, and who really are actuated by the strongest kind of patriotism, will quarrel and rebel, and even fight, for the petty amounts promised them by way of wages, which in themselves neither could tempt them to, nor repay them for, the sacrifices they had cheerfully undergone. Frankly, I have the greatest sympathy with the point of view of the unpaid soldiers or sailors of the past, and I quite understand their demands and complaints under such circumstances.

Perhaps there is an association of ideas between fighting for the liberties of one's country and demanding one's dues. Both are a revolt against injustice and oppression. The mind of the common sailor, especially of that day, was not calculated to draw nice distinctions, and he could see little difference between fighting for liberty and demanding that the country whose independence he periled his life to establish should show the small appreciation of his devotion involved in paying his scanty wages and not withholding his lawful prize money. Jones struggled for rank, station, reputation, opportunity; these men could aspire to no higher station than they already filled, and their corresponding effort was for the money justly due them.

The Richard's men had lost practically everything except the clothes they stood in when their ship went down, and their personal needs were necessarily very great. The original crew of the Alliance were under the impression that Jones had reserved from the small sum he had received at Amsterdam a considerable portion for himself. There is not the slightest evidence to warrant this supposition. The commodore was the most prodigal and generous of men, and his whole career evidences his entire willingness to devote his own personal property to the welfare and wages of his men. He finally persuaded the crew to get under way by promising to run direct to L'Orient, where he hoped they would undoubtedly receive their prize money. With this understanding the crew consented to work the ship to that point, and their departure was accordingly taken on the 28th.

When the vessel was fairly at sea, however, Jones summoned the officers to the cabin and proposed that they should cruise two or three weeks in those waters before making their promised port. I am afraid that the commodore allowed the possibility of taking some valuable prizes and perhaps another British frigate to incline him to break his promise to his men. His interview in his cabin with his officers was an interesting one. With all the eloquence of which he was a master—and he was able to speak convincingly and well on congenial subjects—he placed before them the possibilities presented, appealed to their patriotism, their love of fame, and as a last resort pointed out the further monetary advantage of another rich prize—Iago's argument! If they were successful in taking another frigate they would shed still greater luster upon their names, and put money in their pockets. The officers, however, bluntly refused to be persuaded. They emphasized the mutinous and discontented state of the crews, who had only sailed under Jones' positive promise to take them immediately to L'Orient; pointed out that many of the men had not proper clothing with which to endure the severe winter weather, and that they themselves were in a destitute condition.

Their natural reluctance to fall in with his plans infuriated Jones. Rising from the chair upon which he had been sitting, with an emphatic stamp of his foot he dismissed them with a sneering contempt in the following words:

"I do not want your advice, neither did I send for you to comply with your wishes, but only by way of paying you a compliment, which was more than you deserve by your opposition. Therefore, you know my mind; go to your duty, each one of you, and let me hear no more grumbling!"

The Alliance cruised for some days to the westward of Cape Finisterre, but, as the quarreling between the two crews ran higher than ever, and as Jones had failed to keep his promise, thus adding to their discontent, when they fell in with the American ship Livingstone, laden with a valuable cargo of tobacco, Jones gave over his attempt, and decided to convoy her to L'Orient, where he arrived on the 10th of February, 1780. That he should gravely have contemplated action with a British frigate with his ill-conditioned ship and mutinous crew shows the confidence he felt in his own ability. I have no doubt that, unprepared as she was, if the Alliance had fallen in with an English ship Jones would have been able to persuade his men to action, and with anything like an equal force the results would have been satisfactory.

CHAPTER XIV.

HONORS AND REWARDS—QUARREL WITH LANDAIS—RELINQUISHES THE ALLIANCE.

The tremendous nervous strain which Jones had undergone, the constant labor and exposure necessitated by the circumstances of his hard cruising and fighting, and the recent exposure in the severe winter weather had broken down his health. His spirit had outpaced his body, and in a very ill and weak condition, with his eyes so inflamed that he was almost blinded, he went on shore in search of rest. Meanwhile preparations were made thoroughly to overhaul the Alliance and load her with a large quantity of valuable and much-needed military supplies which had been purchased for the army of the United States, among them the battery which had been cast for the Bon Homme Richard, which had arrived after her departure.

Hard by the Alliance in the harbor lay the handsome Serapis. With perfectly natural feelings Jones longed to get possession of her again. He wrote immediately to Franklin, detailing the repairs necessary to put the Alliance in shape, which were very extensive and correspondingly expensive, and asked that he might have leave to sheath the Alliance with copper, and that the Serapis might be purchased and turned over to him. He hoped that the repairs to the Alliance might be made by the French Government, perhaps that they would also give him the Serapis. As the condition of the Alliance had been justly attributed by Jones to the negligence and incompetence of Landais, and not to any accident of the cruise under the auspices of France, there did not seem to be any good reason for having the ship repaired at the expense of the French Government. Franklin stated that the whole expense would have to fall upon him, and begged him in touching words to be as economical as possible, as his financial resources, as always, were limited. For the same reason it was impossible to secure the Serapis.

He says:

"I therefore beg you would have mercy on me; put me to as little charge as possible, and take nothing that you can possibly do without. As to sheathing with copper, it is totally out of the question. I am not authorized to do it if I had money; and I have not money for it if I had orders."

As the demand in America for the military supplies which Franklin had procured was pressing, Jones was ordered to hasten the repairs to the Alliance. In spite of Franklin's strict injunction to economize, Jones proceeded to overhaul, refit, and remodel entirely the frigate in accordance with his ideas and experience. As his ideas were excellent and his experience had been ample, when the repairs had been completed they left nothing to be desired. But the bills were very heavy. Franklin protested, but paid. As a matter of fact, it must be admitted Jones did not stint himself when it came to outfitting a ship—or anything else, for that matter. His experience with the Ranger, the Richard, and the Alliance had naturally disgusted him with inadequately provided ships of war. The beautiful little boat was the superior of any of her size upon the ocean, and subsequently, under the command of Captain John Barry, she did brilliant and noteworthy service. If it had not been for Jones she would have been worthless.

The charge of extravagance, however, is fairly substantiated. Jones was, in fact, as indifferent in the spending of other people's money as he was with his own, and I have no doubt the bills, although he paid them, almost broke the harassed commissioner's heart. Jones, however, was in a very different position from that he had occupied previously. He had demonstrated his capacity in the most unequivocal manner. He was not a man to be dealt with slightingly, nor did Franklin, who undoubtedly cherished a genuine admiration and regard for him, which the sailor fully reciprocated by an enthusiastic admiration amounting to veneration, wish to do anything to humiliate him.

While the repairs were progressing the financial status of the crew was in no way amended. There was no money forthcoming to them on the score of wages; the sale of the prizes was delayed, and serious differences arose between the agents of the crews, de Chaumont as representing the king, and Jones himself. Finally, in order to further the settlement of the matter, Jones decided to go to Paris and see what he could do personally to hasten the sale of the prizes, and perhaps secure some funds with which to pay the wages of the crews, in part at least.

Early in April, therefore, he left the Alliance at L'Orient and repaired to the capital. From one point of view it was an unwise thing to do, for he left behind him a discontented and mutinous crew, which only his own indomitable personality had been able to repress and control. It is likely, however, that affairs at L'Orient would have remained *in statu quo* had it not been for the advent of Arthur Lee. This gentleman is perhaps the only member of the famous family whose name he bore upon whose conduct and character severe judgment must be passed. Jealous, quarrelsome, and incompetent, his blundering attempts at diplomacy had worked more harm than good to the American nation. By his vanity and indiscretion he had continually thwarted the wise plans and brilliant policy of Franklin, with whom he had finally embroiled himself to such an extent that it became necessary for him to return home. Not only had he lost the esteem of Franklin, but through his petty meanness he had also forfeited the confidence of Congress, which had superseded him by John Jay at the court of Spain, to which he had been accredited previously.

Franklin desired Jones to give him a passage home in the Alliance. Jones had a great dislike to his proposed passenger. When his draft upon the commissioners for twenty-four thousand livres had been dishonored, it was largely through the influence of Lee that the money had been refused him. Lee was fully acquainted with the circumstances which caused Jones to apply, and he might have secured payment. At least that was the opinion of Jones. With his usual frankness, Jones had not hesitated to express his opinion to Lee in a very tart letter, which had not improved the situation. In the face of the request of Franklin, Jones had no option but to receive Lee and his suite on the Alliance. He objected, however, most strenuously to allowing the ex-commissioner to take his carriage and other equipage on the frigate, stating with entire accuracy that articles of such bulk would take up much room, which could be better devoted to other and more important freightage. This, no doubt, further incensed Lee against Jones. He was ever inclined to put his personal comfort before the welfare of his country.

Landais had been summoned, as we have seen, to Paris. The commissioners, with the documents prepared in the Texel before them, had discussed his case, and had decided to send him to America for trial. Franklin, who had not yet expressed any public judgment in the premises, though his private opinion was well known, had presented Landais with a sum of money for his voyage to the United States, and the whole correspondence, including the charges, had been transmitted to Congress.

Arthur Lee, with his usual captious spirit, and inspired by his hatred of Jones and the desire to disagree with Franklin at the same time, had dissented from the view and decision of his colleagues. He had maintained that Landais was legally entitled to continue in the command of the Alliance, and that Franklin had not the power to supersede him—a contention not substantiated by the facts, nor, as was afterward shown, supported by Congress itself.

When Jones went to Paris, therefore, Lee, realizing his opportunity, at once began to foment additional disorder in the already demoralized crew. Coincident with Jones' departure, Landais also made his appearance. Had Lee summoned him? Lee did not hesitate to express the opinion to that gentleman himself, his officers, and crew, that Landais was legitimately entitled to the command of the Alliance, and could not be removed therefrom except by specific direction of Congress. Things, therefore, developed with painful rapidity at L'Orient, until Landais addressed a note to Franklin demanding that he be reinstated in the command of the Alliance—a curious procedure for a man who claimed that Franklin was without power to displace him!

Meanwhile Jones was having a brilliant reception in France. While he had incurred the hostility of the French naval officers, who fancied that he had deprived them of commands to which they were better entitled, and in the enjoyment of which he had gained distinction through opportunities which might possibly have fallen to them and which they might have embraced, he was everywhere received with the highest honors, as well by the court as the people. To the populace, indeed, he was a hero who had humbled the enemy whom they hated with the characteristic passion of Frenchmen. Franklin took him to call upon his old tormentor, the dilatory de Sartine, and, owing perhaps to naval prejudice, his first reception was extremely cool; but, as it became evident that he was a popular hero, the tone of the minister was lowered, and his actions were modified, so that he afterward extended him a warm welcome and professed extreme friendship for the commodore. The king and queen accorded him the favor of an audience, and his majesty, falling in with the popular current, was pleased to declare his intention of presenting him with a magnificent gold-mounted sword, to be inscribed with the following flattering motto:

"VINDICATI MARIS LUDOVICUS XVI.
REMUNERATOR STRENUO VINDICI."[34]

He also signified his royal purpose, should the Congress acquiesce therein, of investing Jones with the cross of the Order of Military Merit, a distinction never before accorded to any but a subject of France, and only awarded for heroic conduct or conspicuous and brilliant military or naval services against the enemy. Nothing could have been more grateful to a man of Jones' temperament than the appreciation of the French people, and these evidences of admiration and esteem from the hand of the king. On his previous visit to Paris, after the capture of the Drake, he had been made much of; in this instance his reception greatly surpassed his former welcome. He became the lion of the day, the attraction of the hour. Great men sought his company, and held themselves honored by his friendship; while the fairest of the ladies of the gay court were proud to receive the attentions of the man who had so dramatically conquered the hated English. In all these circumstances he bore himself with becoming modesty. On one occasion he was invited to the queen's box at the opera. When he entered the theater he was loudly cheered, and at the close of the act a laurel wreath was suspended over his head, whereupon he changed his seat. This natural action has been quaintly commented upon by various biographers, and the statement is made that for many years it was held up before the French youth as an exhibition of extraordinary modesty!

One of the most admirable of Jones' traits was a chivalrous devotion to women. To a natural grace of manner he added the bold directness of a sailor, which was not without its charm to the beauties of Versailles, sated with the usual artificial gallantry of the men of the period. Jones spoke French rather well, and had a taste for music and poetry. There were, therefore, many who did not disdain to draw the "sea lion" in their train. On account of the favors he had received he was a person of distinction at the court. Among his voluminous correspondence which has been preserved are numbers of letters to and from different women of rank and station, dating from this period and from his prolonged stay in Paris after the war had terminated. Among others, he corresponded with a lady who, after the romantic fashion of the time, at first endeavored to hide her identity under the name of Delia. Between Jones and Delia there seems to have sprung up a genuine passion, for the letters on both sides breathe a spirit of passionate, heartfelt devotion. It has been discovered that Delia was but another name for Madame de Telison, a natural daughter of Louis XV, with whom Jones frequently corresponded under her own name, and who is referred to in his biographies as Madame T—, and the identification is definite and complete. He was catholic in his affections, however, for he by no means confined his epistolary relations to the gentle and devoted Madame de Telison.

It is interesting to note that in all these letters there is not a single indelicate or ill-bred allusion. That is what would be expected to-day, but when we remember that so great an authority as Robert Walpole suggested that everybody at his table should "talk bawdy," as being the only subject every one could understand, the significance of his clean letters is apparent. In his correspondence, except in the case of Aimée Adèle de Telison, he never appears to have passed beyond the bounds of romantic friendship. In later years, however, it is possible to infer from his letters that Madame de Telison bore to him a son, whose history is entirely unknown. Among others who honored him with their friendship were three women of high rank, the Duchess de Chartres, Madame d'Ormoy, and the Countess de Lavendahl, who painted his portrait in miniature.

An English lady, Miss Edes, sojourning in France at this time, thus refers to him in two letters which she wrote for publication in the English journals:

"The famous Paul Jones dines and sups here often; he is a smart man of thirty-six, speaks but little French, appears to be an extraordinary genius, a poet as well as hero; a few days ago he wrote some verses extempore, of which I send you a copy. He is greatly admired here, especially by the ladies, who are wild for love of him; but he adores the Countess of Lavendahl, who has honored him with every mark of politeness and distinction.

"'Insulted freedom bled; I felt her cause,
And drew my sword to vindicate her laws
From principle, and not from vain applause.
I've done my best; self-interest far apart,
And self-reproach a stranger to my heart.
My zeal still prompts, ambitious to pursue
The foe, ye fair! of liberty and you;
Grateful for praise, spontaneous and unbought,
A generous people's love not meanly sought;
To merit this, and bend the knee to beauty,
Shall be my earliest and latest duty.'

"Since my last, Paul Jones drank tea and supped here. If I am in love for him, for love I may die. I have as many rivals as there are ladies, but the most formidable is still Lady Lavendahl, who possesses all his heart. This lady is of high rank and virtue, very sensible, good-natured, and affable. Besides this, she is possessed of youth, beauty, and wit, and every other form of female accomplishment. He is gone, I suppose, for America. They correspond, and his letters are replete with elegance, sentiment, and delicacy. She drew his picture, a striking likeness, and wrote some lines under it which are much admired, and presented it to him. Since he received it he is, like a second Narcissus, in love with his own resemblance; to be sure, he is the most agreeable sea wolf one would wish to meet with."

In all this, however, Jones did not for a moment neglect the business which had called him to Paris. He moved heaven and earth to effect the sale of the prizes, bringing to bear all his personal popularity and making use of his new-found friends, both men and women, to accomplish the desired results. In all his attempts he was zealously supported by Franklin, who, I have no doubt, greatly enjoyed the popularity of his *protégé.*

Finally, on the last day of May, having received positive assurance that the prizes would be sold and distribution made immediately, he set out for L'Orient. On leaving Paris he carried with him a personal commendation from Franklin and a letter from de Sartine to the President of Congress, as follows:

"PASSY, *June 1, 1780.*

"Samuel Huntington, Esq., President of Congress.

"SIR: Commodore Jones, who by his bravery and conduct has done great honour to the American flag, desires to have that also of presenting a line to the hands of your Excellency. I cheerfully comply with his request, in recommending him to the notice of Congress, and to your Excellency's protection, though his actions are more effectual recommendations, and render any from me unnecessary. It gives me, however, an opportunity of shewing my readiness to do justice to merit, and of professing the esteem and respect with which I am, etc. B. FRANKLIN."

From M. de Sartine to Mr. Huntington, President of the Congress of the United States:

"VERSAILLES, *May 30, 1780.*

"Commodore Paul Jones, after having shown to all Europe, and particularly to the enemies of France and the United States, the most unquestionable proofs of his valor and talents, is about returning to America to give an account to Congress of the success of his military operations. I am convinced, Sir, that the reputation he has so justly acquired will precede him, and that the recital of his actions alone will suffice to prove to his fellow citizens that his abilities are equal to his courage. But the king has thought proper to add his suffrage and attention to the public opinion. He has expressly charged me to inform you how perfectly he is satisfied with the services of the Commodore, persuaded that Congress will render him the same justice. He has offered, as a proof of his esteem, to present him with a sword, which can not be placed in better hands, and likewise proposed to

Congress to decorate this brave officer with the cross of Military Merit. His Majesty conceives that this particular distinction, by holding forth the same honours to the two nations, united by the same interests, will be looked upon as one tie more that connects them, and will support that emulation which is so precious to the common cause. If, after having approved the conduct of the Commodore, it should be thought proper to give him the command of any new expedition to Europe, His Majesty will receive him again with pleasure, and presumes that Congress will oppose nothing that may be judged expedient to secure the success of his enterprises. My personal esteem for him induces me to recommend him very particularly to you, Sir, and I dare flatter myself that the welcome he will receive from Congress and you will warrant the sentiments with which he has inspired me."

While all this had been going on, however, Franklin had been having serious trouble with the men of the Alliance. On the 12th of April the officers dispatched a letter to Franklin demanding their prize money and wages. Franklin had previously advanced them twenty-four thousand livres, and he wrote them that everything was being done to hasten the sale of the prizes, and that they would have to be content with what he had given them, and receive the balance when they reached the United States. On the 29th of May Landais wrote, repeating his application of the 17th of March, and inclosing a mutinous letter signed by one hundred and fifteen of the crew of the Alliance, declaring that they would not raise an anchor nor sail from L'Orient till they had six months' wages paid to them, and the utmost farthing of their prize money, including that for the ships sent into Norway, and until their legal captain, Pierre Landais, was restored to them.

Landais had added the phrase "until their legal captain, P. Landais, is restored to us," himself. With this letter was another communication from fourteen of the original officers of the Alliance, to the effect that the crew were in favor of Landais, who was a capable officer, whose conduct had been misrepresented, and whom they considered themselves bound to obey as their legal captain. These officers can not be relieved of a large share of the odium attaching to the conduct of the Alliance during the battle between the Richard and the Serapis. The reason for their dislike of Jones is therefore apparent. To carry out their designs they had circulated among the crew statements to the effect that Jones had received the prize money and was enjoying himself at their expense. The fine Italian hand of Mr. Lee is to be seen in the documents they forwarded to Franklin. Franklin's reply to this disgracefully insubordinate batch of letters was remarkable for its tact, acumen, and good sense. After keenly expressing his surprise that the very officers who had testified against Landais a short time before, and whom Landais had stated were all leagued against him, were now desirous of being placed again under his command, he writes as follows:

"I have related exactly to Congress the manner of his [Landais'] leaving the ship, and though I declined any judgment of his maneuvers in the fight, I have given it as my opinion, after examining the affair, that it was not at all likely either that he should have given orders to fire into the Bon Homme Richard, or that his officers should have obeyed such an order should it have been given them. Thus I have taken what care I could of your honour in that particular. You will, therefore, excuse me if I am a little concerned for it in another. If it should come to be publicly known that you had the strongest aversion to Captain Landais, who has used you basely, and that it is only since the last year's cruise, and the appointment of Commodore Jones to the command, that you request to be again under your old captain, I fear suspicions and reflections may be thrown upon you by the world, as if this change of sentiment may have arisen from your observation during the cruise, that *Captain Jones loved close fighting*,[35] but that Captain Landais was skilful in keeping out of harm's way; and that you, therefore, thought yourself safer with the latter. For myself, I believe you to be brave men and lovers of your country and its glorious cause; and I am persuaded you have only been ill-advised and misled by the artful and malicious representations of some persons I guess at. Take in good part this counsel from an old man who is your friend. Go home peaceably with your ship. Do your duty faithfully and cheerfully. Behave respectfully to your commander, and I am persuaded he will do the same to you. Thus you will not only be happier in your voyage, but recommend yourselves to the future favours of Congress and of your country."

At the same time he specifically directed Landais to refrain from meddling with the men or creating any disturbance on the Alliance at his peril. To this letter Landais paid no attention. This was the situation when Jones reached L'Orient. Franklin wrote him concerning the letters and batch of documents from Landais and the crew, which had arrived after his departure, and advised him what had been done in consequence. The commissioner had procured an imperative order to the authorities at L'Orient for the arrest of Landais, who was to be tried for his life as an emigrant without the king's permission. Franklin also directed Jones to withhold from the signers of the mutinous letter any portion of the money he had advanced on account of the prizes, and he added the firm and decided injunction that if any one was not willing to trust his country to see justice done him he should be put ashore at his own charges to await the sale of the prizes.

The situation was most critical, and that Franklin appreciated it fully is shown by the following citation from one of his letters to Jones:

"... You are likely to have great trouble. I wish you well through it. You have shown your abilities in fighting; you have now an opportunity of showing the other necessary part in the character of a great chief, your abilities in policy."

Before this letter was received, however, matters had risen to a climax, which resulted in the ejection of Jones and the assumption of the command by Landais. Immediately he arrived at L'Orient, Jones hastened to get ready for leaving. The Ariel, a small ship of twenty guns, had been loaned by the French Government to carry such supplies as could not be taken on the Alliance. Several American vessels with valuable cargoes were awaiting his departure also, to sail under his convoy.

Jones had gone on board the Alliance as usual, as his duty demanded, and had been received respectfully and his orders promptly obeyed. On the morning of the 13th of June, being now for the first time informed of the mutinous action of the crew and the letters to Franklin, he mustered the crew and caused his commission and Franklin's first order to him to take command of the ship in the Texel, and his last one, to carry her to Philadelphia, to be read to the men. He then addressed the seamen, pointing out to them the obligations they had assumed, the consequences of a refusal to obey him on their part, and urged them to a faithful performance of their duty. He asked them, if any one had any complaints to make against him, that they be made now. No reply was made to this address, and no complaints were brought forward. The men were then dismissed to their stations.

Shortly after this incident Jones went ashore. Landais was advised of the whole situation immediately, and sent a letter to Degges, the first lieutenant, ordering him to assume the command of the ship and retain it in the face of Jones or any one else until Landais should receive an answer to his demand to Franklin to be replaced in the command of the Alliance. When he received this order, Landais stated that he would at once come on board and take over the ship. Degges mustered the crew again and read this letter. The adroit suggestions of Mr. Lee and the insinuations as to Jones' alleged betrayal of their interests by making off with the prize money had so worked on the feelings of the men that they at once declared for Landais, who, on being notified, promptly repaired to the ship and formally assumed command.

Dale and the officers of the Richard on the Alliance, who had not been aware of these last proceedings, for they had been adroitly timed for their dinner hour when they were below, were apprised of Landais' arrival by the cheering on deck. They protested against his assuming command, and were all sent ashore without ceremony. Mr. Lee seems to have suggested and approved of the action of Landais; indeed, without his sanction the latter would never have dared to take command of the ship.

On the afternoon of the same day Jones dispatched a letter to Franklin by express, relating the circumstances, and then immediately followed in person, which was an unnecessary thing to do. On his arrival at Paris he found that peremptory orders had already been sent post haste to L'Orient to detain forcibly the Alliance, and reiterating the command to arrest Landais. Franklin, appreciating the meddling of Lee, withdrew his request to Jones to receive him as a passenger, and stated that he might return to America in some of the other ships going home under the convoy of the Alliance. Finding nothing more to be done, after staying but two days, Jones returned to L'Orient as quickly as possible. He arrived on the morning of the 20th of June, having been absent six days.

During this time the Alliance had been warped out of the inner roads into the narrow strait called Port Louis, which was inclosed by rocks and commanded by batteries, which she would have to pass before she could reach the outer roads of Groix. The peremptory orders to stop the ship had not arrived, but the commander of the port under his previous orders had caused a barrier to be drawn across the narrow strait of Port Louis, and had ordered the forts to sink the frigate if she attempted to pass out. When Jones arrived, a boat was sent off to the ship by the port officer, carrying the king's order for the arrest of Landais. He positively refused to surrender himself. Franklin's latest orders to Landais and the officers and men were then delivered, and were treated with equal contempt.

All this was another evidence of Landais' folly, for the Alliance was completely in Jones' power. He had but to give the word to have caused the batteries to open fire and sink her. She could neither have escaped nor made adequate reply. Indeed, it is probable, from the character of her captain, officers, and crew, that she would have made little or no fight. But, according to Jones' specific statement, for France, the avowed ally of America, to have opened fire upon an American ship, and to have killed and wounded American sailors, would have been a terrible misfortune, a thing greatly to be deplored, and to be avoided if possible, lest the present friendly relations between the two countries should be impaired by this action. The aid of

France was vital to the American cause at this juncture, and it was patent that every effort should be made to promote harmony rather than sow discord; therefore Jones reluctantly requested the commander to secure his batteries, open the barrier, and allow the Alliance to get through the strait. The French officers accordingly, in the absence of other orders, stopped the preparations they had made to detain the frigate, and expressed their admiration for the magnanimity of Jones in allowing the Alliance to go free. As soon as he received permission, Landais warped the Alliance through the passage between the rocks and anchored in Groix roads. Safe out of harm's way, he had reached a position from which he really could defy Jones and France at last, and defy them he did, more boldly than ever.

It is impossible entirely to approve of Jones' conduct in this complicated affair. He might have gone on board the Alliance the day of the outbreak and confronted Landais. His own personality was so strong that it seems probable he could have regained possession of the ship in despite of anything the weak Landais could say or do. However, if the spirit of the men had been so turned against him that in his judgment this would have been impracticable, he certainly had the situation entirely in his own hands when the Alliance lay under the guns of the batteries. It was not necessary for the batteries to open fire. If he had simply kept the pass closed Landais would have been unable to get away, and it is difficult to see how he could have avoided surrendering himself and yielding up his ship eventually. All that would have been necessary for Jones to do would be to have patience; that was a thing, however, of which he had but little throughout his life. If he did not desire to wait, he could have opened fire upon the ship, taking the risk of a rupture, or allowing the blame, if any arose, to fall upon those who had put him in command of the Alliance originally, and had continued him therein. I venture to surmise that the first broadside would have brought down the flag of the Alliance. In this action he would have been entirely within his rights. If Jones really wanted her, he could have easily secured possession of the ship.

Instead of doing any of these things, he let Landais and the Alliance go. For this he is distinctly censurable. It is, perhaps, not difficult to see why he permitted her to escape. I have no doubt he loathed the officers and men upon her. He was probably sick of the sight of her. He could contemplate with no satisfaction whatever a cruise upon her, especially with Arthur Lee as a passenger, and he was a gentleman whom it would have been difficult to dispose of.

There was, it has been surmised, still another and more pertinent reason. The Serapis was still in the harbor. She had just been purchased by the king. Jones' desire for her was as strong as ever—stronger, if anything. Upward of five hundred tons of public stores and munitions of war still remained to be taken to America. The Ariel could not begin to carry it all. His dream was to beg or borrow the Serapis, which, in conjunction with the Ariel, should transport the stores to the United States, and then be refitted for warlike cruising under his command. If he retained the Alliance this hope would vanish. When the Alliance was warped out of the harbor he promptly wrote to Franklin suggesting this plan. Meanwhile, he kept up a hot fire of orders and letters upon Landais, who, being now out of his power, treated his communications with silent contempt. When Jones directed that his personal baggage be sent off from the Alliance, Landais sent it to him in disgraceful condition, trunks broken open, papers scattered, and much of his private property missing.

On the 28th he wrote to Landais ordering him not to sail without his permission, and directing him to send eighty of his best seamen riggers to assist in equipping the Ariel. Landais sent him twenty-two people, of whom he wished to be rid, with an insolent note. When Jones wrote to him for the balance of the men he had ordered, Landais would not allow the officer carrying the order to come on board. A few days after this he sailed for America, with many of the men of the Bon Homme Richard, who still adhered to Jones, and who refused to assist him in getting the ship under way, in irons in the hold.

To close a troublesome subject, it may be stated that the Alliance reached Boston in August. The peculiar conduct of Landais on this cruise so alarmed the officers and jeopardized the safety of the ship, that by the advice of the meddlesome Lee—who was in this single instance justified in his suggestions —he was summarily deprived of the command of the ship on the plea of insanity, and kept closely confined till they reached Boston. No one was more incensed against him than his whilom upholder and defender, Lee. Landais was formally tried by court-martial when he arrived in the United States and dismissed the service. He got off lightly. He should have been hanged from the yardarm of his own ship as an example and a warning to mutinous traitors.

CHAPTER XV.

THE CRUISE OF THE ARIEL.

Early in the month of July Jones received the sword which had been bestowed upon him by the king. He commented enthusiastically upon its beauty and its value, saying that it had cost twenty-four hundred dollars—a large sum for that day. The month was passed in preparing the Ariel for departure, and in a vigorous correspondence with Franklin and his friends, feminine and otherwise. On the 2d of August, in a note to the Prime Minister, the Count de Vergennes, Jones informed him that he was nearly ready to sail. The last of July Franklin had sent him his final dispatches with the Count de Vauban, who expected to sail with him, but for unexplained reasons Jones did not take his departure until the 4th of September, when the Ariel was warped out to the open roads of Groix. From the 4th of September to the 7th of October he was detained, partly by contrary winds and partly by a rumor, to which, perhaps, he should not have given credence, that further dispatches were to be sent to him. On the 7th of October, at two o'clock in the afternoon, he weighed anchor and put to sea, convoying three merchant ships. The wind, being from the north-northwest, blew fair for their departure, and the weather was mild and pleasant.

The next morning the wind shifted and came in violent squalls from the southward. The ship was not yet clear of the land. The island of Groix lay about fifteen miles to the northeastward, and, as the weather became very thick and the wind increased until it was blowing a tremendous gale, they soon lost sight of the shore to the leeward. In spite of their efforts, they were unable to make any headway against the storm, and were accordingly carried down toward the Penmarque Rocks, a series of sharp, low reefs, jagged needles of the sea, terminating the southeastern extremity of the peninsula of Brittany, among the most dangerous in the world. The ship was in that position above all others dreaded by the mariner—drifting upon a lee shore in a gale of wind. The Ariel had been put under close-reefed fore and main sails, and her head laid to the northwest in the hope that she might stretch along and clear the reefs; but the wind, increasing to a perfect hurricane, in the language of Mackenzie, "smothered" the ship, at last obliging Jones to furl the courses and prevented him from showing even a storm staysail.

In the report of the officers it is stated that the storm had become so violent that "the lee fore yardarm was frequently under water; the lee gangway was laid entirely under water, and the lee side of the waist was full." The water in the hold flowed into the cockpit, notwithstanding the utmost efforts of the chain pumps. The ship was very heavy laden, and lay deep in the water, dipping her yardarms with every roll. As the tempest rose in violence it became impossible to tell just where they were, as the murky darkness of the storm hid every landmark. It was evident, however, from an inspection of the compass that they were still drifting toward the shore. This fact was confirmed by the rapid shoaling of the water, a fact Jones established by personally taking successive casts with the hand lead. There was no room to veer and get the ship headed the other way. If there had been, the result would probably have been no different. In the face of such a storm she would have continued to drift toward the reef. Their progress to leeward was frightfully rapid. The ship was leaking badly, and one of the chain pumps had become choked and refused to work. Destruction seemed inevitable. In all his varied experiences Jones had seen nothing like the storm. In his report he says that never before did he fully conceive the awful majesty of a shipwreck. In their distress, as a last resort, he determined to anchor.

A hasty consultation was had among the officers on the quarter-deck, and this desperate resort was agreed upon. At eleven o'clock in the morning the best bower anchor was let go with thirty fathoms of cable. The effect was not perceptible. The ship was not brought to, and continued to drift broadside on toward the land in the trough of the sea. She dragged her anchor as if it had been a straw. Two other cables were spliced on and veered out. Still she drove on. The pressure of the gale upon the bare spars was tremendous. The wind roared through the top-hamper with amazing velocity. The masts quivered and buckled under the awful strain to which they were subjected; the standing rigging to windward stood out as taut and rigid as if it had been cut from bars of steel. As the frigate lay in the trough of the sea the mighty waves tossed her about like a cockboat. Broad sheets of foam swept over the deck, washing away everything not tightly secured. To relieve the pressure and get the ship to ride to her anchor, Jones now ordered the weather shrouds of the foremast to be cut, and the wind instantly snapped off the mast above the deck; with all its weight of spars and rigging it fell to leeward and carried away the other bower anchor and a kedge anchor, and smashed up the head badly.

This afforded some relief, for immediately after the anchor took hold and the ship gradually swung head to the wind at last. Her drift toward the rocks was not entirely checked, but while they were hesitating as to what to do next, the mainmast, the heel of which had been jerked out of its step by the violent motion of the ship, so that it had been vibrating to and fro like a smitten reed, parted just where it entered the main deck. The wind hurled the immense mass of timber and cordage aft, where it fell across the decks, carrying with it the mizzenmast, smashing the lee quarter gallery, and generally wrecking the after part of the vessel. The ship was thus stripped of her spars except the bowsprit, and they could do no more. If she did not bring to her anchor and cease her drag toward the rocks, over which the breakers could now be seen crashing with terrible force, and with a roar heard above the mad noises of the tempest, they were lost. They hastily cleared the wreck as they were able, letting it drift to leeward, and waited with still hearts and bated breaths for the next happening. No mere seamanship, no human skill could save them now. They were in God's hands. Since their other anchor had been lost by the fall of the foremast, if their present anchor gave way they were helpless. Fortunately the stripped ship, relieved of the tremendous pressure of the wind upon her top-hamper, at last rode to her anchor, and her drift on the rocks was stopped. For the present they were saved. They could do nothing now but wait and trust to the strength of the iron fluke and the hempen cable. Fortunately, both held.

For two days and three nights the Ariel swung to that single anchor, and passively endured the tremendous buffeting of wind and waves within a short distance of the mighty reefs upon which, if she had struck, every soul on board must have perished. For the greater part of this time the motion of the mastless ship was so violent that the most experienced seaman could not keep his legs upon the deck. On the 12th the gale had sufficiently moderated to permit the crew to erect jury masts under which they could regain the harbor. The cable was hove short, but the anchor could not be weighed, as it was probably caught upon a rock. Indeed, nothing but a rock hold would have saved them; so the cable was cut, and the battered Ariel limped back to L'Orient, which she reached on the 13th of October. The gale was one of the most severe with which that storm-bound coast had ever been visited within the memory of man. The whole shore was strewed with wrecks and the bodies of drowned men. The merchant ships of the convoy were lost, with hundreds of other vessels. That the Ariel, in the most dangerous position which could possibly have been imagined even, escaped without loss of life was due to the Providence of God and the brilliant seamanship of her captain. Long afterward Richard Dale wrote thus of his commander's conduct in these trying circumstances:

"Never saw I such coolness and readiness in such frightful circumstances as Paul Jones showed in the nights and days when we lay off the Penmarques, expecting every moment to be our last; and the danger was greater even than we were in when the Bon Homme Richard fought the Serapis."

Two months were required to put the Ariel in shape for sea once more. All the arms which she was carrying out for the use of the army had been so damaged by water as to be useless. They were left behind and their place supplied by other cargo. During this interval, when not occupied in superintending the repairs to the ship, Jones amused himself with his usual prolific correspondence. He had also a spirited encounter with one Thomas Truxtun, afterward the distinguished naval officer, at that time master of a privateer called the Independence. Truxtun entered the harbor of L'Orient flying a pennant, the use of which was restricted by act of Congress to regularly commissioned vessels of war, except in the case of privateers cruising alone. A sharp correspondence was carried on between Jones and Truxtun, who was a mere boy at the time. Truxtun at first refused to haul down the offending pennant, but was finally induced to do so by Richard Dale and two heavily armed boats' crews from the Ariel. Jones was not to be trifled with, and Truxtun received a good lesson in subordination and obedience to law—always of value to a privateer.[36]

While the Ariel was being refitted, Jones, with his usual longing for a first-class ship of war—a thing he never enjoyed during the whole course of his life—through some influential friends made an attempt to get the French Government to lend him the new and handsome frigate Terpsichore, but his request, as usual, was not complied with. Just before the Ariel sailed, Jones gave a grand entertainment on board of her, to which he invited all his friends, which closed with an exercise at general quarters, followed by a representation of battle, which greatly alarmed his fair visitors.

On the 18th of December he took his departure once more. His last letters to Madame d'Ormoy are very characteristic of Jones in his capacity as a squire of dames, and well indicate his feelings at this time:

"I can not leave France without expressing how much I feel myself honoured and obliged by the generous attention that you have shown to my reputation in your journal. I will ever have the most ardent desire to merit the spontaneous praise of beauty and her pen; and it is impossible to be more grateful than I am for the very polite attentions I received at Paris and Versailles. My particular thanks are due to you, madam, for the personal proofs I have received of your esteem and friendship, and for the happiness you procured me in the society of the charming countess, and other ladies and gentlemen of your circle. But I have a favour to ask of you, madam, which I hope you will grant me. You tell me in your letter that the inkstand I had the honour to present to you, as a small token of my esteem, shall be reserved for the purpose of writing what concerns me; now I wish you to see my idea in a more expanded light, and would have you make use of that inkstand to instruct mankind, and support the dignity and rights of human nature."

In another letter to the same lady he says:

"It is impossible to be more sensible than I am of the obligation conferred on me by your attentions and kind remembrance, joined to that of the belle comtesse, your fair daughters, and the amiable ladies and gentlemen of your society. I have returned without laurels and, what is worse, without having been able to render service to the glorious cause of liberty. I know not why Neptune was in such anger, unless he thought it was an affront in me to repair on his ocean with so insignificant a force. It is certain that till the night of the 8th I did not fully conceive the awful majesty of tempest and shipwreck. I can give you no just idea of the tremendous scene that Nature then presented, which surpassed the reach even of poetic fancy and the pencil. I believe no ship was ever before saved from an equal danger off the point of the Penmarque rocks. I am extremely sorry that the young English lady you mention should have imbibed the national hatred against me. I have had proofs that many of the first and finest ladies of that nation are my friends. Indeed, I can not imagine why any fair lady should be my enemy, since, upon the large scale of universal philanthropy, I feel, acknowledge, and bend before the sovereign power of beauty. The English may hate me, but *I will force them to esteem me too.*"[37]

The voyage was uneventful. Jones chose the southern passage, which was less frequented by ships than the more direct route; the value of his cargo being so great and the force of his vessel so small, he did not wish to run any risk of being captured on this cruise. When they had reached a point about twelve hundred miles east of Florida and nine hundred miles north of Barbadoes, in latitude 26° N., longitude 60° W., they were chased by a sail, which appeared to be a large frigate. Jones, for the reasons mentioned, endeavored by crowding sail on the Ariel to escape—his reputation for courage and intrepidity was sufficiently high to allow him to run away without any imputation being warranted by this action—but the stranger had the heels of the Ariel, and gradually overhauled her. Night came on before she came within range, and Jones hoped to run away from her in the darkness; but his efforts to elude his pursuer were unavailing, and when day dawned she was still close at hand.

The wind fell during the morning, and the two ships maintained their relative positions all day. Toward evening the breeze became stronger again, and the stranger began to draw up on the Ariel. As she came nearer, Jones discovered that she was not so formidable a vessel as he had imagined, and he determined to effect her capture. Making a great show of endeavoring to escape, therefore, he cleared ship for action, sent his men to quarters, and permitted his pursuer to overhaul him. She ranged alongside the lee beam just at nightfall. Both ships were flying the English flag. Jones was ready for action, the other ship was not. The quartermaster of the Ariel, whose duty it was to hoist the flags, had unfortunately allowed one end of the halliards to escape him. Jones had intended, as the stranger ranged alongside, to haul down the English flag and substitute the American colors, then, crossing the enemy's bows, pour in a broadside and capture her by boarding; but this petty neglect, or trifling accident, on the part of the quartermaster made it impossible to haul down the flag at the appointed time, so the opportunity was lost and the project had to be given over. Vessels of war, when maneuvering for position, frequently sail under strange colors, but it is a point of honor, invariably observed, which, so far as my knowledge goes, has not been disregarded in civilized warfare—if that phrase be permissible—to fight under one's own flag.

Having lost his opportunity from this unfortunate mischance, Jones necessarily entered into a conversation with the other ship, while he made preparations for further maneuvering. What is known in sea parlance as "a regular gam" ensued. The conversation lasted for some time, during which he discovered that their pursuer was the Triumph, an American-built ship of twenty guns, Captain John Pindar, an equal match for the Ariel. She was a British privateer, though Jones and his men considered her a man-of-war. Pindar probably told them so to increase his prestige. After learning all that he could about English affairs in America from the garrulous captain of the privateer, who must have been extraordinarily stupid, Jones directed him to lower a boat and come on board with his commission to prove that he was really an Englishman. Pindar refused to do this, and Jones, watch in hand, said he would allow him just five minutes for reflection as to the disastrous consequences of a refusal to comply with this request. During this interval the Englishman endeavored to clear ship for action, his men not having gone to quarters before—a great piece of carelessness and neglect.

At the expiration of the appointed time, Pindar still proving obdurate, Jones backed his ship on the weather quarter of the Triumph, put his helm up, crossed her stern, and poured in a broadside which raked her at short range and naturally did much execution. He then ranged alongside the lee beam of the privateer, and for ten minutes poured in a vigorous fire. The resistance of the enemy, at first spirited, had grown more feeble, until at the end of that time Pindar hauled down his flag and begged for quarter, saying when he surrendered that half his crew were killed or wounded. The Ariel's men left their stations and gave three cheers, but the erstwhile stupid Pindar proved to be a more wily antagonist than they imagined. His ship had gradually moved ahead of the Ariel during the contest, and now, suddenly putting up his helm and throwing out his studding sails, he ran off dead before the wind, with all his killed and wounded. The unsuspecting and astonished Americans on the Ariel endeavored to follow the man who had so cleverly eluded them, but their overloaded ship was no match in sailing for the swift privateer, which soon made good her escape in the night.

Jones was naturally much disgusted at the outcome of this engagement, and in his journal he properly comments upon Pindar's action as follows:

"The English captain may properly be called a knave, because, after he surrendered his ship, begged for and obtained quarter, he basely ran away, contrary to the laws of naval war and the practice of civilized nations."

Jones stated that he never had seen a ship better fought by a crew than the Ariel had been in this instance. However, the usual conspiracy to rise and take the ship was discovered among the English members of the crew later on. It was thwarted by his vigorous measures, and on the 17th of February, 1781, the Ariel dropped anchor in the harbor of Philadelphia, just three years, three months, and sixteen days from the departure of the Ranger at Portsmouth.

CHAPTER XVI.

CAREER IN THE UNITED STATES TO THE CLOSE OF THE WAR.

When Jones arrived at Philadelphia, the Board of Admiralty was engaged in investigating the delay in bringing the stores from France. Franklin, Jones, and Landais were under discussion. For his share in the performance, and for other actions mentioned, Landais had already been punished, as we have seen. Jones, therefore, was at once summoned before the board, but before he reported to them they dismissed the summons and instead requested him to answer in writing an exhaustive series of questions covering his actions from the time of his arrival at L'Orient the year before. Jones immediately set about preparing his replies, meanwhile sending Franklin's note and De Sartine's letter to the President to Congress, which, on the 27th of February, adopted the following resolutions:

"*Resolved*, That the Congress entertain a high sense of the distinguished bravery and military conduct of John Paul Jones, Esq., captain in the navy of the United States, and particularly in his victory over the British frigate Serapis on the coast of England, which was attended with circumstances so brilliant as to excite general applause and admiration.

"That the Minister Plenipotentiary of these United States, at the Court of Versailles, communicate to his Most Christian Majesty, the high satisfaction Congress has received from the conduct and gallant behaviour of Captain John Paul Jones, which have merited the attention and approbation of his Most Christian Majesty, and that his Majesty's offer of adorning Captain Jones with a Cross of Military Merit, is highly acceptable to Congress."

In accordance with the permission conveyed by these flattering resolutions, the French Minister, M. de la Luzerne, gave a splendid entertainment, to which the members of Congress and the principal citizens of Philadelphia were invited. Before this distinguished company, in the name of the king, the commodore, wearing his beautiful sword, was invested with the cross of a Knight of the Order of Military Merit. It is stated that Jones habitually wore this decoration thereafter, and referred to himself, and desired to be addressed, by the title of Chevalier, which was conferred with it.

On the 28th of March, having carefully considered his answers to the questions, the board declared itself as fully satisfied that the delay had not been owing to Jones or Franklin, and stated to Congress in an enthusiastic document that the conduct of Jones merited some distinguished mark of approbation. In accordance with this recommendation, on the 14th of April the following resolution was passed:

"That the thanks of the United States, in Congress assembled, be given to Captain John Paul Jones, for the zeal, prudence, and intrepidity with which he hath supported the honour of the American flag; for his bold and successful enterprises, to redeem from captivity the citizens of these States, who had fallen under the power of the enemy; and, in general, for the good conduct and eminent services by which he has added lustre to his character and to the American arms.

"That the thanks of the United States, in Congress assembled, be also given to the officers and men who have faithfully served under him from time to time, for their steady affection to the cause of their country, and the bravery and perseverance they have manifested therein."

The thanks of Congress, the highest honor an officer can receive, were given to but five other officers during the Revolution—viz., to Washington, for the capture of Boston; to Gates, for taking Burgoyne; to Wayne, for the storming of Stony Point; to Morgan, for the victory at the Cowpens; and to Greene, for his success at Eutaw Springs. Jones, therefore, stood in distinguished company.

On the 19th of May, to all of these honors was added a further evidence of esteem, which was perhaps as valuable as any that he had received. It came in the shape of the following letter from Washington:

"SIR: My partial acquaintance with either our naval or commercial affairs makes it altogether impossible for me to account for the unfortunate delay of those articles of military stores and clothing which have been so long provided in France. Had I any particular reasons to have suspected you of being accessory to that delay, which I assure you has not been the case, my suspicions would have been removed by the very full and satisfactory answers, which you have, to the best of my judgment, made to the questions proposed to you by the Board of Admiralty, and upon which that board have, in their report to Congress, testified the high sense which they entertain of your merit and services.

"Whether our naval affairs have, in general, been well or ill conducted it would be presumptuous for me to determine. Instances of bravery and good conduct in several of our officers have not, however, been wanting. Delicacy forbids me to mention *that particular one* which has attracted the admiration of all the world, and which has influenced a most illustrious monarch to confer a mark of his favour which can only be obtained by a long and honourable service, or by the performance of some brilliant action.

"That you may long enjoy the reputation you have so justly acquired is the sincere wish of, Sir, your most obedient and very humble servant,

"GEORGE WASHINGTON."

An attempt was made in Congress to promote him to the grade of rear admiral—which he certainly deserved—and a resolution to that effect was introduced. Owing, however, to jealousy among certain other officers whom he would have superseded, the effort fell through. This would have settled the long and tiresome contention on the question of relative rank, and naturally would have been most agreeable to Jones. However, the matter was settled in a more indirect but perhaps equally satisfactory way.

On the 23d of June, Robert Morris became Minister of Marine in succession to the Board of Admiralty, which was abolished, and on that same day Congress resolved to take a ballot three days later to designate the commander of the America, a magnificent ship of the line, building at Portsmouth, which was then believed to be nearly ready for launching. On the 26th of June, the ballot being taken, it was found that Paul Jones had been unanimously chosen for the position. Since the act of Congress on the 15th of November, 1776, made a captain of a ship of from twenty to forty guns equal to a lieutenant colonel, while a captain of a ship of forty guns and upward was made equal to a colonel, and as he was the only officer intrusted with so large a command, Jones was thus in effect placed at the head of the navy list. He certainly belonged there. With his usual good sense he notes in his journal his satisfaction, as follows:

"Thus Congress took a delicate method to avoid cabal and to do justice. It was more agreeable to Captain Jones to be so honourably elected captain of the line than to have been, as was proposed by the committee, raised at once to the rank of rear admiral, because Congress had not then the means of giving a command suitable to that rank."

By direction of Robert Morris, at this time he presented his accounts to Congress. He had received no pay and but little prize money since his entry into the service, and, as has been stated, had advanced large sums of money from his private funds for the payment of officers and crew. The Government indebtedness to him amounted to some twenty-seven thousand dollars, but no money was forthcoming, consequently on the 28th of July he was actually compelled to ask for an advance of four hundred pounds to pay current expenses and small debts in Philadelphia, and enable him to proceed to New Hampshire and enter upon his duties. This he appears to have received. He stopped *en route* at New Rochelle, where he was handsomely entertained by Washington and de Rochambeau, both of whom he had great pleasure in meeting. As he received a hint at the army headquarters that his decoration and title might be obnoxious to the sturdy New Englanders, he thereafter discontinued wearing the cross for a space. He reached Portsmouth toward the last of August, and found that the America was still on the ways and would not be ready to put to sea for months. This was a great disappointment to him, but he set to work with his usual zeal to further the work of getting the ship ready for launching.

During his wanderings he had collected a most valuable professional library, and he now found leisure to devote a good part of his time to study, some of the results of which appeared in the improvements which he carried out on the America. As usual, he also resumed his correspondence. In his letters of this period are many excellent suggestions looking to the welfare and future development of the naval service. Many of these suggestions were subsequently adopted in the service. The following letter, dated August 12, 1782, which he received from John Adams, then minister at The Hague, is pleasant reading:

"The command of the America could not have been more judiciously bestowed; and it is with impatience that I wish her at sea, where she will do honour to her name. Nothing gives me so much surprise, or so much regret, as the inattention of my countrymen to their navy; it is a bulwark as essential to us as it is to Great Britain.[38] It is less costly than armies, and more easily removed from one end of the United States to the other.

"Rodney's victory has intoxicated Britain again to such a degree that I think there will be no peace for some time. Indeed, if I could see a prospect of half a dozen line of battle ships under the American flag, commanded by Commodore John Paul Jones, engaged with an equal British force, I apprehend the event would be so glorious for the United States, and ay, so sure a foundation for their prosperity, that it would be a rich compensation for a continuance of the war."

When Jones heard of the movement which resulted in the surrender of Cornwallis at Yorktown, he had expressed a desire to serve as a volunteer in the army for the campaign under Lafayette. He pined for action always. On this subject he received the following affectionate letter from that gallant Frenchman:

"December 22, 1781.

"I have been honoured with your polite favour, my dear Paul Jones, but before it reached me I was already on board the Alliance, and every minute expecting to put to sea. It would have afforded me great satisfaction to pay my respects to the inhabitants of Portsmouth, and the State in which you are for the present. As to the pleasure to take you by the hand, my dear Paul Jones, you know my affectionate sentiments, and my very great regard for you, so that I need not add anything on that subject.

"Accept of my best thanks for the kind expressions in your letter. His Lordship's [Lord Cornwallis] downfall is a great event, and the greater as it was equally and amicably shared by the two allied nations. Your coming to the army I had the honour to command would have been considered as a very flattering compliment to one who loves you and knows your worth. I am impatient to hear that you are ready to sail, and I am of opinion that we ought to unite under you every Continental ship we can muster, with such a body of well-appointed marines [*troupes de mer*] as might cut a good figure ashore, and then give you plenty of provisions and *carte blanche*."

It would appear from the letters that both Adams and Lafayette held a similar opinion of the capacity of the great commodore.

On the occasion of the rejoicings at Portsmouth over the surrender of Cornwallis he ventured to assume his cross of knighthood again, and, finding that no objections were made, he continued to wear it on all occasions, and he also resumed the title of Chevalier. The fall, the winter, and the following summer passed quietly and pleasantly for the little captain, busily engaged in writing, waiting, working, planning, and drawing. On the whole I think this must have been, after Paris, the happiest period of his life. He made many friends, and was much looked up to by the people of Portsmouth and vicinity. There was a spice of excitement about his work as well, which relieved the monotony, for the enemy conceived various projects to destroy the America, which could not be put in operation owing to the vigorous watchfulness of Jones, who armed and drilled and exercised his workmen for guarding the ship. The birth of the French Dauphin was celebrated elaborately in the summer of 1782.

Toward the last of August the ship was about ready for launching, and Jones cherished high hopes of soon getting to sea in her. Unfortunately, however, a squadron of French ships of the line, under the Marquis de Vaudreuil, entered the harbor of Boston at this time, and one of them, named the Magnifique, was stranded on a rock and lost. Congress, by a resolution dated the 3d of September, presented the America to the French king as a recompense for the loss of the Magnifique, and on the 4th of September Morris sadly acquainted Jones with the decision. To be compelled to turn over the great ship, in which he had hoped to do such brilliant service, to the French was a tremendous disappointment to the commodore, but he wrote in so noble and magnanimous a manner to Morris on the subject that the latter at once said to him that the sentiments which he had expressed would always reflect the highest honor upon his character. In fact, Jones' words made so strong an impression upon the mind of Morris that he immediately submitted his letter to Congress.

The America was launched on the 5th of November. The operation of getting her into the water was a difficult one on account of the peculiar lay of the land opposite the ways, but Jones accomplished it with his usual skill and address. When the ship was safely moored he turned her over to the Chevalier de Martigne, the former captain of the Magnifique, and on the next day he started for Philadelphia. The America was reputed to be one of the most beautiful and effective ships afloat.

Morris, who was a great admirer and an old friend of Jones, now desired to place him in command of that vessel which had been the object of his desire for so many years, the frigate Indien, which, by a queer combination of circumstances, had finally been brought to Philadelphia. The King of France, having no use for the ship, had lent her to the Chevalier de Luxembourg, who had entered into a business arrangement with a certain sea captain named Gillon, who was employed by the State of South Carolina to command a small naval force which had been equipped for the protection of her coasts, Gillon assuming the title of commodore.

The Indien, now called the South Carolina, had been a rather fortunate cruiser. Gillon had captured a number of merchantmen, and had joined in another successful expedition to New Providence. He had then proceeded to Philadelphia. As he was indebted to the United States for advances of large sums of money, and as he had made no accounting to the Chevalier de Luxembourg for his share of the prizes, it was thought by Robert Morris and Luzerne, the French Minister, who represented Luxembourg, that if they could get control of this frigate, by placing it under Jones' command with other ships, they could create a formidable force to cruise against the enemy.

But Gillon contrived to evade the legal process by which the claimants sought to insure the payment of their dues, and, in spite of the efforts made to detain him, he succeeded in carrying the Indien to sea, where she was promptly captured just as she cleared the capes of the Delaware by the Diomede, the Astrea, and the Quebec, three English frigates stationed particularly to intercept her.

Disappointed again in his hope of getting a command by these untoward circumstances, Jones requested permission to embark as a volunteer in the squadron of De Vaudreuil, which was destined to take part in a proposed grand expedition to France and Spain against Jamaica. Morris forwarded Jones' request to Congress with a strong recommendation, and that body at once passed the following resolutions:

"*Resolved*, That the agent of marine be informed that Congress, having a high sense of the merit and services of Captain J. P. Jones, and being disposed to favor the zeal manifested by him to acquire improvement in the line of his profession, do grant the permission which he requests, and that the said agent be instructed to recommend him accordingly to the countenance of his Excellency, the Marquis de Vaudreuil."

Admiral de Vaudreuil was graciously pleased to receive the chevalier on his flagship, the Triomphante, where he treated him with the highest consideration, even sharing his cabin with him. The expedition came to nothing, and though Jones probably enjoyed ample opportunity for observing the handling of the fleet, he saw no actual service, to his great disappointment; instead of which he became seriously ill with intermittent fever. At Porto Cabello, on the 4th of April, 1783, he received the news of the signing of the treaty of peace, and this stern warrior, who was supposed to live only for fighting, thus expressed himself concerning the subject:

"The most brilliant success, and the most instructive experience in war, could not have given me a pleasure comparable with that which I received when I learned that Great Britain had, after so long a contest, been forced to acknowledge the independence and sovereignty of the United States of America."

Jones shortly thereafter left the French fleet and returned to Philadelphia, where he arrived on the 18th of May, 1783. He was still very ill. He carried with him the two following letters to the French Minister from de Vaudreuil and the Baron de Viomenil, who commanded the land forces on board the fleet.

From the Marquis de Vaudreuil:

"M. Paul Jones, who embarked with me, returns to his beloved country. I was very glad to have him. His well-deserved reputation caused me to accept his company with much pleasure, and I had no doubt that we should meet with some occasions in which his talents might be displayed. But peace, for which I can not but rejoice, interposes an obstacle which renders our separation necessary. Permit me, sir, to pray you to recommend him to his chiefs. The particular acquaintance I have formed with him since he has been on board the Triomphante makes me take a lively interest in his fortunes, and

I shall feel much obliged if you find means of doing him services."

From the Baron de Viomenil:

"M. Paul Jones, who will have the honour of delivering to you, sir, this letter, has for five months deported himself among us with such wisdom and modesty as add infinitely to the reputation gained by his courage and exploits. I have reason to believe that he has preserved as much the feeling of gratitude and attachment toward France as of patriotism and devotion to the cause of America. Such being his titles to attention, I take the liberty of recommending to you his interests, near the President and Congress."

He was in some doubt as to his future career, but for the present the state of his health rendered it necessary for him to abstain from active duty. As a matter of fact, there was practically no American navy in existence at the close of the war, and no duty for him to undertake. The commodore's constitution was much shattered, and the wasting fever still clung to him. He removed, therefore, by the advice of his physician, to the village of Bethlehem, Pennsylvania, where he passed the summer in rest and retirement, and his health gradually improved under the careful treatment he received. He seems to have had in mind the project of settling down and forming an establishment somewhere, and marrying "some fair daughter of liberty," and he wrote to some friends in regard to an estate he desired to purchase near Newark, New Jersey. However, the design fell through, mainly because he was unable to realize upon his resources, as his expense account had not been paid by Congress, and no prize money was yet forthcoming. While awaiting the complete restoration of his health he prepared several plans for organizing a navy for the new country, all of which are distinguished by his usual insight and skill. Many of the plans, including the germ of a proposed naval academy in the shape of a school-ship filled with cadets, were adopted with profit to the naval service and the country in after years. But the new nation was too poor and the central government too weak at that time to accept any of these suggestions. Finally, by an act of Congress, dated November 1, 1783, in accordance with the report of a committee of which Mr. Arthur Lee was a member—singular revolution of time which put him in the position of upholding Jones!—he was appointed a special commissioner to solicit and receive the money due from France for the prizes taken by the Bon Homme Richard and his squadron. He was, of course, to act under the direction of the American Minister, Franklin, and was required to give bond to the amount of two hundred thousand dollars for the faithful performance of his duty. It is an evidence of his high reputation for probity and honor that he found no difficulty in securing signers to his bond.

CHAPTER XVII.

PRIZE AGENT IN FRANCE AND DENMARK—LAST VISIT TO THE UNITED STATES—A BLOT ON THE ESCUTCHEON—FAMOUS PASSAGE OF THE BALTIC.

On the 10th of November Jones sailed from Philadelphia to Havre in the packet Washington. Being detained by contrary winds, however, he put into Plymouth on the 30th of November, his first visit to England, save as an enemy, for many years. He there left the ship and went to London for a conference with Adams, the minister, who informed him that his dispatches for Franklin probably contained instructions for concluding the commercial treaty with England, and advised him to hasten. He therefore repaired immediately to Paris, where he arrived on the 4th of December. He was most kindly received by the Maréchal de Castries, the new Minister of Marine, and by the king and queen. Society, too, welcomed him with open arms. He immediately set about the task which had been allotted to him, with his characteristic energy. For a year and a half he successfully combated the various efforts of the French Government to make deductions from the amount realized from the sale of the prizes on one pretext or another, and on the 23d of October, 1784, de Castries at last approved of the account.

There were further delays, as usual, and the matter dragged until January, 1785, when he wrote to de Castries as follows:

"From the great number of affairs more important that engage your attention, I presume this little matter which concerns me, in a small degree personally, but chiefly as the agent of the brave men who served under my orders in Europe, may have escaped your memory. My long silence is a proof that nothing but necessity could have prevailed on me to take the liberty of reminding your Excellency of your promise."

As usual, his persistence at last received its reward in the shape of an order on the Royal Auditor at L'Orient for the money. He set out for L'Orient in July, and there stirred up a further nest of troubles, which, however, he managed to triumph over by the display of his usual qualities, and at the end of September, 1785, the account, amounting to one hundred and eighty-one thousand livres, etc., was paid to him.[39] He charged no commission for collecting this money, but his expenses for the period of his sojourn in France were placed at the large sum of forty-eight thousand livres; to this was added thirteen thousand livres as his share of the prize money, making a total of sixty-one thousand livres, which he appropriated to himself. After paying certain persons then living in France who were entitled to share in the prize money, he turned over to Thomas Jefferson, who had succeeded Franklin, the sum of one hundred and twelve thousand livres, to be returned to the United States for the use of the officers and men entitled to participate in the distribution.

The charges that he made for his personal expenses were certainly very large, but there is not the slightest reason to infer, as has been insinuated, that he falsified the account—every reason to think the contrary, in fact. I have no doubt that he actually spent all that he claimed to have done—probably more, for he was as apt to spend as he was to fight—but the amount is greatly in excess of what should have been properly expended, or at least charged against the total for legitimate living expenses. As I have stated, however, he was supremely indifferent to money, his own or other people's, and it passed easily through his hands; although, so far as is known, he avoided debts and promptly paid his bills. He had great ideas as to the exalted nature of his position and the dignity of the country he represented, and he did not stint himself in anything. It was an expensive court, and he ruffled it royally with the best. He moved as an equal in an extravagant and gay society, and he allowed no considerations as to economy to restrain him from standing among the freest and highest. We need not censure him too severely in the premises, for the account was afterward investigated by Congress and his expenditures approved.

During his long stay in France the fertile mind of the chevalier was busied with various projects to advance his fortunes, among which was a design which he conceived in conjunction with the famous navigator and explorer Ledyard, who had gone around the world with the more famous Captain Cook. The two men proposed to engage in the fur trade in the then comparatively unexplored and unknown waters of the Pacific Ocean. The affair assumed a considerable state of forwardness, but was finally dropped on account of lack of necessary funds, the expenses proving much greater than either of the projectors had imagined they would be. In view of the vast fortunes which have been made subsequently in pursuance of this very idea, the conception throws an interesting light upon the keen business quality of the commodore's mind.[40] As a light relaxation he had his bust made by the celebrated sculptor Houdon, copies of which he presented, with wide generosity, to a number of his friends. The bust was made at the instance of the French Masonic lodge of Three Sisters, of which he was an honored member.

Early in 1787, upon the advice of Jefferson, he determined to repair to Denmark to see what he could do to further the payment of the claim for indemnity, amounting to forty thousand pounds, caused by the delivery of the prizes of his famous squadron to the English at Bergen. He had reached Brussels on his journey to Copenhagen when he decided to return to America for two reasons: In the first place, Jefferson had no authority to approve the account of the commodore in the matter of prize money recently received from France. He had simply acted as a medium of transmittal of the balance handed him to the United States. The Treasury Board of Audit, to which the account and the accompanying balance had been submitted, strongly disapproved of the large item covering personal expenses, and Jones, when he heard their views, felt it incumbent upon him to return to America immediately to insure the acceptance of his statement and the adjustment of the account. In the second place, another motive for his return was on account of lack of funds. He had expected to receive at Brussels remittances from some investments in bank stock in the United States to enable him to proceed to Copenhagen, but they were not forthcoming. It would appear that he had spent all of his prize money, etc., which indicates his careless extravagance in monetary matters.[41] Accordingly, he abandoned his Danish trip for the time, and returned to the United States in the spring of 1787.

His explanations of his personal expenditures, while they may not have convinced the auditors, were apparently satisfactory to Congress, to which the matter had been referred, for his accounts were soon approved, and Congress did him a singular honor in passing the following resolutions, which certainly could never have been adopted if there had been in the minds of any of the members the least cloud upon his financial reputation:

"*Resolved*, That a medal of gold be struck, and presented to the Chevalier Paul Jones in commemoration of the valor and brilliant service of that officer in the command of a squadron of American and French ships under the flag and commission of the United States, off the coast of Great Britain, in the late war; and that the Honourable Mr. Jefferson, Minister Plenipotentiary of the United States at the court of Versailles, have the same executed with the proper devices."

The fact that eight years had elapsed since the event commemorated shows that this action of Congress was not the result of any sudden enthusiasm, but was deliberate and therefore more valuable. In addition to this unique tribute to his worth and services, the same august body addressed the following personal letter to the king, Louis XVI:

"Great and beloved Friend: We, the United States, in Congress assembled, in consideration of the distinguished mark of approbation with which your Majesty has been pleased to honour the Chevalier John Paul Jones, as well as from a sense of his merit, have unanimously directed a medal of gold to be struck and presented to him, in commemoration of his valour and brilliant services while commanding a squadron of French and American ships, under our flag and commission, off the coast of Great Britain in the late war.

"As it is his earnest desire to acquire knowledge in his profession, we cannot forbear requesting your Majesty to permit him to embark in your fleets of evolution, where only it will be probably in his power to acquire that knowledge, which may hereafter render him most extensively useful.

"Permit us to repeat to your Majesty our sincere assurances that the various and important benefits for which we are indebted to your friendship will never cease to interest us in whatever may concern the happiness of your Majesty, your family, and people. We pray God to keep you, our great and beloved friend, under his holy protection.

"Done at the City of New York, the sixteenth day of October, in the year of our Lord 1787, and of our sovereignty and independence the twelfth."

This was presumably a reply to the official communication of De Sartine which has been cited before. So far as I know, Jones remains to this day the only officer so commended. Before this action of Congress he had written the following letter to Jay, the Secretary of State, which may have suggested the official letter to the French king:

"… My private business here being already finished, I shall in a few days re-embark for Europe, in order to proceed to the court of Denmark. It is my intention to go by the way of Paris, in order to obtain a letter to the French Minister at Copenhagen, from the Count de Montmorin, as the one I obtained is from the Count de Vergennes. It would be highly flattering to me if I could carry a letter with me from Congress to his most Christian Majesty, thanking him for the squadron he did us the honour to support under our flag. And on this occasion, sir, permit me, with becoming diffidence, to recall the attention of my sovereign to the letter of recommendation I brought with me from the court of France dated 30th of May, 1780. It would be pleasing to me if that letter should be found to merit a place on the journals of Congress. Permit me also to entreat that Congress will be pleased to read the letter I received from the Minister of Marine, when his Majesty deigned to bestow on me a golden-hilted sword, emblematical of the happy alliance, an honour which his Majesty never conferred on any other foreign officer... .

"It is certain that I am much flattered by receiving a gold sword from the most illustrious monarch now living; but I had refused to accept his commission on two occasions before that time, when some firmness was necessary to resist the temptation; he was not my sovereign. I served the cause of freedom, and honours from my sovereign would be more pleasing. Since the year 1775, when I displayed the American flag for the first time with my own hands, I have been constantly devoted to the interests of America. Foreigners have, perhaps, given me too much credit, and this may have raised my ideas of my services above their real value; but my zeal can never be overrated.

"I should act inconsistently if I omitted to mention the dreadful situation of our unhappy fellow citizens in slavery at Algiers. Their almost hopeless fate is a deep reflection on our national character in Europe. I beg leave to influence the humanity of Congress in their behalf, and to propose that some expedient may be adopted for their redemption. A fund might be raised for that purpose by a duty of a shilling per month from seamen's wages throughout the continent, and I am persuaded that no difficulty would be made to that requisition."

This is the first mention of a matter which had recently come to his notice, and ever after engaged his attention—the dreadful situation of the Americans held captive in the Barbary States. The first public agitation for the amelioration of their unfortunate condition came from him, and the glorious little struggle by which the United States, a few years after his death, broke the power of these pirates, and alone among the nations of the world made them respect a national flag, had its origin in the love and sympathy of Paul

Jones for the prisoner wherever he might be—a significant fact generally forgotten.

On the 25th of October Congress passed some strong resolutions on the subject of the failure of Denmark to pay the claim referred to above, and instructed Jefferson to dispatch the Chevalier Paul Jones to prosecute the claim at the Danish court, stating, however, that no final settlement or adjustment must be made without the approval of the minister. There was a decided difference between the two commissions with which Congress honored Jones.

In the first instance, in France, he was simply to obtain what had been actually received by the French Government from the sale of certain prizes; the amount in question was not in negotiation save for some allowances or deductions which did not greatly affect the total one way or the other. In other words, he was simply to collect, if he could, a just and admitted debt, and, after deducting expenses, divide it in accordance with a certain recognized principle so far as his own share, or the share of any one in Europe, was concerned, and remit the balance to Congress for action. In the second instance, he was charged with the more delicate and responsible work of pressing a claim for heavy damages based on the estimated value of prizes which the Danish Government had illegally returned to their original owners, the whole transaction on their part constituting an unfriendly and unlawful act, which could easily be magnified into a *casus belli*. In the first case he was to collect a bill for forty thousand dollars; in the second, to secure an admittance of obligation, establish the justice of a claim for five times the first amount, and force a payment. The second commission was the more honorable because the more responsible, and is another proof of the continued and, in fact, increased confidence in him which was felt by Congress.

The propriety, therefore, of associating him with Thomas Jefferson, by requiring the approval of the latter to any final settlements, can not be questioned. It can not be considered in any sense as a reflection upon Jones. It was the usual and common practice under such important circumstances to associate several negotiators to conduct the affair. The action was unfortunate, however, as it was made a pretext by the Danish Government for delaying the settlement. They had already compromised their contention of the legality of their action in giving up the ships by offering to settle with Franklin for ten thousand pounds, which offer had been refused.

One other incident of his stay in his country—the last visit he was destined to pay to it, by the way—brings upon the scene for the last time one of the principal actors in the drama of Jones' life. During his stay in New York, in the month of October, he was conversing with a friend while standing on

Water Street, when Captain Landais, who had made his home in Brooklyn since his dismissal from the navy, approached them. Jones' back was turned, and when Mr. Milligan, his friend, told him of the advent of the Frenchman, he continued his conversation without turning around. Landais approached slowly, wearing a vindictive smile. When a few yards away from the two gentlemen, he halted, spat upon the pavement, remarked, "I spit in his face," and passed on. Mr. Milligan asked Jones if he had heard Landais' remark, and he replied that he had not. Nothing further was said about the incident at that time. Landais, however, circulated reports of the meeting derogatory to Jones' character, and in reply the chevalier published a statement of the occurrence signed by Mr. Milligan, and added that his respect for the public had induced him to establish the falsity of Landais' report by the testimony of the only witness present; he also stated that he should not condescend to take notice of anything further which might be said or done by his antagonist. From this circumstance arose the rumor that he had been publicly insulted—caned, in fact—without resenting it![42]

During this period Jones, as usual, kept up his correspondence, especially with Madame de Telison, with whom his relations had evidently reached that intimate point to which I have referred on page 276. On June 23d she advised him of the death of her friend and protectress at court, the Marquise de Marsan. He wrote immediately, commending her to Jefferson, and at once dispatched the following letter to the lady herself:

"NEW YORK, *September 4, 1787.*

"No language can convey to my fair mourner the tender sorrow I feel on her account! The loss of our worthy friend is indeed a fatal stroke! It is an irreparable misfortune, which can only be alleviated by this one reflection, that it is the will of God, whose providence has, I hope, other blessings in store for us. She was a tried friend, and more than a mother to you! She would have been a mother to me also had she lived. We have lost her! Let us cherish her memory, and send up grateful thanks to the Almighty that we once had such a friend. I can not but flatter myself that you have yourself gone to the king in July, as he had appointed. I am sure your loss will be a new inducement for him to protect you, and render you justice. He will hear you, I am sure; and you may safely unbosom yourself to him and ask his advice, which can not but be flattering to him to give you. Tell him you must look on him as your father and protector. If it were necessary, I think, too, that the Count d'A—, his brother, would, on your personal application, render you good services by speaking in your favour. I should like it better, however, if you can do without him. Mr. Jefferson will show you my letter of this date to him. You will see by it how disgracefully I have been detained here by the Board of Treasury. It is impossible for me to stir from this place till I obtain their settlement on the business I have already performed; and, as the season is already far advanced, I expect to be ordered to embark directly for the place of my destination in the north. Mr. Jefferson will forward me your letters. I am almost without money, and much puzzled to obtain a supply. I have written to Dr. Bancroft to endeavour to assist me. I mention this with infinite regret, and for no other reason than because it is impossible for me to transmit you a supply under my present circumstances. This is my fifth letter to you since I left Paris. The two last were from France, and I sent them by duplicates. But you say nothing of having received any letters from me! Summon, my dear friend, all your resolution! Exert yourself, and plead your own cause. You can not fail of success; your cause would move a heart of flint! Present my best respects to your sister. You did not mention her in your letter, but I persuade myself she will continue her tender care of her sweet godson, and that you will cover him all over with kisses from me; they come warm to *you both* from the heart!"

The Count d'A— referred to was the Count d'Artois, subsequently King Charles X. Madame de Telison was his natural aunt, and that Jones should fear any evil consequence to her from her speaking to him is a hideous commentary on the morals of the times. Mackenzie infers the possibility that the Marchioness de Marsan was really the mother of Madame de Telison, and from the assurance that she would have been a mother to him also, had she lived, he thinks it possible that Jones might have contemplated marrying his correspondent. The godson was possibly Jones' own child. Shortly after this, correspondence with Madame de Telison ceased temporarily. But when Jones finally returned to France their relations were resumed. Before he died he provided for her, and she was with him to the end.

On the 11th of November Jones left America for the last time, taking passage at New York on a vessel bound for Holland. He was landed in England, however, and after another interview with Adams at London, he repaired to Paris on the 11th of December, and presented his dispatches to Jefferson. Jefferson now communicated to him a project which had been under discussion between himself and de Simolin, the Russian ambassador at Versailles, looking to a demand for the services of Jones by the Empress Catherine II of Russia. Some recent disasters to the Russian fleet in the Black Sea in the war which she had been waging against the Turks had caused the minister to consider the possibility of securing the services of the distinguished sea captain. No definite action was taken by either party at that time, although Jones, after some persuasion, expressed his willingness at least to consider the situation. Indeed, the prospects were sufficiently brilliant to have dazzled any man; but nothing came of the matter then. Jones had other business to attend to. At the close of January, 1788, he received his credentials from Jefferson, and on the morning of the 2d of February, the day of his departure for Denmark, he breakfasted with a Mr. Littlepage, chamberlain to the King of Poland, and the Russian Minister, who informed him that he had seriously proposed to his sovereign that Jones be intrusted with the command of the Black Sea fleet. He had, in fact, written to her as follows:

"That if her Imperial Majesty should confide to Jones the chief command of her fleet on the Black Sea, with *carte blanche*, he would answer for it that in less than a year Jones would make Constantinople tremble."

He also informed the commodore that the empress had been much impressed with the proposition, and was disposed to look favorably upon it.

Jones in reply said that he would undertake the command, under certain conditions, if the empress continued in the same mind, and set out with high hopes for Copenhagen. He reached that city on the 4th of March, and was royally received by the king and queen and principal people of the country; but in spite of every effort he found it utterly impossible to procure a satisfactory settlement of the claim. The shuffling Danish Government seized upon the flimsy pretext that he was not a plenipotentiary, since his powers were limited by the clause referred to above, and that since Congress had required that everything be referred to Paris, and final action should be taken at that point, there was no use negotiating with an agent. Completely thwarted in his attempts by this unfortunate clause, and having received a definite summons through Baron Krudner, the Russian ambassador at Copenhagen, to repair to Russia, Jones transferred the negotiations to Jefferson at Paris, which was, in fact, all he could do under the circumstances, and prepared to assume his new command.[43] On the 8th of April, 1788, he wrote to Jefferson as follows:

"SIR: By my letters to the Count de Bernstorf, and his excellency's answer, you see that my business here is at an end. If I have not finally concluded the object of my mission, it is neither your fault nor mine; the powers I received are found insufficient, and you could not act otherwise than was prescribed in your instructions. Thus it frequently happens that good opportunities are lost when the supreme power does not place a sufficient confidence in the distant operations of public officers, whether civil or military. I have, however, the melancholy satisfaction to reflect that I have been received and treated here with a distinction far above the pretensions of my public mission, and I felicitate myself sincerely on being, at my own expense (and even at the peril of my life, for my sufferings from the inclemency of the weather, and my want of proper means to guard against it on the journey, were inexpressible; and I believe, from what I yet feel, will continue to affect my constitution), the instrument to renew the negotiation between this country and the United States; the more so as the honour is now reserved for you to display your great abilities and integrity by the completion and improvement of what Dr. Franklin had wisely begun. I have done, then, what perhaps no other person would have undertaken under the same circumstances; and while I have the consolation to hope that the United States will derive solid advantages from my journey and efforts here, I rest perfectly satisfied that the interests of the brave men I commanded will experience in you parental attention, and that the American flag can lose none of its lustre, but the contrary, while its honour is confided to you. America being a young nation, with an increasing commerce, which will naturally produce a navy, I please myself with the hope that in the treaty you are about to conclude with Denmark you will find it easy and highly advantageous to include certain articles for admitting America into the armed neutrality. I persuade myself beforehand that this would afford pleasure to the Empress of Russia, who is at the head of that noble and humane combination; and as I shall now set out immediately for St. Petersburg, I will mention the idea to her Imperial Majesty and let you know her answer.

"If Congress should think I deserve the promotion that was proposed when I was last in America, and should condescend to confer on me the grade of rear admiral from the day I took the Serapis (23d of September, 1779), I am persuaded it would be very agreeable to the empress, who now deigns to offer me an equal rank in her service, although I never yet had the honour to draw my sword in her cause, nor to do any other act that could directly merit her imperial benevolence. While I express, in the warm effusion of a grateful heart, the deep sense I feel of my eternal obligation to you as the author of the honourable prospect that is now before me, I must rely on your friendship to justify to the United States the important step I now take, conformable to your advice. You know I had no idea of this new fortune when I found that you had put it in train, before my last return to Paris from America. I have not forsaken a country that has had many disinterested and difficult proofs of my steady affection, and I can never renounce the glorious title of *a citizen of the*

United States!

"It is true I have not the express permission of the sovereignty to accept the offer of her Imperial Majesty; yet America is independent, is in perfect peace, has no public employment for my military talents; but why should I excuse a conduct which I should rather hope would meet with general approbation? In the latter part of the year 1782 Congress passed an act for my embarkation in the fleet of his most Christian Majesty; and when, a few months ago, I left America to return to Europe, I was made the bearer of a letter to his most Christian Majesty requesting me to be permitted to embark in the fleets of evolution. Why did Congress pass those acts? To facilitate my improvement in the art of conducting fleets and military operations. I am, then, conforming myself to the views of Congress; but the role allotted me is infinitely more high and difficult than Congress intended. Instead of receiving lessons from able masters in the theory of war, I am called to immediate practice, where I must command in chief, conduct the most difficult operations, be my own preceptor, and instruct others. Congress will allow me some merit in daring to encounter such multiplied difficulties. The mark I mentioned of the approbation of that honourable body would be extremely flattering to me in the career I am now to pursue, and would stimulate all my ambition to acquire the necessary talents to merit that, and even greater favours, at a future day. I pray you, sir, to explain the circumstances of my situation, and be the interpreter of my sentiments to the United States in Congress. I ask for nothing; and beg leave to be understood only as having hinted, what is natural to conceive, that the mark of approbation I mentioned could not fail to be infinitely serviceable to my views and success in the country where I am going.

"The prince royal sent me a messenger, requesting me to come to his apartment. His royal highness said a great many civil things to me—told me the king thanked me for my attention and civil behaviour to the Danish flag while I commanded in the European seas, and that his Majesty wished for occasions to testify to me his personal esteem, etc. I was alone with the prince half an hour. I am, with perfect esteem, etc."

It is a quaint letter, but not conspicuous for modesty on the part of the writer. But it is memorable for its passionate and determined assertion of citizenship, and evidence that his entry into the Russian service, temporarily, was due not to his own motion, but to the suggestion of Thomas Jefferson, who highly approved of his acceptance of the offer of Catherine. Inasmuch as his action has been called in question, such approbation as that of Jefferson is of great value. Congress did not confer upon him the desired rank, as should have been done, and, besides, his statement was not quite correct.

Krudner had offered him the rank of captain commandant, equal to that of major general in the army, and placed at his disposal one thousand ducats for the expenses of his journey. He promptly demurred at the proposed rank of captain commandant, or major general, and refused to accept the sum offered for his traveling expenses. It was forced upon him by the insistence of Krudner, however, and he finally received it. He made no use of it at that time, keeping the money intact, and intending to return it in case he should find it necessary on his arrival in Russia to decline the proffered station. He made but few stipulations with her Majesty's agent before entering upon the journey to St. Petersburg, and these were that in the service of the empress he should never be compelled to bear arms against either the United States or France; that he should be at all times subject to recall by Congress; and, as we have seen in his letter to Jefferson, he was particular to assert that under no circumstances would he renounce "the glorious title of a citizen of the United States." The man of the world and the disinterested lover of human liberty had long since come to a local habitation and name, and henceforth he never failed to assert his citizenship in America.

As he left the court of Denmark and entered upon his journey to Russia he carried in his pocket a patent for a pension issued to him by the Danish Government for the sum of fifteen hundred crowns a year, which was presented to him as an acknowledgment of the "respect he had shown to the Danish flag while he commanded in the North Sea," etc.! Curiously enough, the pension is dated the day it was decided to transfer to Paris the negotiations which he had come to further. The transaction is a most peculiar one. The coincidence of dates is, to say the least, unfortunate. The reasons assigned are inadequate, and the statement of cause is puerile. For a negotiator to accept pecuniary reward from the person against whom he presses a claim is a very remarkable thing to do.

It has been urged in justification of his acceptance: First, that he never received any money from it, for the pension was never paid; that, however, was a fact which, while it was potential, was not then actual, and has no bearing upon his acceptance. Second, it has also been claimed that the pension was given because the Danish Government supposed such an evidence of appreciation of the qualities of her appointee would be acceptable to the empress; but if a nice sense of honor would dictate a refusal of the pension, the bestowal could not be considered a compliment, therefore the acceptance could not enhance his reputation. Third, it has been ingeniously surmised that his acceptance of the pension was for the purpose of committing the Danish Government to the payment of the claim; but if that were true, he should have communicated his acceptance and his reasons to Jefferson at once. The fact that the government absolutely refused to conclude negotiations with him, and that he was of necessity obliged to permit the transfer of the negotiations to Paris, takes away some of the odium which attaches to his action, yet it does not completely clear him. As the Russian prospect had matured he was more and more desirous of quitting Denmark, and the transfer of the claim to Paris quite accorded with his wishes.

This is the most painful incident in his career, and I am extremely sorry that it occurred. I do not suppose that he realized the situation quite as it is presented in these pages, or that he imagined it would have so damaging an effect upon his reputation when it became known. His valuation of his own services was so high that it was not difficult to persuade him—or for him to persuade himself—that he was entitled to a pension, or at least that it was not out of keeping with his merits. Though how he had ever shown any particular respect for the Danish flag when he commanded the Bon Homme Richard is a question.

Two circumstances incline me to believe that he was ashamed of it, however, and that he had no primary intention of making use of it. His vanity might lead him to treasure it as an evidence of appreciation, where his sense of honor would restrain him from enjoying it. Of these two circumstances, the first is that he never mentioned it to anybody for three years, and he was never chary of letting the news of evidences of appreciation be disseminated; the second is that he made no attempt to draw anything on it until he was a sick, worn-out, broken man, some years after, when he looked at life under different circumstances and with different eyes. His letter to Jefferson, when he finally did communicate the news to him three years after, is as follows:

"The day before I left Copenhagen the Prince Royal had desired to speak with me in his apartment. His Royal Highness was extremely polite, and after saying many civil things remarked he hoped I was satisfied with the attention that had been shown to me since my arrival, and that the king would wish to give me some mark of his esteem. 'I have never had the happiness to render any service to his Majesty!' 'That is nothing; a man like you ought to be excepted from ordinary rules. You could not have shown yourself more delicate as regards our flag, and every person here loves you.' I took leave without further explanation. I have felt myself in an embarrassing situation with regard to the king's patent, and I have not yet made use of it, though three years have nearly elapsed since I received it."

It is all that he could say for himself. I am glad he had the grace at last to be ashamed. That is the best defense that I can make for him, and I can only close the reference to this unpleasant incident by saying again that I am very sorry indeed that it occurred.

About the middle of April, 1788, he set forth for Stockholm, where, on account of his desire to reach St. Petersburg without delay, he remained but a few hours, and then pressed on to Grislehamn (Gresholm), Sweden, the nearest port to the Aland Islands, *via* which he hoped to cross the Gulf of Bothnia and reach Russia. The ice, however, was so thick that he found it impossible to cross the gulf or even to reach the islands, so he determined to pass through the open Baltic Sea to the southward. He hired an open boat about thirty feet long, and, taking a smaller boat in tow, to be used in case of emergency, he started upon a journey which proved to be one of the most romantic and adventurous of his whole career. Realizing that in the severe winter weather prevailing it would be impossible to get boatmen to attempt the passage, he carefully concealed his destination from the men whom he had employed to ferry him over.

Having first attempted once more to reach the Aland Islands, and thence proceed to the Gulf of Finland, and being balked as before by heavy masses of drifting ice, he started to the southward between the Swedish shore and the ice floes, which, being driven toward Sweden by a strong east wind, scarcely left him a sufficient channel to pass in safety. By nightfall he was nearly opposite Stockholm, and the water seemed clear enough to seaward for him to attempt to cross. The men, by this time alarmed for their safety, determined, in defiance of his orders, to put into Stockholm; but Jones, seizing the helm himself and drawing his pistols, resolutely commanded them to beat out to sea and obey his orders under pain of instant death. He was not a man to be trifled with by a few Swedish boatmen, and by his directions the terrified men headed the boat offshore. The wind fortunately shifted to the westward, and during the whole of the long night, in the midst of a driving snowstorm, they threaded their way through the floating ice, steering for the Gulf of Finland.

Jones had a pocket compass, and the lantern from his traveling carriage enabled him to choose the course. He naturally took command of the boats himself. The next day, baffled again by the ice in an attempt to land on the north shore of the Gulf of Finland, they continued to the westward and southward under circumstances of extreme danger and hardship. The second night was worse than the first. The wind came in violent squalls, and the cold was intense. The second boat was crushed in the ice floes, and the men in it rescued with great difficulty. Their own boat narrowly escaped being crushed between the huge pieces of ice or swamped in the squalls on several occasions. Only by Jones' seamanship and rare skill did they avoid one or the other danger. The men were so terrified as to be helpless between the storm, the cold, and the thought of the incarnate little demon who sat grimly in the stern sheets, pistol in hand, and neither slept nor took rest apparently, and who handled the boat with as much dexterity as if it had been a toy. One thinks instinctively of the little bark which could not sink because it carried Cæsar and his fortunes.

At any rate, after four days of incredible difficulties the passage was made, and the boat landed at Reval, a Russian port on the southern shore of the Gulf of Finland. They had sailed in one way and another about five hundred miles. Those who had known of his departure from Sweden had no thought but that he and all with him had perished in the attempt. He was, as he stated to Jefferson, in wretched health, and the exposure alone might have killed him. That he went on is highly characteristic of him, and exhibits his entire indifference to personal hardships. The passage presents a fine evidence of his audacity. When he determined to do a thing, he never allowed anything to stop him. Having paid the boatmen for the loss of their boat, and remunerated them handsomely for their labors, he dismissed them to return at their leisure, and proceeded to the Russian court, where he arrived on the fourth day of May. His great reputation, his adventurous passage, his strange and attractive personality, and the fact that he stood high in the good graces and enjoyed the favor of the empress, rendered him an object of universal interest and attraction.

On the 6th of May he was presented to the empress, who immediately conferred upon him the rank he coveted, of rear admiral. Catherine treated him with such distinction that he states in his journal that "I was overcome by her courtesies (*je me laissai seduire*), and put myself into her hands without making any stipulation for my personal advantage. I demanded but one favor, that I should never be condemned unheard." Poor fellow! It was the one right —not favor, but rights went by favor then in Russia—which was not accorded him. He little knew what the future that looked so promising had in store for him, but for the present everything was most delightful. He remained, recuperating and preparing for his command, for two weeks, during which period he was magnificently entertained by the highest nobility of Russia and the distinguished foreigners in attendance at the court. Among his papers the cards of many of them are still preserved. There was one exception to his welcome. The English officers in the service of Catherine, and they were many in number and high in quality, affected to describe him as a pirate and a smuggler, and are said to have threatened to resign in a body rather than serve under his command. While I have no doubt as to their feelings, I think it improbable that the threat was ever seriously meant, or that it reached the ears of the empress, for two reasons: first, it was apparently never contemplated that Jones should command the Cronstadt fleet, in which those Englishmen who were highest in rank and reputation were stationed—he had been designated for the Black Sea fleet, and specifically called into service to war against the Turks; and second, it is extremely unlikely that they should have carried such a threat to the throne, for Catherine was not one whom it was safe to threaten for a moment. Such an action in all probability would have resulted in an apology and retraction, or a call for a resignation. It is most improbable that the English protesters would have relinquished the honorable and lucrative positions to which they had attained in the Russian service, with the great opportunities of advancement and pecuniary reward presented, for such a cause. As a matter of fact, Englishmen did serve with credit under Jones' command in the Black Sea, and we hear of no resignations from his squadron there. The story may have gained currency by the gossipy repetition of indiscreet remarks about the court, and from the fact that thirty of the English-Russian officers signed a memorial addressed to Admiral Grieg, their senior in rank, threatening various things if they were associated with Jones. It is hardly possible, however, that Catherine ever saw or heard the petition. At any rate, nothing came of it. Jones enjoyed the anger of the English—he would not have been human if he had not—but as for the rest, he snapped his fingers at them. He could afford to defy them at that hour. He was then in the "high topgallant of his fortunes." In a letter to Lafayette he writes, apropos of this feeling:

"The empress received me with a distinction the most flattering that perhaps any stranger can boast of. On entering into the Russian service her Majesty conferred on me immediately the grade of rear admiral. I was detained against my will a fortnight, and continually feasted at court, and in the first society. This was a cruel grief to the English, and I own that their vexation, which I believe was general in and about St. Petersburg, gave me no pain."

As I have said, I have no doubt as to the feelings of the English officers.

On the 18th of May the admiral left St. Petersburg for Elizabethgrad, the headquarters of Patiomkine. In addition to the sum recently received from Krudner, he was provided with an other purse of two thousand ducats for the expenses of his journey, and his salary was fixed at eighteen hundred roubles a year.[44] As he started for the Black Sea, Catherine handed him this letter:

"SIR: A courier from Paris has just brought from my envoy in France, M. de Simolin, the inclosed letter to Count Besborodko. As I believe that this letter may help to confirm to you what I have already told you verbally, I have sent it, and beg you to return it, as I have not even had it copied, so anxious am I that you should see it. I hope that it will efface all doubts from your mind, and prove to you that you are to be connected only with those who are most favorably disposed toward you. I have no doubt that, on your side, you will fully justify the opinion which we have formed of you, and apply yourself with zeal to support the reputation you have acquired, for valor and skill, on the element on which you are to serve.

"Adieu! I wish you happiness and health.

"CATHERINE."

The letter to Besborodko referred to by Catherine was a request from Patiomkine that Jones might be induced to come immediately to his headquarters, that his talents might be employed in the approaching campaign. Patiomkine promised to to do all in his power to give him an opportunity for displaying his ability and courage,[45] Jones had protested against being under anybody; Catherine refused to consider his protest, hence the reason for her farewell epistle and her inclosure of Patiomkine's promise to be all that he should be to Jones. He arrived at Elizabethgrad on the 30th of May and was most kindly received. But before entering upon the story of his campaign it will be well to consider the situation of the country in which he found himself, and the characters of those with whom he was to be associated in service.

Note with reference to the Danish pension.

The most recent biographer of Paul Jones, whose book was issued simultaneously with this one, makes no mention of the Danish pension, and states that his reasons for omitting any reference to it were "because it was never accepted, never paid, and never was intended to be paid." I am forced to disagree with this statement. Certainly, it never was paid, though what the Danish government may have intended it is impossible to say. Probably if Jones had continued in favor in Russia the pension would have been paid. Certainly the commodore accepted the pension, and he endeavored to procure its payment, and estimated it as an asset in the schedule of property which accompanied his will. See Appendix V, page 473.

CHAPTER XVIII.

IN THE RUSSIAN SERVICE—OTCHAKOFF AND THE CAMPAIGN IN THE LIMAN.

Far to the north is Russia. Extending through no less than one hundred and seventy-three degrees of longitude, and covering forty parallels of latitude, from the Baltic to the Pacific, and from the Black Sea to the Arctic Ocean, with an area of eight and a half million square miles, lies this great lone land. This gigantic empire, touching on the one hand the ice-bound shores of Nova Zembla, and on the other the caravan trails of Bokhara, stretches from the Gulf of Finland in the west to Kamtchatka on the east. Within its boundaries are comprised bleak deserts and fertile plains. Verdant valleys, unscalable mountains, and vast steppes break the monotony of the landscape, and diversify a surface watered by great rivers from the arctic Yenisei to the Oriental Oxus. Great among the powers is this mysterious Colossus, her head white with the snows of eternal winter and her feet laved in the sunlight of tropic streams. The land of the seafarers—so its name indicates—developing enormously and steadily in power, wealth, and civilization, in the nine hundred years which have elapsed since Rurik the Viking first stepped upon its shores, has not yet reached its zenith. It is to-day the home of more diverse nationalities than any other existent country, and foreshadowings of unlimited predominance are apparent. Its sway extends over more races and peoples than any other power has governed since the days of Augustus Cæsar, and the end is not yet. Well do its rulers arrogate to themselves the imperial title of the ancient head of the Roman Empire. Holy Russia, the home of the Orthodox Church, the country of the White Czar, the land of the once despised Slav, yet contains within its borders, in Lithuania, the focal point of that Aryan race which has filled Europe with its splendor. This Russia, the land of the Tartar, the Mongol, the Samoyede, the Cossack, the Finn, and the Pole; this Russia, the land of Ivan the Terrible, of Peter the Great, was now in the hands of a woman—of Catherine II.

The little maiden, born on the 2d of May, 1729, in the quaint old town of Stettin, and of the insignificant house of Anhalt-Zerbst, christened Sophia, was received into the Greek Church on her marriage with Peter of Holstein, grandson of the Romanoff Peter the Great, under the name of Catherine. She had assumed the reins of government after the murder of her wretched impotent husband, against whom she had conspired in conjunction with the Orloffs. When she had deposed and imprisoned him, unable to strike a blow for himself, he had stipulated that in his confinement he might have the undisputed enjoyment of his mistress, his monkey, and his violin! Even these kingly pleasures were soon of little use to him, for on the 18th of July, 1762, but a few days after the revolution which had hurled him from his throne, Peter lay dead in the palace with some ominous and ineffaceable black marks around his throat, telling of the manner of his death from the giant hands of the terrible Orloffs—and his wife was privy to the murder and consenting to it! That her husband had been a knave and a fool—almost a madman—does not excuse her. Catherine was then immediately proclaimed empress in her own right. As the Neapolitan Caraccioli said, the Russian throne was neither hereditary nor elective, but occupative! Catherine occupied it, and as long as she lived Russia knew no other master. The world marveled at her audacity, and trembled for the consequences of her usurpation, but men soon found that, gigantic as had been her assurance, and tremendous as was her task, she was entirely equal to the undertaking. She had a genius for reigning as great as had been exhibited by Elizabeth Tudor—good Queen Bess! In spite of her bad qualities and evil beginning, Russia never progressed more than while under her sway. She fairly divides honor as a sovereign, in Slavonic history, with Peter the Great. True it is that Catherine had "woven out of the bloody vestments of Peter III the most magnificent imperial mantle that a woman had ever worn."

Some one wrote to Madame Vigée le Brun, who essayed to paint her picture:

"Take the map of the empire of Russia for canvas, the darkness of ignorance for background, the spoils of Poland for drapery, human blood for coloring, the monuments of her reign for the cartoon, and for the shadow six months of her son's reign."

A singular and complex character was that of this famous despot, this "Semiramis of the North." Never more than a half-educated woman—and in that she corresponded with her empire—she learned her politics from Montesquieu, drew her philosophy of life from Voltaire, and shaped her morals after Brantôme! A creature of singular contradictions, she loved liberty, favored the struggle of the United States, and ruled an absolute despot; she wrote charming fairy tales for children and rode horseback astride like a man; she was one of the greatest sticklers for morals—in other people —the world has ever known, and yet was herself one of the most colossal examples of unblushing and shameless professional sensuality that ever sat upon a throne. Other rulers and sovereigns have had their favorites, she alone made favoritism a state institution. "What has ruined the country," she naïvely writes, "is that the people fall into vice and drunkenness, and the comic opera has corrupted the whole nation!" As a corrupter by example she surpassed all the comic operas ever written. The morals of Russia, in her day, were rotten from the head downward. Yet in spite of all this she was a great princess. She was allowed to occupy that throne because she made Russia greater with each successive year; not alone by force of arms either, and the Russian destiny makers loved her. Education, the arts, and sciences, all felt the stimulus of her interest and responded to her efforts. Progress was the word of this imperious woman. She had a faculty for ruling as remarkable as her exploitation of favoritism. Yet she governed her empire with a sublime indifference to public opinion, and squandered its revenues in a shameless prostitution of her own person, which ceased only with her death, in 1794, at the age of sixty-five! The fact that Catherine made an official business out of favoritism, and that she was so utterly oblivious to the moral inconsistency of it—for she was a faithful member of the Holy Orthodox Church—seems to lift it upon a plane of its own, so simple and brazen was it.

Upon the chief of her favorites alone she had bestowed more than fifty million roubles, vast estates carrying with them nearly one hundred thousand serfs, and in addition orders, titles, privileges, and decorations innumerable. The name of this favorite was Gregory Alexandrovitch Patiomkine, commonly called Potemkin. He was the second of the great *Vremienchtchick*, as the favorites were called, the word meaning "men of the moment!" He succeeded the gigantic Orloff, whose term as the favorite was longer than that of any successor, for he had enjoyed a tenure of almost ten years—the usual period being about two. Patiomkine's personal association with the empress was only for that short time, when he was supplanted by another object of royal regard. Unlike all the other favorites, Patiomkine was not relegated to prompt obscurity, and he continued to be the power behind the throne for practically the remainder of his life. He was greater than all the others—too great to be done away with, in fact. If he could not be the favorite, he would, like Warwick the kingmaker, make the favorite, and for fifteen years he continued to do so. During this period he swayed the destinies of the empire as a sort of mayor of the palace.

The analogy is not altogether accurate, for Catherine was no supine Merovingian to commit the administration of the state to others while she passed hours of dalliance in the secret chambers of the palace; she was too strong and too great for that, and she always retained her grasp upon the helm; but it is certain that none of her favorites had ever enjoyed such power and wielded it so openly as this princely pander.

As to Patiomkine himself, the world did not know whether he was a genius or a madman. At times he seems to have passed over that slender line which divides these two antitheses of character, and appears now on one side, now on the other. Personally he was a man of huge bulk and great strength, with the natural instincts of an animal and a veneer, more or less strong on occasion, of refinement. He, too, typified Russia, a giant rising through barbarism into the civilization of the century—and not yet arrived, either— now inclining to the one side or the other. Catherine usually chose her favorites among men of great physical vigor. Patiomkine was a giant in size. His vast frame was capable of sustaining the most tremendous hardships. He was a black-haired, swarthy, hot-tempered man, not pleasant to look upon, for he had lost an eye in a fist fight after a drunken revel with the Orloffs. He squinted with the other, and even had not a figure to redeem him, for he was markedly knock-kneed. He, like his mistress and his country, was a creature of contradictions. In his palace in St. Petersburg we find him trifling with the most delicate creations of the most skilled *chef*, and on his journeys eating rapaciously of anything that came to hand. He sent his adjutants thousands of miles for perfumes which caught his fancy, and galloped madly himself across half Europe without rest or sleep for days in pursuance of duty, and then spent weeks in dalliance with his harem.

With the one hand he wrote poetic letters that quiver and thrill with tenderness and beauty, pathos and passion, and with the other he calmly consigned thousands of people to death. One day we find him raging because his soldiers are not better cared for, and on the next day remarking cynically, when the absence of ambulances was brought to his notice, that so much the better—they would not have to bother with the wounded! Sometimes cowardly, sometimes bold to the point of recklessness; atheist and devotee, debauchee and ascetic, coarse and refined, imperious and cringing, brutal and gentle, king and slave, Christian and pagan—his life remains a mystery.

After he died of a frightful attack of indigestion, brought on by gorging himself with coarse food, Catherine's son, upon succeeding to the throne, treated his body with great indignity; and it was not until seventy years later that his remains were discovered and interred in the Cathedral of Kherson. Prince of Taurida, the conqueror of the Crimea, and under Catherine the originator of that tremendous and irresistible Russian policy which will some day replace the Greek cross upon the temple of Justinian in Constantinople, Patiomkine is one of the most remarkable figures in the history of the world.

In the service of the first of these two personages, and under the specific orders of the last, Paul Jones was to make a campaign. It was foredoomed to failure. Jones was not a good subordinate to any one. His temper, his lack of self-control, his pride, and his vanity rendered any ultimate successful association with a man like Patiomkine impossible. Patiomkine had all Jones' faults and a thousand more. They harmonized like flint and steel. To further complicate matters, Jones was to be associated in his command, with the limits of authority not clearly defined between them—always a prolific source of trouble, and certain to cause failure—with Prince Otto of Nassau-Siegen, of whom we have heard before. He had asked to serve under Jones in the Indien, and when that project fell through he had failed to answer Jones' letters, and had treated him with discourtesy and indifference. In Catherine's army and navy thousands of soldiers of fortune found a congenial atmosphere and a golden opportunity. They were all made welcome, and, with anything like success to warrant them, they generally achieved a handsome reward in her generous service. The most noted among them, and one of the most worthless, is this man, whom Waliszewski calls "the last notable *condottierre* of Europe; a soldier without country, without home, and almost without family, his very name is the first of his conquests." His father was the illegitimate son of a princeling, but the Parliament of Paris, in 1756, gave the young Otto, then eleven years of age, the right, so far as they had the power, to bear the name of his ancestors, to which he had no legitimate claim. They could not, however, do anything for his patrimony. He had been a lieutenant of infantry, a captain of dragoons, and finally a sailor under Bougainville when he made his famous voyage around the world. Later he appears as an unsuccessful explorer in Africa. In fact, he was not successful at anything. Unlike Crichton, he did everything equally ill.

In 1779, as a colonel of French infantry, he made an unsuccessful attempt upon the island of Jersey. The next year, in the Spanish service, he commanded, unsuccessfully as usual, some floating batteries before Gibraltar. Among other exploits—and it was his one triumph—he seduced the Queen of Tahiti, so he said, and the reputation of the unfortunate lady found no defenders in Europe. He married a homely Polish countess with a great fortune, and after meddling (unsuccessfully) with all sorts of things got himself appointed to the command of a flotilla of Russian gunboats operating against the Turks.

But to return to the story; the long distance—seven hundred and fifty miles as the crow flies and probably twice that by road—between St. Petersburg and Elizabethgrad, was covered by Jones in twelve days. He was in a hurry, as always, to get to sea. The object of the Prince Marshal's attack was the fortified town of Otchakoff, commonly spelled in contemporary manuscripts Oczakow. This important place was situated on the Russo-Turkish frontier of that day, on the Black Sea, not far from the present city of Odessa, and occupied a commanding position at the confluence of the great river Dnieper and the smaller river Bug. Southward of the mainland the peninsula of Kinburn, a narrow, indented point of land, projects for perhaps twenty miles to the westward, forming a narrow estuary of the Black Sea about fifty miles long and from five to ten miles wide, into which the two rivers pour their vast floods. This estuary is sometimes called the Dnieper Bay, but more commonly the Liman, and the undertaking hereafter described is referred to as the campaign in the Liman. The bay or inlet is very shallow. Sand banks and shoals leave but a narrow, tortuous channel, which is of no great depth at best. The end of the peninsula of Kinburn terminates in a long and very narrow strip of land, a point which reaches up toward the northward and almost closes the opening of the estuary; the distance between the point and Fort Hassan, the southernmost fortification of Otchakoff, is possibly two miles. This narrow entrance is further diminished by a long shoal which extends south from Fort Hassan toward the point, so that, except for one contracted channel, the passage is practicable for vessels of very light draught only.

Otchakoff lies between the Bug and a smaller river called the Beresan, deep enough near its mouth for navigation by small vessels. It was strongly fortified and garrisoned by ten thousand men. While it remained in the hands of the Turks it menaced the Russian communications and rendered it difficult for them to hold the great peninsula of Taurida, now known as the Crimea, which Patiomkine had conquered previously, and from which he had taken the name of Taurichevsky, or Tauricien, or Taurida, with his dukedom. Patiomkine, therefore, decided to besiege and capture this place.

To prevent this, the Turks had re-enforced it by one hundred and twenty armed vessels, ranging from ships of the line to gunboats, under the command of one of the ablest of their admirals, a distinguished old sailor, who had been recalled from service in Egypt, which had been brilliantly successful, to conduct this operation. So long as they could keep open communication by sea with Otchakoff its power of resistance would be prolonged and its capture a matter of extreme difficulty. The object of Jones' campaign was to hold the Liman till Patiomkine could invest Otchakoff, then to defeat the Turkish naval forces in the bay, and to blockade the town. Incidentally he was required to cover the Russian towns on the Dnieper and prevent any descent upon them by the Turks; a hard task for any man with the force available and likely to be placed under his command.

Having stayed but one day at Elizabethgrad, Jones, accompanied by one of the staff officers of Patiomkine, set out for Kherson, which is located near the point where the Dnieper enters the Liman, and is the principal Russian naval depot in that section of the country. The two officers spent but one day at Kherson, but the time was sufficient to develop the fact, as Jones said, that he had entered "on a delicate and disagreeable service."

Mordwinoff, the Russian Chief of Admiralty, treated him with the utmost coolness and indifference, and, though he had been ordered by Patiomkine to give Jones full information as to the situation, he told him nothing of importance, and even failed to provide him with a rear admiral's flag, to which he was entitled. However, the day after his arrival at Kherson, Jones repaired to the town of Gluboca, off which, in one of the deeps of the river between the Dnieper and the mouth of the Bug called Schiroque Roads, his command was anchored. It comprised a single line of battle ship, the Wolodimer—which, on account of its great draught and the shoal water of the Liman, could only mount twenty-six guns—five frigates, five sloops of war, and four smaller vessels, making a total of fifteen sail.[46] The ships were badly constructed, "drew too much water for the navigation of the Black Sea, were too crank to carry the heavy guns that were mounted on them, and sailed badly." They were makeshift craft constructed by people who since Rurik's advent have exhibited surprisingly little aptitude for the sea. I can imagine Jones' disgust and disappointment as he inspected his squadron with a seaman's quick and comprehensive glance. In addition to this force, there was a large flotilla of light-draught gunboats, each carrying a single heavy gun, and sometimes smaller pieces, manned by from thirty to forty men each, and propelled mainly by oars.

The command of the flotilla had been committed to the Prince of Nassau-Siegen, and, although Jones had been repeatedly assured that he was to have supreme charge of all naval operations in the Liman, he found that Nassau exercised an independent command, and instead of being subordinate to him, had only been requested to co-operate with him. Jones' command will be called the squadron, Nassau's the flotilla, hereafter in these pages, to prevent confusion. The squadron had been hitherto under the command of a cowardly Greek corsair named Alexiano, reputed a Turkish subject, who had attained the rank of captain commandant, or brigadier, equivalent to commodore. He was a man of little capacity, great timidity, and was tricky and unreliable in his disposition.

Jones immediately proceeded on board the Wolodimer and exhibited his orders. He found that Alexiano had assembled all the commanders of the ships, and endeavored to persuade them to rebel against his authority. The attempted cabal came to nothing, however, and on receiving a letter from Patiomkine Alexiano relinquished the command to Jones, and with a very ill grace consented to serve as his subordinate—he had to. On the same day in which he arrived, in order to ascertain the topography of the situation, Jones left the Wolodimer and rode over to Kinburn Point, opposite Otchakoff. After a careful examination of the water which he was to defend and the town he was to blockade, so far as he could make it from the shore, he returned to the Wolodimer, and finding, as he says, "all the officers contented," he hoisted his rear admiral's flag on that ship on the evening of the 6th of June, 1788.[47] The Prince of Nassau-Siegen called upon him promptly, and apparently recognized his superiority in rank, if not his right to command. He had an immediate foretaste of the character of his new associates when the prince informed him that if they gained any advantage over the Turks it would be necessary to exaggerate it to the utmost! Jones replied that he had never adopted that method of heightening his personal merits. He might have added that a true recital of his exploits was sufficiently dazzling to need no embellishment by the wildest imagination.

The celebrated General Suvorof was in command of the strong fortress of Kinburn, which was supposed to command the entrance of the Liman, but it was too far inland to menace Otchakoff, or, indeed, to command anything effectively. It is an evidence of Jones' quick perception and fine military instinct that as soon as he inspected the position he discovered the advantage of placing a battery on Kinburn Point, opposite the shoal to which I have referred: and his first act upon assuming the command was to point out to Suvorof, who was perhaps the greatest of all Russian soldiers, the absolute necessity for a battery there. Realizing the fact, Suvorof immediately mounted a formidable battery on the point, and he magnanimously credited Jones with the idea, in spite of the fact that the previous neglect to fortify the point was a reflection on his military skill. Before the guns were in position the capitan pasha as the Turkish admiral was styled, with twenty-one frigates and sloops of war, and several smaller vessels, entered the Liman and anchored before Otchakoff. He was followed by a flotilla of gunboats about equal in number and individual efficiency to the Russian flotilla. The ships of the line and heavier frigates of the Turks, unable to approach near the town, remained at anchor in the open roads to the westward, and as they took no part in the subsequent actions they may be dismissed from further notice. Even as it was, however, the Turkish force greatly overmatched the Russian.

Jones had fifteen ships, the Turks twenty-one, and ship for ship the advantage was entirely in favor of the Turks. In number the two flotillas of gunboats were about the same, and there was not much choice in their quality. The poor quality of Nassau's leadership could hardly be surpassed by any Turk, however incompetent, but the capitan pasha in critical moments led his own flotilla, and, as Jones practically did the same for the Russian gunboats, Nassau's incompetency did not matter so much as it might.

On the 9th of June, having meanwhile received re-enforcements of soldiers to complete the crews, the squadron, followed by the flotilla, got under way and stood toward the entrance of the Liman. The combined force anchored in two lines, the squadron forming an obtuse angle in the channel with the opening toward Otchakoff, so as to be able to pour a cross fire upon any approaching ships. On the right and left flanks in the shallow water divisions of gunboats were stationed, with another division immediately in the rear of the squadron, and a reserve division at hand to re-enforce any threatened point of the line. The station was just in front of the mouth of the Bug, and commanded the entrance to that river and the Dnieper as well, thus protecting Kherson from any attack by the Turks, and affording Patiomkine's troops a free and unimpeded passage of the Bug when they marched to invest the town. The position was most advantageously chosen by Jones. His force was too weak to attack the Turks with any hope of success at present, and he had been ordered by Patiomkine not to enter upon any operation until the Russian army arrived. Absolutely no fault can be found either with his location or his dispositions.

The Turks made no movement to attack them, and Nassau, who was good at proposing aggressive movements when no dangers threatened, suggested that they abandon their position and move forward nearer the town. Nothing would be gained by this maneuver, and opportunities for a successful attack by the Turks would have been greater than in their present position. Jones realized that the Turks must of necessity attack them sooner or later; that no commander could afford to throw away such advantage in force as the Turks enjoyed, when any hour might bring re-enforcements to the Russians, and the battery which Suvorof had completed would prevent further re-enforcements being received by the Turks. So Jones grimly held to his position in spite of Nassau's remonstrances, which were seconded by those of Alexiano, and waited. To wait is sometimes braver than to advance.

Finally one of the reasons for Nassau's desire to advance transpired. He wished to remove from his position near the Turkish shore, upon which batteries were being erected in the absence of any Russian land force to prevent them, which would subject the right wing of his flotilla to a land fire; and he desired to take a position where he would be protected by the new fort at Kinburn Point and by the ships of the squadron. Suvorof had made Jones responsible for the safety of the fort on Kinburn Point, by the way, while awaiting the advance of the army. Having received no orders from Patiomkine, Jones assembled a council of war on the Wolodimer, at which Nassau was present. Jones' supremacy was fully recognized by Nassau. The council approved of the position in which Jones had placed his squadron, and commended his resolution to maintain that position, and in obedience to urgent pleadings from Jones the officers of the flotilla and squadron agreed to co-operate and work together for the common good in the event of being attacked. They did not have long to wait for the inevitable encounter.

On the afternoon of the 18th of June, the Turkish flotilla in two divisions made a dash at the Russian gunboats on the right flank, and a sharp engagement began. The Russians, greatly outnumbered, began to give ground, and, though the reserve was immediately sent to support the right wing, before the dashing attacks of the Turkish gunboats the retreat was not stayed. A battery of artillery which had been unmasked on the adjacent shore also seriously annoyed the extreme flank of the Russians. On account of the shoal water the ships of the squadron could not enter the engagement. Jones, therefore, with his instinctive desire to get into a fight, left the Wolodimer and embarked in Nassau's galley. That commander had entirely lost his head. He could think of nothing to do of value, but implored Jones to send him a frigate —which was impossible, for all the frigates drew too much water; failing this, he threatened to withdraw his right wing, in which case the Turkish gunboats probably would have taken the squadron in reverse, and might have inflicted serious damage. Jones convinced him that a return attack was not only necessary but inevitable, and, as Nassau made no objection, he assumed the direction of the vessels himself. Summoning the unengaged center and left divisions, he brought them up through the squadron to attack the approaching Turkish galleys on the flank. The diversion they caused so inspirited the broken right and reserve divisions that they made a determined stand and stopped their retreat. The capitan pasha, seeing himself in danger of being taken between two fires and his retreat cut off, withdrew precipitately before the center and the left fairly came into action. Had Jones been in command of the flotilla from the beginning, a most disastrous defeat would have been inflicted upon the Turks. As it was, they retreated in confusion, leaving two gunboats in the hands of the enemy.

As the affair had been conducted entirely between the different flotillas, Nassau claimed all the credit for the brilliant maneuvers of the Russians. Jones contemptuously allowed him to make any claims he pleased in his report to Patiomkine, and gave Nassau credit for at least having taken his advice. It would have been better for Nassau's fame if he had continued to take Jones' advice. Having obtained this slight success, Nassau, who knew how well his urgency would look in the reports, again proposed to Jones that they should advance and attack. The Russian army had not yet invested the place, and the success they had gained was so slight that circumstances had not changed. Jones still refused to be moved from the position he had assumed, which the experience of the 18th of June had justified, and calmly awaited the further pleasure of the enemy. It takes a high quality of moral courage for a stranger, who has a reputation for audacity and intrepidity, absolutely to refuse to do that thing to which a subordinate urges him, and which has the appearance of courage and daring; and I count this refusal, in the interests of sound strategic principles, not an unimportant manifestation of Jones' qualities as an officer.

Meanwhile, the Russian army, having passed the Bug, invested the city on the 28th of June, and the Turkish fleet was forced to attack or withdraw. The capitan pasha elected to do the former. Having re-enforced his crews by some two thousand picked men from the great fleet outside the Liman, he advanced down the bay to attack the Russians. The wind was free, and the Turkish fleet came on in grand style, the capitan pasha leading in the largest ship, with the flotilla of gunboats massed on his left flank, making a brilliant showing. Nassau's desire to advance suddenly vanished, and he clamored for a retreat. Jones paid no attention to him, but weighed anchor, and, as it was impossible for him to advance on account of the wind, he waited for the enemy. Fortunately for the Russians, at one o'clock in the afternoon the Turkish flagship, which had been headed for the Wolodimer, took ground on the shoals near the south shore of the Liman. The advance of the fleet was immediately stopped, and the Turkish vessels came to anchor about the flagship.

A council of war was at once convened on the Wolodimer, and Jones at last persuaded the Russians, although inferior in force, to attack the Turks as soon as the wind permitted. During the night the wind fortunately shifted to the north-northeast, and at daylight on the 29th the squadron stood for the Turkish fleet. The Wolodimer led the advance. By hard work the Turkish admiral had succeeded in floating his flagship, but his ships were huddled together without order. Jones immediately dashed at him, opening fire from his bow guns as he came within range. The squadron was formed in echelon by bringing the van forward on the center, making another obtuse angle, with the opening toward the crowd of Turkish ships—in fact, Jones was attempting with his smaller force to surround them. In the confusion caused by the bold attack, the Turks, who seem to have been taken completely by surprise, again permitted the ships of the admiral and of his second in command to take ground. Jones' prompt approach and the heavy fire poured upon them made it impossible to float the stranded ships. They both of them keeled over on the shoal and could make no defense. Their flags were struck, and they were abandoned by their crews. The other Turkish ships were so discouraged by this mishap that they withdrew toward Otchakoff, their flight being accelerated by the tremendous fire poured upon them by the Wolodimer and the other Russian ships. Just as the Wolodimer reached the stranded ship of the capitan pasha, Alexiano, who found himself sufficiently near to the enemy, ordered the anchor of the Wolodimer to be let go without informing Jones. As the order was given in Russian, Jones knew nothing about it until the motion of the ship was stopped.

There was plenty of fight in the Turkish admiral, who seems to have been a very gallant old fellow, for after the loss of the flagship he hoisted his flag on one of the gunboats and brought up the flotilla, which poured a furious fire from its heavy guns upon the right division of Jones' squadron, to which the lighter guns of the ships could make but little reply. The situation became dangerous for the squadron. One of the Russian frigates, the Little Alexander, was set on fire and blown up by the Turkish shot, and the fortune of the day trembled in the balance.

The light-draught gunboats each carried a large gun, heavier, and therefore of greater range, than any on the ships. The shallow water would not permit the ships to draw near enough to the flotilla to make effective use of their greater number of guns. Hence, under the circumstances, the squadron was always at the mercy of the flotilla unless by some means they could get into close action, in which case the ships would have made short work of the gunboats. Jones' position was therefore one of extreme peril—untenable, in fact, without the help of his own flotilla. The Russian flotilla had followed the squadron in a very leisurely and disorderly manner, so slowly that Jones had twice checked the way of his ships to allow them to come within hailing distance. He now dispatched a request to Nassau to bring up his gunboats on the right flank and drive off the Turkish gunboats, thus enabling him to take possession of the two frigates, which had been abandoned by their crews, and continue the pursuit of the flying Turkish ships.

No attention was paid to this and repeated requests, and Jones finally took his boat and went himself in search of Nassau's galley to entreat him to attack the Turkish flotilla. He found Nassau in the rear of the left flank, far from the scene of action, and bent only upon attacking the two ships which were incapable of defense. Unable to persuade him to act, Jones at last appealed to Nassau's second, Brigadier Corsacoff, who finally moved against the Turks and drove them off with great loss after a hard fight. Jones meanwhile returned to the Wolodimer—both journeys having been made under a furious fire, in the midst of a general action, in which upward of thirty-six ships of considerable size and possibly a hundred gunboats were participating—but before he could get under way Nassau, with some of his flotilla, surrounded the two abandoned ships and set fire to them by means of a peculiar kind of a bomb shell called *brandkugels* (hollow spheres, filled with combustibles and perforated with holes, which were fired from a piece called a *licorne*). The Turkish fleet and flotilla, very much shattered, retreated to a safe position under the walls of Otchakoff, thus ending the fighting for that day. Nassau's action was inexcusable. The two ships he so wantonly destroyed would have been a valuable addition to the Russian navy, and, as they were commanded by the Wolodimer and the rest of the squadron, they could not have been recaptured, and could easily have been removed from the shoals.

The Turkish defeat had been a severe one, but the only trophy which remained in the hands of the Russians was the flag of the capitan pasha. A shot from one of the gunboats having carried it away, it fell into the water, whence it was picked up by some Zaporojian boatmen, who brought it to the Prince of Nassau's boat. Jones happened to be on board of it at the time. The flag certainly belonged to him, but he magnanimously yielded it to Nassau in the hope of pacifying that worthless individual. It was by this time late in the afternoon, but Jones gave orders to get under way toward Otchakoff. Now was the proper time to advance and deliver a return blow upon the broken enemy, but now Nassau desired to remain where he was. Jones was inflexible as usual, and determined to finish the job so auspiciously begun. Accordingly, the anchor of the Wolodimer was lifted and she got under way, followed by the remaining ships of the squadron. Having approached as near to Otchakoff as the shoal water permitted, Jones anchored his vessels across the channel in such a position as to cover the passage to the sea. If the Turkish vessels attempted to escape, they would have to pass under the guns of the squadron, and would find themselves within easy range of the formidable battery at Kinburn Point. Nassau's flotilla at last following, the squadron was massed on the right flank.

Map of the Russian Campaign on the Liman.

The Turkish fleet and flotilla were drawn up in line parallel to the Russians, under cover of the Otchakoff batteries; they still presented a threatening appearance, but the severe handling they had received during the day had taken much of the fight out of them. Having disposed his squadron and flotilla to the best advantage, and being unable to proceed further without coming under the fire of the heavy Otchakoff batteries, there was nothing left for Jones but to hold his position and wait another attack.

In order, however, to familiarize himself with the field of future operations, and see if he had properly placed his force, just before sunset he took soundings in a small boat all along the Turkish line within range of case shot from the Otchakoff batteries, and from the Turkish ships as well. His action was a part of his impudent hardihood. His dashing attack had so discouraged the Turks, and his success of the morning had so disheartened them, that not a single gun was fired upon him. Having completed his investigations to his satisfaction, he returned to the flagship.

That night the Turkish admiral attempted to escape with his remaining ships and rejoin his main fleet on the Black Sea outside of Kinburn Point. In an endeavor to avoid Jones' squadron on the one hand, and the battery on the point on the other, nine of his largest ships ran on a shoal. The attempt to escape was made under the fire of the fort and ships, in which the flotillas and Fort Hassan joined. A few of the ships succeeded in getting to sea; the rest were forced to return to their position of safety under the walls of Otchakoff.

When morning came, the plight of the nine ships aground was plainly visible. Suvorof, who had commanded the Kinburn battery in person that night, immediately signaled Jones to send vessels to take possession of the Turkish ships. Jones decided to send the light frigates of his squadron, but it being represented to him by Brigadier Alexiano that the place where the

Turks had grounded was dangerous and the current running like a mill stream with the ebb tide, upon the advice of his captains he turned over the duty of taking possession of the Turkish ships to the flotilla. Alexiano, having received permission, went with the Prince of Nassau.

The boats of the flotilla soon reached the Turkish ships. When they came within range of them they opened a furious fire, to which the latter made no reply. In their helpless position, heeling every way upon the shoal, it was impossible for them to make any defense. They struck their flags and surrendered their ships. The Russian gunboats paid no attention whatever to this circumstance, but continued to fire upon them, drawing nearer and nearer as they realized the helplessness of the Turks. Resorting to *brandkugels* again, they at last set the ships on fire. The hapless Turks in vain implored mercy, kneeling upon the decks and even making the sign of the cross in the hope of touching the hearts of their ruthless and bloodthirsty antagonists. Seven frigates and corvettes were burned to the water's edge with all their crews. It is estimated that about three thousand Turks perished in this brutal and frightful butchery. Nassau and Alexiano enjoyed the situation from a galley at a safe distance in the rear of the attacking force. By chance two of the vessels were not consumed, and were hauled off later and added to the squadron.

Jones viewed the dreadful slaughter of the Turks with unmitigated horror and surprise. A man of merciful disposition and kindly heart, who never inflicted unnecessary suffering, he was shocked and revolted at the ferocity of his new associates. He protested against their action with all his energy, and laid the foundation thereby of an utter breakdown of the relations between Nassau and himself. Besides being horribly cruel, the whole performance was unnecessary. Like the two ships burned the day before, it was possible to have saved them, and they could have been added to Jones' command and would have doubled his effective force. After the destruction of the Turkish vessels Nassau and Alexiano immediately dispatched a report of the operations to Patiomkine. They claimed that the flotilla had captured two and burned nine ships of the line!

Patiomkine, who was at this time extremely fond of Nassau, forwarded this preposterous statement to the empress, with strong expressions of approbation of Nassau's conduct. He gave him the whole credit of the victory, which was entirely due to Jones, and suppressed the fact of his ruthless and reckless destruction of the surrendered ships, which would have been so valuable a re-enforcement to the government. In this report Patiomkine also spoke favorably of the rear admiral, saying that he had done his duty, but that the particular glory of and credit for the success was due to the princeling who had hung on the outskirts and lagged behind when there was any real fighting to be done.

For some ten days the naval force remained inactive, waiting for Patiomkine to complete his investment of the town. On the night of the 8th of July the marshal sent orders to Nassau to advance with his flotilla and destroy the Turkish flotilla under the walls of Otchakoff. Jones was commanded to give him every assistance possible. The weather prevented the carrying out of the orders for a few days. On the night of the 12th of July, however, at one o'clock in the morning, the advance began. The plan of attack had been arranged by the marshal himself, but circumstances prevented its being followed. But that did not matter; Patiomkine was not a military genius, and Jones knew very much better than he what could or should be done in a naval engagement. As it was impossible to use the ships of the squadron, Jones manned all his boats, and led them to tow the gunboats.

As day broke on the 12th of July, the flotilla, having advanced within gunshot distance of the walls, began firing upon the Turkish boats and on Otchakoff itself. After assisting in placing the Russian gunboats in an advantageous position, Jones, with the boats of the Wolodimer, made for five of the enemy's galleys which lay within easy range of the heavy guns of Fort Hassan. These galleys were subjected to a cross fire from the Russian flotilla on one side and Fort Hassan on the other. They were also covered by the guns of the Turkish flotilla and the citadel of Otchakoff. Their position made the attack a most hazardous one. Jones was far in advance of the gunboats, which, under the supine leadership of Nassau, did not manifest a burning anxiety to get into close action. In spite of a furious fire which was poured upon them, Jones dashed gallantly at the nearest galley. It was taken by boarding after a fierce hand-to-hand fight. Turning the command of the galley over to Lieutenant Fabricien with instructions for him to tow her out of action, Jones then assaulted the next galley, which happened to be that of the capitan pasha. This boat lay nearer the fort and was much better defended, but the Russians, under the inspiring leadership of their admiral, would not be denied, and the galley was presently his prize. The cable of this boat was cut without order, and she immediately drifted toward the shore and took ground near Fort Hassan, where she was subjected to a smashing fire from the Turkish batteries close at hand. Jones was determined to bring out the boat as a prize if possible. He caused the galley to be lightened by throwing everything movable overboard, and meanwhile dispatched Lieutenant Fox to the Wolodimer to fetch a kedge and line, by which he could warp her into the channel.

While waiting for the return of this officer he again manned his boats and endeavored to bring up the Russian flotilla. He was partially successful in this attempt, for they succeeded in compelling the three other galleys of the group with which he had been engaged to strike their flags and in forcing the other gunboats to retreat with severe loss. When Fox returned from the Wolodimer a line was run from the galley to the burned wreck of a Turkish ship, but, before the galley could be moved, Jones, who had re-entered his barge, was intensely surprised and annoyed to see fire break out on the two vessels he had captured. They had been deliberately set on fire by the orders of Alexiano. The other three Turkish galleys were also burned by the use of the deadly *brandkugels*. It was brutal cruelty again. Not one was saved from the five galleys except fifty-two prisoners whom Jones personally brought off in his boats from the two which he had captured by hard hand-to-hand fighting. These galleys appear to have been propelled by oars which were driven by slaves on benches, in the well-known manner of the middle ages. As they were Turkish galleys, the slaves were probably captive Christians. They perished with the Turks left on board. Two more ships belonging to the squadron which had endeavored to escape the week previous, were set on fire and burned under the walls of Fort Hassan. The rest of the flotilla effected nothing, and under the orders of Nassau withdrew to their former position.

This action ended the general naval maneuvers which were undertaken. In this short and brilliant campaign of three weeks Jones had fought four general actions, all of which he personally directed. With fifteen vessels against twenty-one he had so maneuvered that the enemy lost many galleys and no less than thirteen of his ships; a few had escaped, and a few were locked up in the harbor, so that the Turkish naval force in the Liman was not only defeated but practically annihilated by Jones' brilliant and successful leadership and fighting. Eleven ships might have been prizes had it not been for the cruelty and criminal folly of Nassau. Jones had captured by hand-to-hand fighting two of the largest of the enemy's galleys. He had shown himself a strategist in his disposition of the fleet at the mouth of the Bug, and later, when he had placed it to command the mouth of the Liman. He had demonstrated his qualities as a tactician in the two boat attacks, and had shown his usual impetuous courage at all times. Nassau had done nothing that was wise or that was gallant. When Jones was not with him his tendency was always to retreat. The orders which brought the flotilla into action which made the brilliant combination on the first day's fight, by which the Turks were outflanked, were issued by Jones himself.

Nassau, like Landais, was "skilled in keeping out of harm's way," and he did not personally get into action at any time. His services consisted in the useless burning of the nine ships and the five galleys, but he had a ready tongue, and he still enjoyed the full favor and confidence of Patiomkine. As soon as the flotilla had retired from the last conflict, he and Alexiano hastened to the army headquarters to report their conquests and exploits. They lost nothing in the telling. In accordance with Nassau's previous statement to Jones, they were very much exaggerated, and the actions of the rear admiral were accorded scant notice.

Patiomkine received the two cowards graciously, and, as usual, forwarded their reports. Jones was not accustomed to this performance, and in ignorance of their actions took no steps to establish the value of his services beyond making a report of what he had done in the usual way—a report quietly suppressed. Two days after Alexiano returned on board the Wolodimer in the throes of a malignant fever, of which he died on the 19th of July. It had been asserted that every Greek in the squadron would immediately resign upon the death of Alexiano, but nothing of the kind took place. The Greeks, like the English and the Russians, remained contentedly under the command of the rear admiral. On the day he died Catherine granted Alexiano a fine estate in White Russia. At the same time Nassau received a valuable estate with several thousand serfs in White Russia, and the military order of St. George. The empress also directed him to hoist the flag of a vice admiral when Otchakoff surrendered. Jones received the minor order of St. Anne, an order with which he would have been perfectly satisfied if the other officers had been awarded nothing more.

All the officers of the flotilla were promoted one step, and received a year's pay with a gold-mounted sword. They were most of them soldiers. The officers of the squadron, who were all sailors, and who had conducted themselves gallantly and well, obtained no promotion, received no pecuniary reward, and no mark of distinction was conferred upon them. They were naturally indignant at being so slighted, but when Jones promised them that he would demand justice for them at the close of the campaign, they stifled their vexation and continued their service.

It is evident that the failure to ascribe the victory to Jones was due to Patiomkine, and his action in giving the credit to Nassau was deliberate. Jones and Nassau had seriously disagreed. The scorn which ability and courage feel for inefficiency and cowardice had not been concealed by the admiral; he had been outspoken in his censure, and not reserved in his strictures upon Nassau's conduct. He had treated the ideas and suggestions of that foolish commander with the indifference they merited, and had allowed no opportunity to pass of exhibiting his contempt—which was natural, but impolitic.

He seems to have made the effort in the beginning to get along pleasantly with Nassau, and to work with him for the good of the service; but, after the demonstration of Nassau's lack of character and capacity in the first action, and after the repeated failure of the prince to maneuver the flotilla in the most ordinary manner, Jones lost all patience with him. Patiomkine had endeavored to establish harmony and good feeling between the two, not only by letters, but by a personal visit which he paid the rear admiral on the Wolodimer on the 29th of June. He did everything on that occasion to persuade Nassau to make an apology for some remarks he had addressed to Jones previously, and, having done so, effected some kind of a reconciliation, but the differences between them were so wide—Nassau was so worthless and Jones so capable, while both were hot-tempered—that the breach between them was greater than before.

Between the two Patiomkine, while not at first unfriendly to Jones, much preferred Nassau. Hence his action. Not only did Patiomkine enjoin harmony, but Littlepage, the American, whom we have seen before as the chamberlain of the King of Poland, who had accepted the command of one of the ships under Jones, also wrote him to the same effect.

Jones received his letter in the spirit in which it was written, and assured the writer that he had borne more from Nassau than he would have done from any other than a madman, and he promised to continue to try to do so. The effort was a failure. Littlepage himself, unable to endure the animosities engendered between the squadron and the flotilla, threw up his command and returned to Warsaw. His parting counsel to Jones showed that he well understood the situation.

"Farewell, my dear admiral; take care of yourself, and look to whom you trust. Remember that you have rather to play the part of a politician than a warrior—more of a courtier than a soldier."

Jones indorsed upon this note the following remark:

"I was not skilled in playing such a part. I never neglected my duty."

To resume the narrative: After the defeat in the Liman, the grand Turkish fleet sailed away from Otchakoff, which was then strictly blockaded by Jones' squadron, assisted by thirty-five armed boats which had been placed under his command. At the end of July the Turkish fleet, having had an indecisive engagement with the Russians at Sebastopol, returned to Otchakoff. Preparations were made by Jones to receive an attack, but none was delivered.

Three ships attempted to run the blockade: one was sunk, and the others got in with difficulty. Nothing of importance happened during the months of August and September, in which Jones continued an effective blockade, although he undertook some minor operations at the request of the marshal.

Patiomkine carried on the siege in a very desultory manner. In accordance with his contradictory nature he sometimes pressed operations vigorously, and then for weeks did nothing. He seems to have had a harem in his camp, which perhaps accounts for his dawdling. Nassau, with his usual boastfulness, sent word to Patiomkine that if he had permission he would take the boats of the flotilla and knock a breach in the walls of Otchakoff big enough to admit two regiments; whereupon Patiomkine asked him wittily how many breaches he had made in Gibraltar, and removed him from his command. He was sent northward, where he still managed to hold the favor of the empress. This did not greatly improve Jones' situation, however, for the relations between him and Patiomkine had become so strained as to be impossible.

On the 24th of October Patiomkine sent him the following order:

"As it is seen that the capitan pasha comes in his kirlangich from the grand fleet to the smaller vessels, and as before quitting this he may attempt something, I request your excellence, the capitan pasha having actually a greater number of vessels, to hold yourself in readiness to receive him courageously, and drive him back. I require that this be done without loss of time; if not, you will be made answerable for every neglect."

Indorsing this insulting document as follows: "A warrior is always ready, and I had not come there an apprentice," Jones immediately returned a spirited answer, part of which is quoted:

"MONSEIGNEUR: I have the honour to transmit to your highness a plan of the position in which I placed the squadron under my command this morning, in conformity to your orders of yesterday.... I have always conformed myself immediately, without murmuring, and most exactly, to the commands of your highness; and on occasions when you have deigned to leave anything to my own discretion I have been exceedingly flattered, and believe you have had no occasion to repent. At present, in case the capitan pacha does resolve on attempting anything before his departure, I can give assurance beforehand that the brave officers and crews I have the honour to command will do their duty 'courageously,' though they have not yet been rewarded for the important services they have already performed for the empire under my eyes. I answer with my honour to explain myself fairly on this delicate point at the end of the campaign. In the meantime I may merely say that it is upon the sacred promise I have given them of demanding justice from your highness in their behalf that they have consented to stifle their grievances and keep silent."

This provoked a reply from Patiomkine and another tart rejoinder from Jones. The correspondence, in which on one occasion Jones had stated that "every man who thinks is master of his own opinion, and this is mine"—good doctrine for the United States, impossible in Russia—terminated by another order from Patiomkine, which closed as follows:

"Should the enemy attempt to pass Oczakow, prevent him by every means and defend yourself courageously."

Jones' indorsement on this document was as follows:

"It will be hard to believe that Prince Potemkin addressed such words to Paul Jones!"

But the patience of the prince had reached its limit, and on the 28th he summarily relieved Jones of his command, and replaced him by Vice-Admiral Mordwinoff, who had received him so coldly when he arrived at Kherson six months before.

The order relieving him is as follows:

"According to the special desire of her Imperial Majesty, your service is fixed in the northern seas; and as this squadron and the flotilla are placed by me under the orders of the vice admiral and the Chevalier de Mordwinoff, your excellency may in consequence proceed on the voyage directed; principally, as the squadron in the Liman, on account of the season being so far advanced, can not now be united with that of Sevastopol."

The northern sea service was only a pretext, but on the 30th Jones replied with the following brief note:

"I am much flattered that her Majesty yet deigns to interest herself about me; but what I shall ever regret is the loss of your regard. I will not say that it is not difficult to find more skilful sea officers than myself—I know well that it is a very possible thing; but I feel emboldened to say that you will never find a man more susceptible of a faithful attachment or more zealous in the discharge of his duty. I forgive my enemies who are near you for the painful blow aimed at me; but if there is a just God, it will be difficult for Him to do as much."

Patiomkine was intensely angered by this note, and he took serious exception to the implication that he had been influenced against Jones by any one. Jones states in one of his letters that when he took leave of Patiomkine a few days afterward, the prince remarked with much anger:

"Don't believe that anyone leads me. No one leads me!" he shouted, rising and stamping his foot, "not even the Empress!"—which was correct. The jesting interrogation with which Catherine closes one of her letters to Patiomkine by saying, "Have I done well, my master?" contained much truth. However, he moderated his tone somewhat in the face of the sturdy dignity of Jones, and, before the admiral started for St. Petersburg, Patiomkine gave him the following letter to the empress:

"MADAM: In sending to the high throne of your Imperial Majesty Rear-Admiral M. Paul Jones, I take, with submission, the liberty of certifying the eagerness and zeal which he has ever shown for the service of your Imperial Majesty, and to render himself worthy of the high favour of your Imperial Majesty."

Having given the officers he commanded, who seem to have become much attached to him, testimonials as to the high value of their services, Jones embarked in a small open galley on the 1st of December for Kherson. He was three days and three nights on the way, and suffered greatly from the extreme cold. He arrived at Kherson dangerously ill, and was unable to proceed upon his journey until the 17th of December. When he reached Elizabethgrad he received word that Otchakoff had been taken by storm the day he had departed from Kherson; over twenty thousand Turks were put to the sword on that occasion. He arrived at St. Petersburg on the 8th of January, 1789, and was ordered to appear at court on the 11th, when the empress awarded him a private interview, at which he presented the letter of Patiomkine. A few days afterward Catherine sent him word that she would wait the arrival of the prince before deciding what to do with him.

CHAPTER XIX.

SLANDERED IN RUSSIA—A SLAVONIC REWARD FOR FAITHFUL SERVICES.

Patiomkine did not reach St. Petersburg until the middle of February, and while waiting for him Jones busied himself with formulating suggestions for a political and commercial alliance between Russia and the United States, one feature of which involved an attack upon Algiers. In addition to holding a large number of American prisoners in captivity, the Algerines had made common cause with the Turks, and had been present in large numbers before Otchakoff. When Patiomkine did arrive, the project was submitted to him, but it was not thought expedient to attempt it at the time, lest it should result in the irritation of England. During this time the commodore wrote to Jefferson and learned for the first time that all the letters he had written since he entered the Russian service had been intercepted. When he examined the official reports concerning his actions, which had been forwarded from the Liman, he found that he had been grossly misrepresented, and the reports were false even to the most trifling details.

His situation was very different from what it had been when he entered St. Petersburg before. Antagonized secretly by Patiomkine, and openly by Nassau and the English at court, his favor appreciably waned. The old story about the insubordinate carpenter whom he had punished in the West Indies was revived, and in its new version the carpenter became his nephew, and it was stated that he had flogged him to death. This was the precursor of a more deadly scandal. His occasional invitations to court functions became less and less frequent, and the coldness in official circles more and more marked. Finally, in the month of April, when he appeared at the palace to pay his respects to the empress, he was refused admittance, and unceremoniously ordered to leave the precincts.

This deadly insult, this public disgrace, which of course at once became a matter of general knowledge, was due to a most degrading accusation made against his character. To discover the origin of this slander is difficult indeed.

In the first flush of his anger Jones specifically charged that his English enemies, whose animosities were not softened by time, were the authors of the calumny. It is impossible to believe that any English officer could descend to such depths, nor is it necessary to credit the report that his disgrace was due to them. The Russian court was as full of intrigue as that of an Oriental despot. Jones was out of favor. He had succeeded in creating powerful enemies for himself in Nassau and Patiomkine. The latter gentleman had negatived a promising plan in the hope of thereby pleasing England, with whom Russia was now coquetting. If he were the instigator of the cabal against Jones, he might have thought the disgrace of the man they hated would gratify the English people. If he could bring this about without compromising himself he would not hesitate to take the required action. Nassau had very strong reasons for hating Jones, who made no secret of his contempt for that pseudo princeling. At any rate, whatever the source or origin, there is no doubt as to the situation.

Jones was accused of having outraged a young girl of menial station, who was only ten years old! The charge was false from beginning to end. It had absolutely no foundation, but with the peculiar methods in vogue in Russia, it was not easy to establish his innocence. He was not only presumed, but was declared guilty, without investigation. The advocate he employed was ordered to abandon his case, and he found himself in the position of one condemned beyond hope with no opportunity for justification. He was ever jealous on the point of his personal honor, and to see himself thus cruelly stigmatized at the close of a long, honorable, and brilliant career nearly drove him frantic. After exhausting unavailingly every means to force a consideration of his case and an examination of evidence which he succeeded in securing with great difficulty, he fell into despair and seriously contemplated suicide. He was not the man that he had been. Already within a few years of his death, although only forty-one, his constitution was so broken that his strength was seriously undermined.

Providence raised up for him a friend in the person of de Ségur, the French ambassador at Catherine's court. This man should be held in eternal gratitude by all Americans—nay, by all who love honor and fair play—for he did not permit himself to be influenced, as is the wont of courtiers, by the withdrawal of royal favor from the chevalier, whom he had known in happier days and under more favorable circumstances. He had been Jones' friend when he had been in the zenith of his career, and he remained his friend in this nadir of his misfortunes. The part that he played in the transaction can be best understood by his own statement, confirmed by two letters written by Jones. The first letter is addressed to Patiomkine. It had been written before the visit of de Ségur:

"ST. PETERSBURG, *April 13, 1789.*

"MY LORD: Having had the advantage to serve under your orders and in your sight, I remember, with particular satisfaction, the kind promises and testimonies of your friendship with which you have honoured me. As I served all my life for honour, I had no other motive for accepting the flattering invitation of her Imperial Majesty than a laudable ambition to distinguish myself in the service of a sovereign so magnanimous and illustrious; for I never yet have bent the knee to self-interest, nor drawn my sword for hire.... .

"A bad woman has accused me of violating her daughter! If she had told the truth I should have had candour enough to own it, and would trust my honour, which is a thousand times dearer to me than my life, to the mercy of the empress. I declare, with an assurance becoming a military character, that I am innocent. Till that unhappy moment I have enjoyed the public esteem, and the affection of all who knew me. Shall it be said that in Russia a wretched woman, who *eloped* from her *husband* and *family* in the country, *stole away her daughter*, lives here in a house of bad fame, and leads a debauched and adulterous life, has found credit enough on a simple complaint, unsupported by *any proof*, to affect the honour of a general officer of reputation, who has merited and received the decorations of America, of France, and of this empire?

"If I had been favoured with the least intimation of a complaint of that nature having found its way to the sovereign, I know too well what belongs to delicacy to have presented myself in the presence of the empress before my justification.

"My servant was kept prisoner by the officers of police for several hours, two days successively, and threatened with the knout.

"After the examination of my people before the police, I sent for and employed Monsieur Crimpin as my advocate. As the mother had addressed herself to him before to plead her cause, she naturally spoke to him without reserve, and he learned from her a number of important facts, among others, that she was counselled and supported by a distinguished man of the court.

"By the certificate of the father, attested by the pastor of the colony, the daughter is several years older than is expressed in the complaint. And the complaint contains various other points equally false and easy to be refuted. For instance, there is a conversation I am said to have held with the daughter in the Russian language, of which no person ever heard me pronounce two words together; it is unknown to me.

"I thought that in every country a man accused had a right to employ advocates, and to avail himself of his friends for his justification. Judge, my prince, of my astonishment and distress of mind, when I yesterday was informed that the day before the governor of the city had sent for my advocate, and forbidden *him*, at his peril, *or any other person*, to meddle with *my cause!*

"I am innocent before God, and my conscience knows no reproach. The complaint brought against me is an infamous lie, and there is no circumstance that gives it even an air of probability.

"I address myself to you with confidence, my prince, and am assured that the friendship you have so kindly promised me will be immediately exerted in my favour; and that you will not suffer the illustrious sovereign of this great empire to be misled by the false insinuations and secret cabals of my hidden enemies. Your mind will find more true pleasure in pleading the cause of an innocent man whom you honour with your friendship than can result from other victories equally glorious with that of Oczakow, which will always rank among the most brilliant of military achievements. If your highness will condescend to question Monsieur Crimpin (for he dare not now *even speak to me*), he can tell you many circumstances which will elucidate my innocence. I am, with profound respect, my lord, your highness's devoted and most obedient servant," etc.

This letter was accompanied by certificates which fully established the character of the wretched woman by whose agency his ruin had been sought. The letter is dignified and touching. It is the passionate protest of an innocent man against an accusation concerning that which he had ever held dearer than life—his honor. It carries conviction with it. Incidentally it throws much light upon the Russian legal methods of that day. Never does Jones appear in a better light. But it was sent to an utterly unresponsive man. Honor, justice, innocence, were idle words to Patiomkine. No reply was made to the note, and Jones abandoned himself to despair. The narrative of de Ségur is taken from his memoirs, and, excepting in some minor details, is substantially correct:

"The American rear admiral was favourably welcomed at court; often invited to dinner by the empress, and received with distinction into the best society in the city; on a sudden Catherine commanded him to appear no more in her presence.

"He was informed that he was accused of an infamous crime: of assaulting a young girl of fourteen, of grossly violating her; and that probably, after

224

some preliminary information, he would be tried by the courts of admiralty, in which there were many English officers, who were strongly prejudiced against him.

"As soon as this order was known every one abandoned the unhappy American; no one spoke to him, people avoided saluting him, and every door was shut against him. All those by whom but yesterday he had been eagerly welcomed now fled from him as if he had been infected with a plague; besides, no advocate would take charge of his cause, and no public man would consent to listen to him; at last even his servants would not continue in his service; and Paul Jones, whose exploits every one had so recently been ready to proclaim, and whose friendship had been sought after, found himself alone in the midst of an immense population; Petersburg, a great capital, became to him a desert.

"I went to see him; he was moved even to tears by my visit. 'I was unwilling,' he said to me, shaking me by the hand, 'to knock at your door and to expose myself to a fresh affront, which would have been more cutting than all the rest. I have braved death a thousand times—now I wish for it.' His appearance, his arms being laid upon the table, made me suspect some desperate intention.

"'Resume,' I said to him, 'your composure and your courage. Do you not know that human life, like the sea, has its storms, and that fortune is even more capricious than the winds? If, as I hope, you are innocent, brave this sudden tempest; if, unhappily, you are guilty, confess it to me with unreserved frankness, and I will do everything I can to snatch you, by a sudden flight, from the danger which threatens you.'

"'I swear to you upon my honour,' said he, 'that I am innocent, and a victim of the most infamous calumny. This is the truth. Some days since a young girl came to me in the morning, to ask me if I could give her some linen or lace to mend. She then indulged in some rather earnest and indecent allurements. Astonished at so much boldness in one of such few years, I felt compassion for her; I advised her not to enter upon so vile a career, gave her some money, and dismissed her; but she was determined to remain.

"'Impatient at this resistance, I took her by the hand and led her to the door; but, at the instant when the door was opened, the little profligate tore her sleeves and her neck-kerchief, raised great cries, complained that I had assaulted her, and threw herself into the arms of an old woman, whom she called her mother, and who certainly was not brought there by chance. The mother and the daughter raised the house with their cries, went out, and denounced me; and now you know all.'

"'Very well,' said I, 'but can not you learn the names of those adventurers?' 'The porter knows them,' he replied. 'Here are their names written down, but I do not know where they live. I was desirous of immediately presenting a memorial about this ridiculous affair, first to the minister and then to the empress; but I have been interdicted from access to both of them.' 'Give me the paper,' I said; 'resume your accustomed firmness; be comforted; let me undertake it; in a short time we shall meet again.'

"As soon as I returned home I directed some sharp and intelligent agents, who were devoted to me, to get information respecting these suspected females, and to find out what was their mode of life. I was not long in learning that the old woman was in the habit of carrying on a vile traffic in young girls, whom she passed off as her daughters.

"When I was furnished with all the documents and attestations for which I had occasion, I hastened to show them to Paul Jones. 'You have nothing more to fear,' said I; 'the wretches are unmasked. It is only necessary to open the eyes of the empress, and let her see how unworthily she has been deceived; but this is not so very easy; truth encounters a multitude of people at the doors of a palace, who are very clever in arresting its progress; and sealed letters are, of all others, those which are intercepted with the greatest art and care. Nevertheless, I know that the empress, who is not ignorant of this, has directed under very heavy penalties that no one shall detain on the way any letters which are addressed to her personally, and which may be sent to her by post; therefore, here is a very long letter which I have written to her in your name; nothing of the detail is omitted, although it contains some rough expressions. I am sorry for the empress; but since she heard and gave credit to a calumny, it is but right that she should read the justification with patience. Copy this letter, sign it, and I will take charge of it; I will send some one to put it in the post at the nearest town. Take courage; believe me, your triumph is not doubtful.'"

The contents of the letter which Jones was advised to copy and send are not now ascertainable, but the following letter was written to the empress; and, while it is so evidently in Jones' own peculiar and characteristic style as to admit of no doubt as to its authorship, he probably embodied in it the suggestions of de Ségur and substituted it for the copy proposed:

"ST. PETERSBURG, *May 17, 1789.*

"MADAM: I have never served but for honour; I have never sought but

226

glory; and I believed I was in the way of obtaining both when I accepted the offers made me on the part of your Majesty, of entering into your service.... I sacrificed my dearest interests to accept an invitation so flattering, and I would have reached you instantly if the United States had not entrusted me with a special commission to Denmark. Of this I acquitted myself faithfully and promptly.... The distinguished reception which your Majesty deigned to grant me, the kindness with which you loaded me, indemnified me for the dangers to which I had exposed myself for your service, and inspired me with the most ardent desire to encounter more.... I besought your Majesty never to condemn me unheard. You condescended to give me that promise, and I set out with a mind as tranquil as my heart was satisfied....

"At the close of the campaign I received orders to return to court, as your Majesty intended to employ me in the North Seas, and M. le Comte de Besborodko acquainted me that a command of greater importance than that of the Black Sea ... was intended for me. Such was my situation, when, upon the mere accusation of a crime, the very idea of which wounds my delicacy, I found myself driven from court, deprived of the good opinion of your Majesty, and forced to employ the time which I wish to devote to the defence of your empire in cleansing from myself the stains with which calumny has covered me.

"Condescend to believe, madam, that if I had received the slightest hint that a complaint of such a nature had been made against me, and still more, that it had come to your Majesty's knowledge, I know too well what is owing to delicacy to have ventured before you till I was completely exculpated.

"Understanding neither the laws, the language, nor the forms of justice in this country, I needed an advocate, and obtained one; but, whether from terror or intimidation, he stopped short all at once, and durst not undertake my defence, though convinced of the justice of my cause. But truth may always venture to show itself alone and unsupported at the foot of the throne of your Majesty. I have not hesitated to labour unaided for my own vindication; I have collected proofs; and if such details might appear under the eyes of your Majesty I would present them; but if your Majesty will deign to order some person to examine them, it will be seen by the report which will be made that my crime is a fiction, invented by the cupidity of a wretched woman, whose avarice has been countenanced, perhaps incited, by the malice of my numerous enemies. Her husband has himself certified and attested to her infamous conduct. His signature is in my hands, and the pastor, Braun, of the district, has assured me that if the College of Justice will give him an order to this effect he will obtain an attestation from the country people that the mother of the girl referred to is known among them as a wretch absolutely unworthy of belief.

"Take a soldier's word, madam; believe an officer whom two great nations esteem, and who has been honoured with flattering marks of their approbation.... I am innocent; and if I were guilty I would not hesitate to make a candid avowal of my fault, and to commit my honour, which is a thousand times dearer to me than my life, to the hands of your Majesty.

"If you deign, madam, to give heed to this declaration, proceeding from a heart the most frank and loyal, I venture from your justice to expect that my zeal will not remain longer in shameful and humiliating inaction. It has been useful to your Majesty, and may again be so, especially in the Mediterranean, where, with insignificant means, I will undertake to execute most important operations, the plans for which I have meditated long and deeply. But if circumstances, of which I am ignorant, do not admit the possibility of my being employed during the campaign, I hope your Majesty will give me permission to return to France or America, granting, as the sole reward of the services I have had the happiness to render, the hope of renewing them at some future day...."

Catherine, to her credit be it stated, took the "soldier's word," examined the convincing proofs, and, being satisfied of his innocence, publicly received him at court again and thus openly vindicated him. New projects immediately began to take shape in his fertile brain. No bodily weakness could apparently impair his mental activity. With a half dozen East Indiamen armed for warlike purposes he offered to cut off the food traffic between Egypt and Constantinople; an idea as old as the days of the Cæsars, when upon the arrival of the corn ships from Alexandria depended the control of the Roman plebeians; but the idea was as good now as it was then, and if he had been intrusted with the meager force he requested he would have compelled the Turks to detach ships from the Black Sea fleet, and thus relieve the pressure on the Crimea.

Count Besborodko was pleased with the project, and promised to submit it to the empress, proposing, at the same time, if this plan fell through, to give him another command in the Black Sea, with an adequate fleet, by which he might force his way into the Mediterranean. About the middle of June, on his applying to this minister again, he was promised an answer in two days as to the pleasure of the empress concerning him. Besborodko stated that Catherine would either give him a command or grant the leave of absence which he had asked in his letter of the 17th. The minister had a court memory, however, and not two days, but many, passed without the information. On the 5th of July Jones wrote again to the minister in the usual direct way he employed when he was irritated, and asked for an immediate declaration of intentions regarding him. It was a high-handed way to address the Russian court, but it brought an immediate reply. On the 8th of July he was officially informed that his request for a leave of absence was granted for two years, with permission to go outside the limits of the empire. His salary was to be continued during that time.

On the 18th of July he had a farewell audience with the empress, who treated him very nicely on this occasion. As he kissed her hand in good-by she wished him *bon voyage*, which was politic but unsubstantial. He did not leave St. Petersburg immediately, and it was not until the last of August that he took his final leave of the Russian capital. During this interval he was detained partly by the difficulty in collecting his arrears in pay and allowances, and partly for the reason that he undertook, in spite of the rebuffs he had received, again to lay before Besborodko and others a project for a war against the Barbary States, which, of course, came to nothing. He left Russia a bitterly disappointed man.

The disinterested friendship of de Ségur had not been exhausted by his previous actions, and he gave additional proofs of his affection by supplying Jones with letters of introduction to the representatives of the French Government at the different courts of Europe which he proposed to visit, and the two following statements addressed to the French Minister of Foreign Affairs:

"ST. PETERSBURG, *July 21, 1789.*

"The enemies of the Vice-Admiral[48] Paul Jones having caused to be circulated reports entirely destitute of foundation concerning the journey which this general officer is about to undertake, I would wish the inclosed article, the authenticity of which I guarantee, should be inserted in the *Gazette de France*, and in the other public papers which are submitted to the inspection of your department. This article will undeceive those who have believed the calumny, and will prove to the friends and to the compatriots of the vice admiral that he has sustained the reputation acquired by his bravery and his talents during the last war; that the empress desires to retain him in her service; and that if he absents himself at this moment it is with his own free will, and for particular reasons, which can not leave any stain on his honour.

"The glorious marks of the satisfaction and bounty of the king toward M. Paul Jones, his attachment to France, which he has served so usefully in the common cause, his rights as a subject, and as an admiral of the United States, the protection of the ministers of the king, and my personal friendship for this distinguished officer, with whom I made a campaign in America, are so many reasons which appear to me to justify the interest which I took in all that concerned him during his stay in Russia."

"Article to be inserted in the Public Prints, and particularly in the Gazette de France.

"ST. PETERSBURG, *July 21, 1789.*

"The Vice-Admiral Paul Jones, being at the point of returning to France, where private affairs require his presence, had the honour to take leave of the empress, the 7th[49] of this month, and to be admitted to kiss the hand of her Imperial Majesty, who confided to him the command of her vessels of war stationed on the Liman during the campaign of 1788. As a mark of favour for his conduct during this campaign the empress has decorated him with the insignia of the order of St. Anne; and her Imperial Majesty, satisfied with his services, only grants him permission to absent himself for a limited time, and still preserves for him his emoluments and his rank."

Jones did not lack other friends either, for M. Genet, Secretary of the French Legation at St. Petersburg, and subsequently Minister from France to the United States—his extraordinary conduct while he enjoyed that office will be remembered—whose father had been an old friend of the commodore's, gave him a most cordial and gratifying letter of introduction to the celebrated Madame Campan, in which he specifically states the unfounded nature of the charges which had been made, and, describing the circumstances in which Jones left Russia, authorized her to correct any rumors to his disadvantage which might be put in circulation at Versailles. He also consented to act as Jones' financial representative, and transmitted to him from time to time such amounts on his pay as he could wrest from the Russian Government.

CHAPTER XX.

LAST YEARS AND DEATH.

The next year of his life the commodore passed in travel. His destination when he left Russia was Copenhagen; perhaps he had in mind the possibility of resuming the negotiations with the Danish Government on the old claim, and it is possible that his deferred pension may have had something to do with this intention. He had no especial place to go; one city was as good as another to him. In his busy wandering life he had never made a home for himself, and, while his mind and heart turned with ever more intensity of affection to the United States, yet he loved America in an abstract rather than a concrete way. The principles for which the United States stood, and upon which they were constituted and organized, appealed to him, but those personal ties which he had formed in his brief sojourn before the Revolution were weakened by absence or had been sundered by death. There was no employment for him there, for his country had absolutely no navy. Besides, he needed rest. He who had fought throughout a long life for liberty and freedom, for honor and fame, was doomed to struggle for that last desire for the few remaining years left him.

He traveled leisurely from St. Petersburg to Warsaw, where he was kindly received at the court of Poland, and where he busied himself preparing journals of his American service and of the Liman campaign, copies of which he sent to Catherine. There, too, he met the great Pole, Kosciusko, and the acquaintance between the veteran sailor and the old soldier of the Revolution speedily ripened into intimacy. Sweden had declared war against Russia. Kosciusko, who was the inveterate enemy of this gigantic empire which finally wrote *finis Poloniæ* across the story of his country, would have been most happy if he could have seen the fleets of Sweden led by so redoubtable a warrior as Jones. But of course such a proposition was not, and could not be, entertained by Jones.[50]

On leaving Warsaw for Vienna, it is suggested that he made the detour necessitated by visiting that point, rather than proceeding directly to Copenhagen via Berlin, at the instigation of Catherine, who desired to remove him from the vicinity of the Swedes. She might not use him herself, but she could not contemplate with any degree of equanimity the possibility of his serving against her. There is not the slightest evidence that he ever thought of entering the service of Sweden. He repels the idea with indignation, and the sole foundation for it arose from Kosciusko's ardent desire. Jones' conduct in the affair is beyond criticism; indeed, he was too ill at that time, although he did not realize it, to be employed by any one. In his papers the following declaration is found. It is undated, and the documents to which it was attached give no clew as to when it was written, or whether it was ever published, but from its contents it must have been prepared while he was on this leave of absence from Russia. It is a notable little document, for it repeats his assertion of American citizenship, expresses his intention of never warring against the United States or France, and clearly defines the tenure of his connection with the Russians:

"NOTICE.

"The Rear-Admiral Paul Jones, desirous of making known unequivocally his manner of thinking in relation to his military connection with Russia, declares:

"1st. That he has at all times expressed to her Imperial Majesty of Russia his vow to preserve the condition of an American citizen and officer.

"2d. That, having been honoured by his most Christian Majesty with a gold sword, he has made a like vow never to draw it on any occasion where war might be waged against his Majesty's interest.

"3d. That circumstances which the rear admiral could not foresee when he wrote on the last occasion make him feel a presentiment that, in spite of his attachment and gratitude to her Imperial Majesty, and notwithstanding the advantageous propositions which may be made to him, he will probably renounce the service of that power, even before the expiration of the leave of absence which he now enjoys."

To return to his trip. After staying some time in Vienna, where he seems to have been received with favor in high social circles, though the illness of the emperor prevented his being presented, he went to Amsterdam via Hamburg. Here he remained for some time, engaged, as usual, in correspondence. He still seems to have cherished the sailor's dream of buying a farm and passing his remaining years thereon, for we find among his letters an inquiry addressed to Mr. Charles Thompson, the Secretary of Congress, about an estate near Lancaster, Pennsylvania, which he thought of purchasing from funds invested in the United States. But in view of his anomalous connection with Russia he thought it well to remain in Europe until it had either ceased or been renewed. This was the time, being in need of funds, that he wrote to his old friend Krudner to endeavor to secure payment of the Danish pension.

Krudner readily undertook Jones' commission, and the Danish

Government promised to pay the pension at Copenhagen to any one whom Jones would authorize to receive it. They never paid it. Krudner always retained his friendship for Jones, and one of his letters closes with these words:

"At all events, I flatter myself, as a good Russian, that your arm is still reserved for us."

At the end of April, 1790, he crossed over to London on some financial business, which he settled to his satisfaction. He remained but a brief time in England—his visits there were always brief and devoid of publicity; he seems to have felt keenly the hatred with which the English regarded him, and under such circumstances his action was wise.

Toward the close of May he returned to Paris, which was perhaps the place where his happiest hours had been spent, and at Paris he continued to reside until the last scene in his eventful history. It was no longer the gay and pleasure-seeking resort of his earlier and happier years. The grim shadow of the Revolution, as yet no larger than a man's hand, was already lowering on the horizon. A year before his arrival the States-General had been summoned for the first time in a hundred and seventy-five years. On the 14th of July, eight months before his coming, the drums of the sections rolled the knell of the Bastile, and a little later still the old feudal constitution, which had endured the vicissitudes of a thousand years of change, was abrogated, and the rule of the people began. Louis XVI, poor puppet of fortune, "imponderous rag of circumstance," was driven hither and thither by the furious blasts of liberated passion charged with centuries of animosity, for a few aimless, pitiful years, and then—the guillotine!

For two years Jones lived in quiet retirement. He made but one other public appearance, in July, 1790, in connection with the first anniversary of the taking of the Bastile. Paris, inspirited with the first breath of freedom, drawn from the first labor pains of the Revolution, determined to celebrate in fitting style this grand anniversary. Different groups of foreigners residing in France sent delegates to appear before the National Assembly and ask permission to take part in the national *fête*. Paul Jones headed the Americans, and made an address to the Assembly. Thenceforward he did nothing of a public character.

His traveling had brought him neither surcease of care nor restoration to health. His hardy constitution, shattered by constant exposure in all weathers and every climate, and worn out by the chafings of his ardent and impatient temperament throughout the course of a career checkered by periods of alternate exaltation and depression, and filled with hopes and disappointments in equal measure, was rapidly yielding to the pains and ailments which were ushering in the fatal moment which should put an end to all his dreams and aspirations. His time, however, was not passed unhappily, and returns from investments provided him with enough for his simple needs. During the stirring hours of the beginning of the Revolution he busied himself in writing his journals, arranging the great mass of papers he had accumulated, and in his never-failing correspondence. Sometimes he attended the Sorbonne, and held discussion with philosophers. Madame de Telison was with him.

He was drawn in two ways by the condition of France. His sympathies were ever with humanity struggling for freedom; but he had received so many marks of favor from the French king, to whom he owed his great opportunities for achievement and advancement, that he could scarcely view with equanimity the dangers and harassments of that unhappy monarch. He was a republican through and through in principle, but by instinct and association, if not by birth, he was one of the proudest and most thoroughgoing of aristocrats—as Washington was an aristocrat. Like many other people, his theory of life and government was different from his practice. Besides, the liberty which the French were striving to establish was already perilously verging on that unbounded license into which it soon degenerated, and that his disciplined soul abhorred. His associates in France were mainly among the Girondists, with whom he was more nearly affiliated than with other political parties.

He did not realize that he was so broken in health, for he still clung to his tenuous connection with Russia, sending repeated letters to Catherine and Patiomkine, with demands, requests, and suggestions of various plans for service. Patiomkine, as usual, took no notice, but the last letter to Catherine having been forwarded through Baron Grimm, she directed him, rather curtly by the way, to inform Jones that if she had service for him she would let him know. After that Jones seems to have discontinued his letters to Russia. He found, however, two new outlets for his restless zeal. Early in 1792, chancing to meet an Algerian corsair, who had captured many Americans now held for ransom in Algiers, he learned much of the unfortunate condition of those unhappy sailors, to whose fate their country was apparently oblivious. The corsair informed him that if these captives were not ransomed promptly they would be sold into slavery. Jones wrote immediately to Jefferson, then Secretary of State, and with all his power urged that something be done for them, either by sending a force to compel restitution or by means of ransom. The letter, as we shall see, was not without result.

The second object of interest was a claim which he entertained against the French Government for salary due him while in command of the Bon Homme Richard and the squadron. The United States had paid him his salary as an officer during that period, but he felt that since his services had been asked by France, and the squadron had been at the charge of the French Government, a further amount was due him from the French, and he wrote to de Bertrand, Minister of Marine, demanding the balance due. The claim was the subject of acrid correspondence, and the matter was pending when he died.[51] From the letters written during the last years of his life I quote portions of three—the first two to his sister, Mrs. Taylor, and the last one to Lafayette:

"AMSTERDAM, *March 26, 1790.*

"I wrote you, my dear friend, from Paris, by Mr. Kennedy, who delivered me the kind letter you wrote me by him. Circumstances obliged me to return soon afterward to America, and on my arrival at New York Mr. Thomson delivered me a letter that had been intrusted to his care by Mrs. Loudon. It would be superfluous to mention the great satisfaction I received in hearing from two persons I so much love and esteem, and whose worthy conduct as wives and mothers is so respectable in my eyes. Since my return to Europe a train of circumstances and changes of residence have combined to keep me silent. This has given me more pain than I can express; for I have a tender regard for you both, and nothing can be indifferent to me that regards your happiness and the welfare of your children. I wish for a particular detail of their age, respective talents, characters, and education. I do not desire this information merely from curiosity. It would afford me real satisfaction to be useful to their establishment in life. We must study the genius and inclination of the boys, and try to fit them, by a suitable education, for the pursuits we may be able to adopt for their advantage. When their education shall be advanced to a proper stage, at the school of Dumfries for instance, it must then be determined whether it may be most economical and advantageous for them to go to Edinburgh or France to finish their studies. All this is supposing them to have great natural genius and goodness of disposition; for without these they can never become eminent. For the females, they require an education suited to the delicacy of character that is becoming in their sex. I wish I had a fortune to offer to each of them; but though this is not the case, I may yet be useful to them. And I desire particularly to be useful to the two young women, who have a double claim to my regard, as they have lost their father. Present my kind compliments to Mrs. Loudon, her husband, to Mr. Taylor, and your two families, and depend on my affectionate attachment...."

"PARIS, *December 27, 1790.*

"I duly received, my dear Mrs. Taylor, your letter of the 16th August, but ever since that time I have been unable to answer it, not having been capable to go out of my chamber, and having been for the most part obliged to keep my bed. I have now no doubt but that I am in a fair way to perfect recovery, though it will require time and patience.

"I shall not conceal from you that your family discord aggravates infinitely all my pains. My grief is inexpressible that two sisters, whose happiness is so interesting to me, do not live together in that *mutual tenderness and affection* which would do so much honour to themselves and to the memory of their worthy relations. Permit me to recommend to your serious *study* and *application* Pope's Universal Prayer. You will find more morality in that little piece than in many volumes that have been written by great divines:

```
"'Teach me to feel another's woe,
   To hide the fault I see;        That mercy I to others show,
   Such mercy show to me.'
```

"This is not the language of a weak, superstitious mind, but the spontaneous offspring of true religion, springing from a heart sincerely inspired by charity, and deeply impressed with a sense of the calamities and *frailties* of human nature. If the sphere in which Providence has placed us as members of society requires the exercise of brotherly kindness and charity toward our neighbour in general, how much more is this our duty with respect to individuals with whom we are connected by the near and tender ties of nature as well as moral obligation. Every lesser virtue may pass away, but *charity* comes from Heaven, and is immortal. Though I wish to be the instrument of making family peace, which I flatter myself would tend to promote the happiness of you all, yet I by no means desire you to do violence to your own feelings by taking any step that is contrary to your own judgment and inclination. Your reconciliation must come free from your heart, otherwise it will not last, and therefore it will be better not to attempt it. Should a reconciliation take place, I recommend it of all things, that you never mention past grievances, nor show, by *word, look, or action*, that you have not forgot them."

"Paris, *December 7, 1791.*

"DEAR GENERAL: My ill health for some time past has prevented me from the pleasure of paying you my personal respects, but I hope shortly to indulge myself with that satisfaction.

"I hope you approve the quality of the fur linings I brought from Russia for the King and yourself. I flatter myself that his Majesty will accept from your hand that little mark of the sincere attachment I feel for his person; and be assured that I shall be always ready to draw the sword with which he honoured me for the service of the virtuous and illustrious 'PROTECTOR OF THE RIGHTS OF HUMAN NATURE.'

"When my health shall be established, M. Simolin will do me the honour to present me to his Majesty as a Russian admiral. Afterward it will be my duty, as an American officer, to wait on his Majesty with the letter which I am directed to present to him from the United States."

Jones appears in a very pleasant light in all of these letters, and I am glad to read the evidences of gentleness and of affection and kindly feeling which they present. In March, 1792, his disease, which had developed into a lingering form of dropsy, became complicated with a disorder of the liver. He grew much worse, lost his appetite, became very jaundiced, and was confined to his bedroom for two months. Under treatment he grew temporarily better, until the beginning of July, when he became suddenly worse again and the dropsy began to manifest itself once more. The disease attacked his chest. His legs became much swollen, and the enlargement extended upward so that he could not button his waistcoat and had great difficulty in breathing.

He was not, as has been asserted, in poverty and want, deserted by his friends. He lived in a comfortable apartment in the second story of No. 42 Tournon Street, and enjoyed the services of one of the best physicians in France, who was, in fact, physician to the queen. Gouverneur Morris, the American Minister, was a warm friend of his, and paid him many visits during his dying hours. He had no lack of other friends either, for he was attended by two gentlemen, ex-American army officers, Colonels Swan and Blackden, and by a French officer, M. Beaupoil. They all seem to have been fond of the little commodore, and to have visited him constantly. They did everything possible to lighten his dying hours. His symptoms became so alarming about the middle of July that Colonel Blackden took upon himself the duty of advising him to make his will and settle his affairs. He put off this action until the 18th of the month. On the afternoon of that day Morris drew up a schedule of his property from Jones' own dictation, and his friends having sent for a notary, he made his will, which was drawn in English by Morris, and transcribed in French by the notary. The will was witnessed by Swan, Blackden, and Beaupoil.[52] In this document—the last of all his writings—dictated in those solemn hours when he looked Death in the face in final glance, the real value of earthly honors and titles became apparent to him; he describes himself with touching simplicity, not as Commodore,

Chevalier, or Admiral—titles he had loved—but in greater words as "*John Paul Jones, a citizen of the United States.*"

At eight o'clock in the evening his friends bade him good by, and perhaps "Good night" were the last words any one heard him speak. They left him seated in his armchair in his parlor in the second story. A short time after their departure the physician arrived to pay his regular evening visit. The armchair was empty, and the door of the chamber adjoining the parlor was open. He walked over toward it and stopped in the entrance, and this is what he saw: the figure of the great commodore lying prone upon the bed, his feet touching the floor and his hands outstretched before him. There was no sound in the still room. The physician stepped softly to the bedside, turned him over, and laid his hand upon his heart. He felt no responsive throb. The little captain of the Bon Homme Richard was dead, worn out, fretted away, broken down, at the age of forty-five! "The hand of a conqueror whom no human power can resist had been laid upon his shoulder, and for the first time in his life the face of Paul Jones was turned away from the enemy."[53] Fitting, indeed, would it have been if from the deck of the war ship the soul of the sea king had taken its flight; but, after all, he was at rest at last—"in peace after so many storms, in honor after so much obloquy."

The peculiar position in which he was found, as I have thought upon it, has suggested to me the possibility that, when he felt the last crisis coming upon him, he may have attempted to sink down by his bedside, that the call of his Maker might find him—as years after it found David Livingstone in the heart of dark Africa—on his knees in prayer. And then sometimes I think—and this is perhaps more likely—that he may have risen to his feet to face death, as was his wont, and have fallen forward when it came. No one can tell. A century has fled away since they found him there, but the sorrow of it all is still present with me as I write. An exile from his native land, far from the country of his adoption, in the prime of life, he dies. There was not a woman with him to whisper words of comfort, to give him that last touch of tenderness that comes from a woman's hand. Alone he had lived—alone he died. Oh, the pity of it! The man of the world, become the citizen of the new republic, had found another country—let us hope a heavenly one. He did much and he suffered much, and for such we may be sure there is much charity, much forgiveness.

By the terms of his will all his property, amounting to some thirty thousand dollars, was left to his two surviving sisters and their children—the same to whom he had sent those sweet words counseling forbearance and consideration. The fact that he had shown but little of the one and had received but little of the other in his life only accentuates his sense of their need. One other honor his country had in store for him, but it arrived too late. He had been long buried when a commission appointing him to negotiate the release of the prisoners in Algiers arrived in France. It was an honor he would have appreciated, and in carrying it out he would have found a congenial task.

The National Assembly honored his memory by sending a deputation, headed by its president, to represent them at his funeral, which took place on the second day after his death, at eight o'clock in the evening. All his friends, including the Americans, were there as well. A French Protestant clergyman named Marron conducted the services and delivered a eulogy, but one sentence of which is worthy of quotation: "The fame of the brave outlives him; his portion is immortality."

It has been determined recently that the interment was made in the little cemetery reserved for those who died in the Protestant faith, situated at the corner of the Rue de la Grange aux Belles and Rue des Écluses Saint Martin —then in the suburbs, now in the heart of the city. The cemetery was officially closed on January 1, 1793. A canal was afterward cut through it and buildings erected upon the other, lots. The exact location of Jones' grave is unknown, and, as there were at least ten thousand people buried there, it would probably be a matter of great difficulty to find it, should the effort be made; and the expense would be considerable. The body, clad in an American uniform, was incased in a leaden coffin, with sword,[54] etc., and unless all the elements have been dissipated by the action of the water it might be possible to identify his remains. Certainly there is no question, if satisfactory settlement could be had, that his remains should be brought to the United States, with all naval honors, here to be suitably interred and his grave marked by an appropriate monument. So far as I know, there has not even been so much as a memorial tablet erected to his memory in any part of the great country toward whose independence he contributed so much. A serious and ungrateful omission this, and, whether his remains be found or not, it is to be hoped that it may be soon rectified.[55]

CHAPTER XXI.

PERSONAL APPEARANCE—CHARACTERISTICS—WAS HE A PIRATE?—FAREWELL.

Paul Jones was a small, slender man, somewhat under the middle stature, or about five feet five inches in height. As is frequently the custom with seamen, who pass much of their lives between decks, his shoulders were slightly rounded, and at first glance he seemed smaller than he was. In physique he was active and graceful, well proportioned and strong. Many portraits of him exist, some of them gross caricatures, representing him as the proverbial pirate of early days clad in fantastic costume, his belt bristling with pistols and knives, and depicting him in the act of slaying some terrified and helpless sailor; but it is from such representations as the painting by Peale,[56] the bust by Houdon, the naval medal, and the miniature by the Countess de Lavendahl, that we get a correct idea of his appearance. His features were regular; his nose was straight, prominent, and slightly enlarged at the tip; his lips were elegantly curved. His head was well proportioned, and set firmly upon his shoulders; in spite of his stoop he held it erect, which gave him an intent, eager expression. His large black eyes were set deep in their sockets under heavy, arched eyebrows; in moments of action they sparkled with fire and passion. His hair was black and plentiful, and the darkness of his complexion had been intensified by years of exposure to wind and weather. His hands and feet were small and of good shape. He was always particular in his dress, which was of material as rich and in cut as elegant as his means permitted. Without being handsome, therefore, he was a man of distinctly striking and notable appearance in any society.

His habitual expression was thoughtful and meditative. His face was the face of a student rather than that of a fighter. As it looks out at us from the canvas of the past in Peale's portrait, there is a little touch of wonder and surprise in the soft, reflective eyes. The mystery of life is there. We feel that the man is speculating upon us, measuring us, wondering who and what we are. There is a gentle gravity about the face which is most attractive. In the profile on the medal and in the Houdon bust other qualities predominate. You catch a glimpse of the proud, imperious, dashing sailor in the uplifted poise of the head, the tense, straight line of the lips, and the firm, resolute chin; and there is a suggestion of humor, grim enough, in the whole face. The Countess de Lavendahl apparently depicts him in the role of a lover, fashionably attired and arrayed for conquest. In each of these representations we have the broad, splendid brow which typifies the mind that was in him. It is probable that these different portraits were each good likenesses, and that each artist, in accordance with his insight, wrought into his presentment what he saw in the man.

A man of abundant self-confidence, he was not easily embarrassed, and we find him at home as well in the refined and cultivated colonial society of North Carolina as upon the decks of a ship manned by the rudest and roughest of men. He bears himself with easy dignity at the courts of Russia and France, and is not discomfited in the presence of king, queen, or empress. His manners were easy and polite. There was a touch of the directness of the sailor and the fighter in his address, I doubt not, but his behavior was certainly that of a gentleman—quiet, dignified, somewhat haughty, but pleasing. This is established by the testimony of those who knew him, including the Englishwoman mentioned above; by traditions which have come down to us; by the fact that he was admitted into the most exclusive circles in various courts of Europe, and that he retained the place which had been accorded him through years of acquaintanceship. He has been called low, brutal, common, and vulgar, but such accusations are incompatible with the position he occupied. He might have been received, of course, but he never would have been not merely tolerated, but admired and sought after, if the charges were correct.

In saying this, I do not wish to be understood as being oblivious of his faults. As occasion has demanded, I have not hesitated to call attention to them. He was irritable and impatient, captious and quarrelsome, at times variable and inconsistent. We find him addressing a superior at one time in terms that are almost too respectful, and in his next communication writing with a blunt frankness of a superior to an inferior. This frequently caused him trouble, inasmuch as he usually had to deal with men who were his superiors in birth and station, though not to be compared with him in talents and education. The limitations of his humble origin account for this variant attitude to the world's so-called great.

His great fault was his vanity. It was a weakness, like some of his other qualities, colossal. It manifested itself in every way that vanity can manifest itself. No defense can be uttered. We recognize the fact and note it with pain, but in the presence of his great qualities pass it by, after calling attention to the strange fact that other and more famous sailors, including the greatest man who ever fought a ship or squadron, Lord Nelson, were under the spell of the same weakness—and other greater weaknesses. No character in history is without weakness. There was but One who manifested no weakness, not even on a cross.

His mind was a well-furnished one. From boyhood he had cultivated the studious habit with which he was endowed in large degree, with the assiduity and perseverance of a Scotsman. He was thoroughness itself; whatever he attempted he did so well that he usually left nothing further to be desired. His brain was alert and active. He was quick-witted, and not devoid of humor, although there is always a touch of sternness in his persiflage. His letters fall into two classes. When he wrote under pressure of strong emotion or excitement, he expressed his personality with his pen as adequately as he did in his actions; his remarks were short, sharp, direct, logical, and in good taste; his style was vigorous and perspicuous. On the other hand, he frequently descended, especially when addressing women, into verbosity, and verbosity of that most intolerable species known as fine writing—witness his letter to Lady Selkirk. As a phrase maker many of his sentences ring with his spirit. "I do not wish to have command of any ship that does not sail fast, for I intend to go in harm's way"; "I have not yet begun to fight"; "I have ever looked out for the honor of the American flag"; "I can never renounce the glorious title of a citizen of the United States," are some of his sayings which have passed into history, and might appropriately serve for inscriptions on the four sides of his monument, when a too tardy people pay him the honor of erecting one.[57]

He spoke French well and wrote it better. He found no difficulty in making himself understood in France, and that language was used entirely in his Russian campaign. In an age when everybody scribbled verse he wrote poetry which is creditable to him. It has been remarked that it was much better verse than Nelson wrote. Like many other naval officers of that day, he played the flute and had a taste for music. He was undoubtedly a member of the Presbyterian Church by baptism in infancy, and although, so far as is known, he was not actively in communion with any religious organization during his life, he was in no sense an irreligious man. "They that go down to the sea in ships that do business in great waters," who see "the works of the Lord, and his wonders in the deep," are rarely ultimately indifferent to religion. They are superficially careless, perhaps, but they are neither skeptics nor atheists.[58] Nothing could be sweeter and more gentle than his letters to his sisters with their unequivocal recognition of the Power above which shapes our ends.

In a day when seamen—and no less the naval officer than the merchantman—considered a capacity for picturesque and plentiful profanity a mark of professional aptitude, he was distinguished by refraining from oaths and curses. Mark the words: "Do not swear, Mr. Stacy—in another moment we may all be in eternity—but let us do our duty." Uttered in the heat of action, and in a critical moment, the sentence is as rare as it is beautiful, and it somehow reminds me of the dying words of Nelson in the cockpit of the Victory. He was clean-mouthed and clean-hearted. I do not wish to say that he was immaculate, a saint, or anything of that sort, but there is no man of similar upbringing, who lived in his day, and under such circumstances, whose life appears to be cleaner. There is a total absence of sensuality in his career. In over thirteen hundred letters which have been examined, there is not a coarse or indelicate allusion; no *double entendre* ever sullies his pages, and the name of no woman is mentioned save in terms of respect. It is probable that his amour with Madame de Telison passed the bounds of Platonic friendship or romantic admiration, and it is possible that they did have a child; but even this is by no means certain, and the conclusion may do him an injustice.

When one remembers that from a tender age he was deprived of those gentle restraints imposed by pious and loving family ties, his character is remarkable. I have observed in much experience with men that when the check put upon humanity by the Church, by association with good women, and by keeping in touch with law-abiding society is removed, and men are assembled far from these things in camps or ships, where the principal requirement is a stern obedience to law, and the atmosphere strictly masculine, they are apt to think, say, and do things to which they would never descend under ordinary circumstances. Jones had been a sailor—an apprentice boy at that—at twelve years of age; for sixteen years thereafter he had never been off blue water for more than a few months. Five years of that time he had been on a slaver, beginning as third mate at sixteen and quitting as chief mate at twenty-one, and of all the degrading, brutal influences to which humanity could be subjected there was nothing that equaled the horrors of a ship in the slave trade. The tough moral fiber of the Scotsman stood him in good stead here, for the thing which with a boy's indifference he could countenance, he could not endure as a man.

And this brings us to another of his qualities, which awakens our interest— his intense love of liberty. Probably it began with the slave trade; at any rate, it was always and everywhere present with him. Practically his first military effort was an attempt to set free American prisoners, and his last commission from the United States was the appointment to effect the release of the unfortunate Americans held by the Barbary States. Thus he fought not merely for the establishment of civil liberty and national independence, but with an eye single to the individual prisoner, and his spirit was sufficiently catholic to make him kindly disposed even when the prisoners were trophies of his prowess. His pleading at L'Orient, when he was left with the dishonored draft, mutinous crew, and over one hundred prisoners, was as much for those Englishmen whom the fortune of war had thrown into his power as for his own people.

Like most men of fierce passions and quick temper, he did not long cherish animosities. He was not a good hater, and this very quality sometimes led him into mistaken kindness. He was a humane man, in no sense the cruel and bloodthirsty warrior of popular imagination. He is thankful, for instance, after the descent on Whitehaven, that there was no loss of life on either side, and we have no reason to doubt the genuineness of his outburst of gratitude when peace was declared, although it left him without occupation.

He had a good head for business also. In spite of his roving life he succeeded in amassing considerable property, and his success as a trader before he entered the naval service had been better than the average. In fact, his merchant services resulted in an unbroken line of testimonials not only to his capacity but to his probity and trustworthiness as well. As a negotiator or diplomatist he was open, straightforward, persistent, and unusually successful. A solid foundation of good qualities must have been laid by his homespun mother in those twelve years in which she watched over and shaped the future character of the boy.

While he was too much of a wanderer ever to form those deep and abiding social ties which are the delight of old age and reflection—though to youth matters of indifference—yet his various duties brought him into intimate association with great men all over the world, and there is a universal testimony from them as to his worth. They were not blind to his faults, but they saw the worthiness of the man beneath them. Franklin, the keen philosopher and diplomat, who knew him best, esteemed him most; but Robert Morris, the incorruptible financier; Thomas Jefferson, the great Democrat; Gouverneur Morris, the accomplished man of the world; John Adams, the shrewd statesman; and Washington, the first of them all, esteemed and admired him, and considered themselves honored in his friendship. Richard Dale, his great subordinate, who had been with him in times that tried men's souls, entertained the most devoted feelings of attachment toward him, and Cooper, who knew Dale personally, tells us that to the day of his death he never lost his affectionate regard for his old captain. The terms of their intimacy when not on duty permitted Dale to address Jones by the friendly name of Paul, and Cooper chronicles the peculiar tenderness with which he uttered the word in his old age.

Among the French who respected and admired him, the gallant and impetuous Lafayette is pre-eminent. That warm-hearted representative of the haute noblesse of France sought opportunities for service with the commodore, and never failed to express his affection for him in the most unequivocal words. Among others were Rochambeau, the soldier; Malesherbes, the great advocate, defender of his king; the Baron de Viomenil, who led the French assaulting column at Yorktown; and Admirals d'Orvilliers, de Vaudreuil, and d'Estaing. Among other foreign friends were van der Capellen, the Dutch statesman and diplomat and friend of America; of Russians, Krudner and Grimm; and the immortal Kosciusko, of Poland. His acquaintance with these men was no mere passing contact, but was intimate and personal; and his relations in most instances were not temporary and casual, but lasting and permanent. Laughton, the English authority in naval history, in his famous sketch entitled "Paul Jones, 'the Pirate'"[59] says that Jones' moral character may be summed up in one word—detestable! He calls him a renegade and a calculating liar, incapable of friendship or of love, and says that, "Whenever his private actions can be examined, they must be pronounced to be discreditable; and as to many others that appear to be so, there is no evidence in favor except his own unsubstantial and worthless testimony." It is not an indictment against Jones alone that Professor Laughton so lightly writes, but against the great men who, with infinitely better opportunities for observation than any of his biographers have enjoyed, have not been slow to call him their friend. Is it to be conceived for a single moment that Franklin, Jefferson, Lafayette, the Morrises, or any of the others, would have associated with, corresponded with, and publicly praised a vulgar blackguard? Would such a man, however successful, have been admitted to any society whatsoever? Or, having in the first flush of joy at the news of his tremendous victory been so admitted, could such a man have retained his position for thirteen years—until he died, in fact? Nonsense! He looked like a gentleman; he wrote like a gentleman; whenever his words have been recorded we find he spoke like a gentleman, and he certainly fought like one.

Never was a man so calumniated. His actions were so great that intense interest was felt in his career from the day of his arrival in Europe, and after his death quantities of sketches of him appeared, many of which are still extant. They are of the chap-book order—the dime novel of the day—and usually contain an awe-inspiring picture, and relate a tale in which smuggling, gambling, falsehood, theft, rape, murder, and everything else that is vile, are included. Laughton seems to have arrived at his estimation of Jones by accepting these scandalous tales as authentic, and building his biography of material culled from these disgraceful and discredited sources. No man can conceal his real character for any great length of time, especially a man in official station, who lives in the white light of public criticism. If Jones were the creature that Laughton describes him, it would appear somewhere in some serious page of his own. He was a most voluminous correspondent—Philip II was not a more indefatigable letter writer than he—and he spoke of the subjects under discussion with a sailor's frankness. Why is it that none of these things are evident? He was foolish sometimes, but never base. It is too late to write down in a few careless words the great men who entertained so high an opinion of the commodore. But Professor Laughton is not alone in his opinions. Indeed, his conclusions appear to represent a general English sentiment. So great a novelist as the gentle Thackeray calls Jones a traitor, and the popular opinion even in this day does not seem to have changed. In the current number of the London Academy[60] he is again called a "pirate." Let us settle this question at least.

What is a pirate? Says President Woolsey: "Piracy is robbery on the sea, or by descent from the sea upon the coast, committed by persons not holding a commission from, or at the time pertaining to, any established state. It is the act (1) of persons forming an organization for the purpose of plunder, or with malicious intent; but who, inasmuch as such a body is not constituted for political purposes, can not be said to be a body politic; (2) of persons who, having in defiance of law seized possession of a chartered vessel, use it for the purpose of robbery; (3) of persons taking a commission from two belligerent adversaries. The reason for ranking these latter among pirates is that the *animus furandi* is shown by acting under two repugnant authorities. It has been held by some that a vessel which takes commissions even from two allies is guilty of piracy, but others regard such an act only as illegal and irregular."[61]

Chancellor Kent calls piracy "robbery, forceful plunder, or murder by marauders on the high seas *in the spirit and intent of universal hostility.*" The Century Dictionary defines it as follows: "Specifically in the law of nations, the crime of depredations or willful and aggressive destruction of life and property, committed on the seas by persons having no commission or authority from any established state. As commonly used, it implies something more than a simple theft with violence at sea, and includes something of the idea of general hostility to law."

By any of these definitions can Paul Jones be called a pirate? It will be readily seen that the charge hangs upon the question as to whether Jones held a commission from an established state. In fact, the determination of that point settles the matter. He was regularly commissioned a captain in the navy of the United States, as we have seen.[62] Was the United States an established power, a sovereign state? The United States began to be with the Declaration of Independence. To quote Woolsey again: "The sovereignty of a state dates from its *de facto* existence, and does not depend upon its recognition by foreign powers. Thus the sovereignty of the United States was complete from July 4, 1776, not 1782, when the English Government recognized, not granted, its independence." If the United States had not a legal existence as a sovereign power competent to wage war, and therefore to issue commissions to naval officers, until the treaty of peace, England would have granted independence thereby, instead of which she recognized a long-accomplished fact. Moreover, the British Government, long before peace was declared, had conceded belligerent rights to the revolted colonies, after much protestation.

But necessary privileges of belligerency are those of raising forces and commissioning officers whose status as individual belligerents is determined by the recognition. None of the American prisoners taken from time to time were hanged as rebels or traitors, nor would such action have been permitted by the British people, if it had been seriously entertained by the king. Even if they had captured Paul Jones, the English, in all their fury, would not have dared to treat him as a pirate. Upon the point of law there is no justification for the charge. Paul Jones' commission was as valid a document as any under which a naval officer ever sailed. The sovereignty of the United States had been recognized long before the termination of the war by France, Spain, and Holland, and Frederick the Great, by opening the port of Dantzic to American ships, had practically committed himself to that side; although the failure of any or all of these to do so would not have abrogated our *de facto* existence as a nation.

But, turning from the subject of the commission as established, let us examine the other phases involved in the charge. Piracy consists of murder and robbery in a spirit of universal hostility toward humanity (the *animus furandi* of Woolsey's paragraph). Jones directed his attacks at England alone. There was no killing unless in open combat; no robbery except by taking ships and property in open warfare, and surely Jones' conduct with regard to Selkirk's plate was not that of a robber or a pirate! By the law of nations a pirate, whatever his nationality, is subject to the jurisdiction of any country. Thus, an English pirate caught by the French Government, or a French pirate caught by the English Government, would be summarily dealt with without the slightest reference to the country of his nationality. If Jones had been a pirate France would either have made short work of him, or else have incurred the odium of humanity as an abettor of piracy.

His acts were not those of an irresponsible person or a body of people who sent him forth with malicious intent, but were undertaken for distinctly political purposes at the instance of an undoubted body politic. These purposes were: (1) The protection of our coasts by showing the vulnerability of the coasts of England. (2) The stoppage of the ravages on our seaboard, by demonstrating some of their horrors in the land of the ravagers. (3) The securing of prisoners by which the principle of exchange should be established, and thus our citizens released from a captivity in which they were treated with scant regard to the laws of humanity. (4) The breaking up of the enemy's commerce and the impairment of his material resources, so that the burden of consequences would induce him to end the war and recognize our independence. (5) The making of a diversion in the north which would facilitate the proposed grand operations of the French and Spanish fleets in the south. These are legitimate motives in the highest sense. They are of the deepest importance, and they constitute a brief catalogue of his accomplishments. Add to the list the shattering of British prestige by his hard and successful fighting, and mention the way he contrived to force the Netherlands finally to declare for the United States, and we have a catalogue of achievements of which any one might be proud.[63]

There was no thought in Jones' mind of private gain. Prize money had accrued from captures from time immemorial, but Jones was ambitious of distinction, and as anxious to worthily serve his country as Farragut or Sampson, and the question of prize money was purely a minor one with him. If gain had been his object, a privateering commission which he was urged to accept in France—and which he could undoubtedly have received in America —but which he rejected with disdain, would have given him greater opportunity than he ever enjoyed of acquiring wealth. His whole career, in fact, shows him to have been absolutely indifferent to money. He never hoarded or amassed it, and, though he received large sums from time to time, he usually spent it in generous profusion as fast as it came in. Had professional advancement been his sole desire, he would have accepted the rank of *Capitaine de Vaisseau*—that is, a captain of a ship of the line—which d'Orvilliers had offered to procure for him, from which he might have progressed to the highest naval rank, instead of which he chose to remain in command of the petty little Ranger. How Laughton can deny his enthusiasm for America when, with but little hope of reward, he periled his liberty and his life in her service, and absolutely refused under any circumstances to withdraw from that service, I fail to understand.[64]

He did not, in defiance of law, charter a vessel for the purpose of waging private war. On the contrary, his ship was provided by the French king, and commissions for those officers who had not been commissioned directly by Congress, as had Jones himself, were issued by Franklin, who possessed the unquestioned power to do this by the specific action of Congress. Indeed, such was Franklin's power, that when he displaced Landais from his command he did not hesitate to overrule a commission issued by Congress under circumstances of peculiar importance, and he was upheld by that body when his action was called in question.

Nor did Jones take a commission from two belligerent adversaries—that is, he had no commission from England which he threw up to accept that of the United States. He had never served in the English navy in any capacity. There were officers in the United States land service who had held English commissions and yet accepted American commands, but Jones was not one of them. He had never, until he entered the Russian service, sailed under any commission save that of the United States, and one of the noblest acts of his life was his indignant repudiation of a French letter of marque when his acceptance of it was considered the only way of saving his head. Nothing could induce him to declare the Alliance a French ship in those hazardous moments in the Texel when he was menaced by the Dutch fleet on one side and the English fleet on the other, nor would he even temporarily hoist the French flag on that ship. He did not even commit the so-called illegal and irregular act of accepting a commission from two allies, for he refused a French commission again and again. This certainly constitutes a clear and overwhelming refutation of the charge of piracy. Indeed, on the question of piracy, Jones' own ingenious comment is not without interest. Laughton has called attention to it in the following words:

"Paul Jones strongly objected to the word as applied to himself; he had, he said, looked in the dictionary and found the definition of pirate to be 'an enemy against mankind.' Now, he was not the enemy of mankind, but only the enemy of England. With a *tu quoque* argument, not wanting in ingenuity, he urged that, as England was then at war with the whole of America, the greater part of Europe, and much of Asia, not to speak of a part of Africa, she, in point of fact, came as near being the enemy of mankind as could well be conceived—that England was therefore the pirate, not Paul Jones."

Why was it that the English called him a pirate, put a price on his head, and attempted to compass his death or capture by private hands? Why was it that he evoked such widespread animosity, and became the object of a hatred which has not exhausted itself to this day? Surely not because he had been a British subject! All who fought on the American side had been British subjects. Jones had removed to America and had determined to settle there before the war broke out. Why should any one attempt to insinuate that the same feelings which actuated Adams, Washington, and Patrick Henry did not operate to make him espouse the colonial cause? He was as fond of freedom as they, and as anxious to promote it.

Many of the most distinguished colonists were not only British subjects, but they had worn the king's uniform, fought under the king's flag, and eaten the king's bread; as, for instance, the great Washington. Richard Montgomery, an Irishman, who laid down a life valuable to his adopted country when he fell in the assault on Quebec, had been a British officer; and there were many others, some of whom, like the traitor Charles Lee and the worthless Gates, were actually half-pay officers in the British army when they entered the American service!

Among the naval officers, the heroic Biddle, who matched the little Randolph, of thirty-two small guns, against the huge line of battle ship Yarmouth, and fought until his ship was blown to pieces, and he and all his crew were lost except four men, had been a midshipman in the British navy with Nelson. Stout old John Barry, who commanded the Alliance when he captured the Atlanta and the Trepassy, and fought the last action of the war by beating the frigate Sibylle, of superior force, was an Irishman.[65] The most bigoted Englishmen to-day speak of those men with respect which they will not accord to Jones. Why is this?

The reason for the strange exception lies in the brilliant success with which he cruised and fought. The English claimed and exercised an absolute and practically undisputed supremacy on the high seas. Their arrogant navy for more than a hundred years had been invincible. In single ship actions they had always conquered. No enemy had landed on their shores for over a century. They could stand being beaten on land—they were accustomed to it. With few notable exceptions England does not produce great soldiers—Carlyle feelingly refers to the average English commander as a "wooden hoop pole wearing a cocked hat"[66]—but such a line of sailors as had sprung from their shores has never been equaled in the history of the world. Such sea leadership and such sea fighting has never been exceeded, or even equaled, by any nation.[67]

The capture of the Serapis was a trifling circumstance; it did not impair the naval efficiency or abridge the maritime supremacy of England an appreciable degree; but it had a moral significance that could not be misunderstood by the nations of the world. They saw and approved.[68] English ships had been beaten in fair fight, in one instance by a ship of equal, and in the other instance of inferior, force. The English coasts, in spite of swarms of great ships of the line, had been shown to be as vulnerable as any other.[69] The affront had been to her pride, and never since the days that brave old Tromp—gallant Dutchman, for whose character I have the greatest admiration—swept the narrow seas with a broom at his masthead, and actually entered the Thames under that same provoking emblem, had England suffered such naval humiliation. The English cheek tingles still from the blow dealt upon it by the hot-handed sailor. Naturally, they did not love Paul Jones. The hatred, which after a hundred years still rankles, is evidence of what they feel—and what he did! As for us, we love the bold little captain for the enemies he has made.

It has been stated by unthinking people that the Bon Homme Richard was a privateer or a letter of marque: in one case an armed vessel owned by private individuals and authorized, under certain restrictions, to cruise at private expense to prey upon the commerce of the enemy; in the other case, an armed vessel engaged in trade, but possessing the right to capture ships of the enemy should she happen to fall in with them. There is nothing disgraceful about either of these commissions, though, to be sure, their essence consists in making war for individual gain. The Bon Homme Richard was purchased and converted into a man-of-war by the French Government, and then loaned to the American Government for the time being. De Chaumont acted only as the representative of the king—that is, of the Government. There was no question of individual gain in the matter. The money for the sale of the prizes was received, and the share of Jones was paid, by the French Government. Therefore it was a Government ship, not a private vessel. France and the United States were allies in a war against England when she was commissioned, and the transaction was customary and legitimate. The Bon Homme Richard was as bona fide an American man-of-war as the Constitution. Of course, there could be no exception to the status of the Ranger or any of the earlier ships in which Paul Jones sailed.

I have considered the personal character and professional status of Paul Jones, now let me say a few words as to his qualities as an officer. Here at last we reach a field in which there is practically little disagreement. First of all, he was a thorough and accomplished seaman. His experiences had been many and varied. His handling of the Providence in the Gut of Canso, of the Alfred along the coast of Cape Breton, his splendid seamanship in the Ariel in the terrific gale off the Penmarques, his daring passage of the Baltic amid the winter gales and ice, not to speak of the way he maneuvered the Richard in the battle with the Serapis, all tell the same story of skill and address. Not only did he understand the sailing of ships, but he acquired no small familiarity with the principles of naval architecture. Witness his remodeling of the Alliance, the improvements he introduced in the America, and the skillful way he managed the launching of that ship. Some of his suggestions were radical, and some of the principles he laid down were embodied in shipbuilding by naval architects until the advent of the ironclad age.

He was a stern disciplinarian, and usually managed to work his very indifferent crews into something like fair shape. In none of his commands did he have a first-class crew of American seamen, such as the 1812 frigates exhibited. His sway on his ships was absolute. His officers were generally creatures of his own making (Simpson being an exception), and completely under his domination; with few exceptions, like Dale, whom he loved and respected, they were poor enough. In his passionate impatience with their stupidity or inefficiency, he sometimes treated them with great indignity, even going to the length of kicking them out of the cabin when they displeased him.[70] He was a fierce commander, who brooked no interference, needed no suggestions, and had no tolerance for ignorance and incapacity. Notwithstanding all this, he was a merciful captain in an age in which the gospel of force, punctuated by the cat-o'-nine-tails, was the only one in vogue on ships of war. He resorted but rarely to the practice of flogging, and in comparison with most commanders of the period his rule was not intolerable. He did not, however, inspire affection in his crews; they respected his talents, trusted to his skill, and admired his courage, but nothing more. His men were drilled and exercised incessantly, and target practice was had as frequently as the poverty of his supplies permitted. His ships were all notably clean and orderly.

As a commander we may consider his achievements from three points of view: as a strategist, as a tactician, and as a fighter. Strategic operations tend to bring you where sound policy dictates you should be, while tactical maneuvers refer to the manipulation of your force at the point of contact. A man may be a brilliant strategist and a poor tactician, or the reverse; or he may be both, and yet not be a hard, determined fighter. Jones was all three in large measure. His strategic conceptions were excellent. His successful destruction of the fishery industry at Canso, and his attempt upon the coal fleet in the Alfred; the brilliant plan which would have resulted in the capture of Lord Howe by d'Estaing if it had been carried out in time; the project he conceived for taking the homeward-bound East Indiamen by capturing St. Helena as a base of attack, and the other enterprises he urged upon the French Government indicate these things; but the conception which lifted him above the ordinary sea officer was his acute realization of the great principle that should regulate commerce destroying, which is one of the legitimate objects of warfare, and merciful in that it tends to end the conflict, and is aimed at property rather than life.

His idea was that, to be successfully accomplished, it could not be committed to the cruiser or commerce destroyer, but that attacks on centers of trade must be made by forces sufficiently mobile to enable them to cover great distances rapidly, and sufficiently strong to defeat any reasonable force, and then crush the enemy's commerce at vital points. A single ship may catch a single ship upon the high seas, or from a fleet in convoy perhaps cut out two or three; but a descent upon a great body of shipping in a harbor—unprotected as were the harbors of those days—would result in an infinitely greater loss to the enemy. Mahan has demonstrated that the necessary preliminary to the destruction of the enemy's commerce is to batter his navy to pieces—then it is at one's mercy. So far as I know, Jones is the only sailor of his day, or of many subsequent days in any navy, who had a glimmer of an idea in this direction; and, without detracting from Mahan's originality, in a limited sense Jones forestalled him. Mahan, indeed, gives him full credit for his genius on this very point.

The beginning of strategy is to determine the vital point at which to aim, and Jones began well. He tried to carry out his idea of commerce destroying with the Ranger in the Irish Channel, and he came near enough to success to demonstrate the absolute feasibility and value of his conception, given adequate force to carry it out. He had a greater force, of course, under his partial command in his famous cruise in the Bon Homme Richard, but the peculiar constitution of that squadron, which was an assemblage of co-operative ships rather than a compact body responsive and obedient to one will, also prevented him from carrying out his plans. Suppose, for instance, that the Alliance had obeyed his orders, and that the Vengeance, the Cerf, and the privateers had remained with the Pallas under his command, and that all had been well officered and manned! He would have taken the Serapis in half an hour or less, and the great Baltic fleet, worth millions of dollars, would have been at his mercy. What he attempted at Leith he could have carried out at Newcastle and Hull.

The largest force under his command was the Russian squadron in the Liman. He chose his admirable position there with an eye to its strategic possibilities, and it was due to him, and not to the trained and veteran soldier Suvorof, that the fort was placed on Kinburn Point, which practically determined the fate of Otchakoff, since it prevented the Turks from re-enforcing their fleet, and kept them from escaping after Jones had defeated them. Fortune never gave him an opportunity, but it can not be doubted from what he did accomplish with an inferior force that if he had been given a chance he would have made a name for himself as a sea strategist not inferior to that of Nelson or Sampson.

As a tactician he was even more able—perhaps because he enjoyed better opportunities. It was seamanship and tactics which enabled him to escape from the Solebay, and it was seamanship and tactics by which he diverted the Milford from the pursuit of his prizes and insured their safety. His tactics when he fought the Drake were admirable. In his famous battle with the Serapis they were even more striking. One never ceases to wonder how he succeeded in maneuvering his slow, unwieldy ship so as to nullify the greater speed and gun power of the Serapis. His action in laying the Bon Homme Richard aboard the English frigate was the one chance that he had of success, and he made that chance himself.

His tactics in the Liman were even higher than elsewhere. It was he who so maneuvered the boats of the flotilla on June 17th as to precipitate the flight of the Turks; it was he who again, on June 28th and 29th, so placed his ships that he drove the Turks from their stranded flagships. It was he who dispatched the flotilla to clear the right flank, which would have enabled the Russians to take possession of the two frigates if Nassau had not foolishly burned them. It was he who, by his splendid disposition of his ships and the battery on the point, forced the Turkish ships to take ground upon the shoals, in their attempt to escape, where Nassau destroyed them. On the other hand, he was never reckless. He coolly calculated chances and judiciously chose the right course, and he was happy in that the right course was usually the bold and daring one.

In the third capacity of an officer, there is no question as to his willingness and ability to fight. No one ever called him a coward. He certainly exhibited the very highest reach of physical bravery. It was not the courage of the braggart, for he was not continually thrusting it in the face of people on all occasions. Having established his reputation, he was content to rest upon it, and did not seek opportunity—which he did not need—for further demonstration. Nothing could surpass the personal courage and determination with which he fought his ships. Unlike most commanders, who confine their efforts to direction, he labored and fought with his own hands.

We find him heading the boarders on the forecastle of the Richard, and, pike in hand, repelling those from the Serapis; he assists in lashing the two ships together; he takes personal command of the quarter-deck guns, one of which, with the assistance of a few resolute souls, he dragged across the deck from the unengaged side. When the Ariel was drifting in deadly peril upon the Penmarques, with his own hand he heaves the lead. At Kinburn, after repeated efforts to get the galley fleet to move, he leads it forward himself. To ascertain the depth of water, he goes in a small boat under the walls of Otchakoff, within easy range of the cannon. He takes his barge on the Liman in the midst of the hottest engagement, and rows about through the contestants. When the assault is made on the flotilla under the walls of that town, he leads in person, and captures two gunboats by boarding. At Whitehaven, alone he confronts a mob and keeps them in check until the fire which he started himself has gained sufficient headway. The bullying of the Dutch admiral in the Texel can not move him a single foot.

While he did not always exhibit the same amount of moral courage, yet in some very interesting situations he showed that he possessed it in large measure. His physical courage was, of course, natural. His moral courage seems to have arisen in part from an absolute confidence in his own ability and an habitual reliance upon the accuracy of his own judgment. He showed this moral courage when, at the peril of his commission, he assumed the responsibility of piloting the Alfred to her anchorage in the Bahama expedition. He showed it particularly when, after assuming the proper position demanded by good strategy in the opening of the Liman campaign, he refused to be moved from it by the representations of such fire eaters as Nassau and Alexiano. His declining to hoist the French flag, or to sail under a French letter of marque, were evidences of this quality, and he showed it again by sending a present to Louis XVI in the dark days of the Revolution, when respect to the king in his hours of humiliation marked a man immediately.

On the other hand, he showed a sad lack of moral courage if de Ségur's statement be true that he found him, pistol in hand, in his apartments in St. Petersburg, apparently contemplating suicide. Moral courage is perhaps a more universal requisite for true greatness of character than any other virtue, and he did not rise in this sphere quite to the height he attained in the others. In other words, he was greater as a commander and as an officer than as a man.

As a commander he made mistakes. What commander did not? His quickness to imagine or to resent a slight was marred by too great a willingness to forgive. His treatment of the mutinous Simpson was entirely too gentle and forgiving for the maintenance of that discipline necessary to the welfare of the service. It was certainly a mistake to yield to Landais' importunities and leave the advantageous situation off Limerick, and, as I have stated, the excuse was worse than the action. His failure to keep his promise to his men after leaving Corunna in the Alliance was a more serious blunder. There are few professions in which the word of an officer is so implicitly relied upon by his inferiors as in the naval service. The lives of the crew are so entirely in the hands of the officers that without confidence the situation is impossible. His extravagant outfitting of the Alliance was also a wrong to Franklin under the circumstances. His method of dealing with the mutiny on the Alliance and with Landais' successful attempt to get command of her was weak, and can only be explained by the postulation that he did not really desire to get possession of her; but even the explanation leaves him in a bad position. His dawdling at L'Orient is also censurable. This, however, is a small catalogue in view of what he attempted and accomplished. Otherwise in his campaigns and in his military life he made no blunders.

He has been severely censured for choosing localities with which he was familiar from childhood as the scene of his military operations. The war of the Revolution was practically a civil war, with all the rancorous passions attendant thereon superadded to those ordinarily engendered in conflict. In America, friend met friend in deadly hatred, and not one royalist or rebel hesitated to use his local knowledge for the advancement of his cause. In accordance with his duty, by his oath as an officer, Jones was bound to put all the information as well as the ability he possessed at the services of the country under whose flag he fought. He was not born at Whitehaven, and, while he had sailed from the port many times, he had no special attachment for the place and people which comes from long association in society and business. When he made his famous descent upon the place it was seven years since he had set foot in it. At any rate, he was only doing in England what other people on both sides were doing in America without censure, and he was doing it with so much more respect to the laws of civilized warfare, and with so much more mercy, that there is no comparison between his forays and those, let us say, of Lord Dunmore, for instance, or Mowatt at Portland. The journal of an officer of the Serapis, who was killed in the action, was found after the battle was over. He had been under Dunmore's command in Virginia at the outbreak of the Revolution, and such a tale of maraudings, accompanied by destruction of property, murdering, and outraging of women as the volume contained would have been incredible had it not been confirmed by the statement of hundreds of witnesses in America. None of this kind of warfare was waged where Jones commanded.

A century and a decade, lacking two years, have elapsed since the lonely little commander entered upon his long, long rest; and the country whose first banner was hoisted by his hands at the masthead of the Alfred, whose permanent standard was flung to the breeze by the same hands from the truck of the Ranger, whose ensign was first saluted by one of the greatest powers of the world through his address and determination, whose flag was made respectable in the eyes of the world by the desperate gallantry with which he fought under it, which alone among the powers that sailed the sea through him demonstrated its ability to meet successfully the Mistress of the Ocean, has done nothing to perpetuate the memory of this founder of the Republic and rescue him from oblivion. The place of his grave is known, but squalid tenements and cheap stores have been erected over his remains. Commerce, trade, and traffic, restless life with its passions, noble and ignoble, flows on above his head, and it is probable that so it will be until the end of time. "So runs the world away!"

It is all so mournful in some strange way. In spite of his glory and his heroism, in spite of his strenuous life and his strugglings, the note that lingers in my mind as I write these concluding words is one of sadness. I read of hopes that brought no fruition; of plans made and abandoned; of opportunities that could not be embraced; of great attempts frustrated by inadequate means; of triumphs forgotten. I see a great life that might have been greater, a man of noble qualities marred by petty faults, and yet I love him. I can not tell why exactly, but the words of Solomon come into my mind as the vision of the little captain appears before me, dying alone of a broken heart, fretted away —*Vanitas vanitatem.*

And yet he did not live in vain, and his exploits shall live forever in the minds of his countrymen. So long as we possess that masculine virility which is the heritage of a great nation whose rugged coasts are washed by thousands of leagues of beating seas; so long as the beautiful flag we love waves above the mighty Republic, which, true to the principles of its founders, stands in every quarter of the globe for freedom of person, for liberty of conscience, for respect to law, so long shall the story be told of the little captain from the far land who loved these things, and who fought so heroically to establish and to maintain them.

9 783752 348873